PETALS

from

MARS

A Memoir of Resilience
and Triumph over Adversity

JUDIE DZIEZAK

*I dedicate this book to the inner strength—
the light within—of you, the reader.*

"You have power over your mind—not outside events. Realize this, and you will find strength."

— Marcus Aurelius
   Emperor of Rome and stoic philosopher

Author's Note

Hello! Thank you for picking up *Petals from Mars*. This memoir is about triumph over adversity. It is about finding the key to standing in your own power, strengthening your resilience, and moving forward toward success without withering or hardening your heart to life's challenges.

Please be forewarned: The first section ("The Whisper") and Part I of the book depict triggering and painful moments from my abusive childhood. I felt this necessary to show you my roots, so you know where I come from.

I invite you to walk with me through this book. These pages reveal challenges, victories, and powerful tools distilled from them for healing, embracing who we are deep down, and evolving into our greatness. Know that our circumstances and experiences do not define us; they do not limit us.

My hope is to inspire you to reach for the stars. You have an incredible power within—an inextinguishable light, an inner strength—that you can access at will whenever needed. May your light shine through and shape your life to be as you wish. May all your experiences, including the adverse and traumatic, imbue you with wisdom, grace you with resilience, and affirm your confidence that you can overcome anything.

May you cast your light brightly and far, melting obstacles in your path, so you succeed in all you do and fully actualize into the being you are meant to be. You are more powerful than you know. You are amazing.

Judie Dziezak, JD, MS

Contents

PROLOGUE   1

  A Whisper   3

  Fast-Forward to the Future ...   7

PART 1—SETTING ROOTS   13

  My Family   15

  Santa Claus   22

  Blame   26

  The Actress and the Nurse   29

  The Seemingly Inconsequential Toothbrush   33

  Meltdown   38

  The Struggle to Stay Here   42

  Birthday Presents   45

  That Damn Nun! and Making Too Much Noise 50

  Curiosity about Mom's Behavior   53

  Mesmerizing Immersion   55

  The Circus   61

  Strategically Folded Arms   64

  Annoying, but Effective   67

  Bunnies   71

  You Stink!   74

The Hairdresser   77

Math, Butterflies, and Bees   79

Immersion in Tranquility   81

Snowball Cookies: A Trigger   86

Shhh . . . Siblings' Secret   91

Boob Time   94

Phone Marathon: "She's crazy!"   96

Running on Empty   99

An Ice Cream Cone   103

Guests Unwanted   107

An Alter Ego   109

The Nun and a Sliver of Insight   112

College, Not a Question Mark   116

"Brainwashed"   119

PART 2—SPROUTING   123

College: Freshman Year   125

A Push to "F-A-I-L"   130

The Displaced Blessing   132

A Merging of Two Worlds   137

The Intruder   141

A Cruel Joke?   148

Bittersweet Ending of College   150

Bitten by Rats   152

Repeat: "Do Not Comprehend"   155

The Toxicology Lab   161

A Turning Point   163

A Magical Christmas   167

A Police Arrest Averted   173

Stance toward Bullies   176

The "Mmmm . . ."   178
Lace Panties   181
A Delicate Tango   186

PART 3—GROWING   189
Making Bombs   191
Growth Spurt in Confidence   193
Debut into the World of Men   196
Who, Me?   198

PART 4—BUDDING   203
A Leap   205
A Bayonet through the Heart   207
Look Out: Female Flying Solo   213
Menacing   215
Bags   217
The Crowbar   219
I Got This   222
Tempest in the Teapot   227

PART 5—BLOOMING   231
Debut into Law   233
An Olive Branch   239
Reflecting on Loss   242
Litigator   246
Bringing Family up to Speed   247
What was *THAT*?   249
A Surprisingly Warm Family Welcome   253
Loved the Job   256
The Allure of Ideas   259

Change in Focus: Mom in Trouble 263

A Stolen Key? 268

The Grasshopper Tattoo 271

The Money Drip and the Fateful Key 276

A Crusade for a Cause 278

Stakeout and "Wanted" 281

The Saboteur: A Foiled Stir-Up 284

A Sense of Peace 286

The Vanishing Purses Act 289

Sticky Matters 290

"You Don't Think So?" 294

Transitioning of Mary Keefe 301

Something Amiss 304

Tying Up Loose Ends 310

A Dance with My Soul: Taking a Stand 313

A Hit on My Life 319

The Teensy Fish—An Augur? 328

Mixed Messages 331

Sidelined 333

Needed: A Woman's Presence 335

Today's Winning Concept Is . . . 338

The Gaslight 340

The Switcheroo 343

Intelligence + Competence = Fired 347

Final Visit and the Cemetery Call 350

Two Weeks' Notice 356

Doing It My Way 362

A Near Miss 364

Evolving: 180-Degree Shift 372

PART 6—BLOSSOMING FULLY   375

     One Step Forward, Two Steps Inward   377

     What Have I Learned?   379

AFTERWORD   383

     A Reflection on Trauma in a Parent   385

Acknowledgments   389

Resources   391

About the Author   393

Follow-Up Note to the Reader   395

PROLOGUE

PROLOGUE

A Whisper

1966

A thunderous tornado of chaos plunged full speed through the door into the bedroom I shared with my sister. It snapped my attention away from hemming a jumper, opening into a tumultuous sequence of disoriented, nonsensical bustle. I was ten years old.

Mom and I were home alone. It was she who barged into my shared room. She was coming at me with full steam. She forcefully ripped off my top and pants, with me resisting. She started pulling off my underpants. As I kicked my legs vigorously, she gave up on that and doggedly dragged me by my arms through the hall into the kitchen, my legs buckling beneath me as I struggled to gain traction.

"What are you doing? Why are you doing this?" I screamed.

Mom did not answer. Did she not hear my pleas?

She was a strong, big-boned woman about three times my weight; I was bone-skinny. I managed to wriggle one arm free, but her strength overpowered my grip on door frames and kitchen chairs. Two chairs toppled over as I tried to obstruct her haul through the kitchen. I knew I couldn't stop her; I could only buy time. Thoughts raced frantically through my mind; what was the endgame of Mom's plan? I feared she was going to throw me down the steep basement stairs. That door was open; so was the back door. Both doors met at a ninety-degree angle. Which one would it be?

To my relief, she chose the back door. Forcibly, she threw me outdoors—with me wearing only the underpants that I had to fight for. If she'd had her way, I would have been stark naked.

With her thrust, I shot past the wood porch, flying over its nearly four-foot span from the door. I caught myself from tumbling down its stairs. Quickly, I scurried back up to the porch, its width of almost ten feet hugging nearly half the back of the house.

Mom shut both the outer screen door and the heavy, inside wood door. Quietly. I heard the lock click. Through the door, I could hear her laughing euphorically, "Everyone is looking at you! You should be so ashamed! They're all laughing at you!"

Inured to the content of her comments by now, I quickly scanned the area. The only person outdoors was a neighbor boy, Matt, who was one grade ahead of me in school. He was working with his friend on a motor in his backyard two houses down, about sixty-five to seventy feet away. They were not aware of me.

With a clear head, I sat down on the porch's green wood floor a few feet from the door, along its same wall. My back pressed against the rough, brown wood shingles on the outside wall, absorbing its heat from the day. Making my body small, I hugged my knees in so no one would see me topless. I became invisible.

Our next-door neighbor, Rick, would soon come home from work. He would see me at this spot, his view interrupted by widely spaced, narrow, green posts rising from the porch floor that, with a banister, hemmed the porch. He, I felt, would bring a blanket or something to cover me, as I suspected he was aware of Mom's mental state. I was not worried. My thoughts sought to understand why Mom threw me outside, nearly naked. I knew she was sick, but what was she hoping to accomplish?

Watching birds dip in and out of Rick's bird bath, I passed the time, waiting for whatever might come next. Two feral cats gracefully slunk across the alley toward our garage from the direction of a junkyard behind Rick's property, undoubtedly scavenging for food. Matt and his friend, the only ones outdoors, were still absorbed in their project.

It must have been only five to ten minutes when the inside door cracked open barely an inch. From a few steps behind the screen door, out of view from anyone outdoors, Mom whispered surreptitiously, "You can come in now."

Why is she whispering? I thought. *She is always loud and brash. And loves attention. Mom does* not *whisper. So why now?*

Inside, I beelined to my shared bedroom without either of us exchanging a word.

There, I mulled over her actions. Mom did not slam the door shut when she threw me out: she closed it *softly*. And she *whispered*. Mom *never* whispers. She amplifies. From that, I reasoned that she had wanted to remain unseen and unheard by anyone who might see me outdoors.

But why? I believe she had hoped I would make a scene and pound on the door, so she could loudly reprimand me—"Get back in the house!"—and tell everyone that I had run outside wearing only underpants and she had to pull me in.

"Scenes" were common across the street where a neighbor boy, much older than me, lived. He would chase his mother in front of their house with a kitchen pot or an aerosol can of whipped cream. Mom said he was crazy.

Mom doesn't want to be outdone, I reasoned. *Why else would she strip me of my clothes and throw me outdoors with only underpants?* Her actions told me she wanted to be able to brag to the neighbors that her daughter was crazier than the kid across the street.

Not to be outdone and to keep her name in the ring. That was the "why."

Fast-Forward to the Future ...

2013

Raising his glass, my husband, John Smith, toasted me at dinner at the Rosebud. "To your success. To your grace. To your understated tenacity. May success and happiness continue to flow from your dreams." A soft, echoing clink resounded as our champagne glasses met. The effervescent bubbles tickled my nose.

He set down his glass on the white linen tablecloth as a waiter passed behind him. The lean architecture of his cheekbones contrasted against his discursive, ample eyebrows. Wearing a serious expression, he played with the stem of the glass, twirling it with his fingers. He glanced down. As his eyes came up to meet mine, he said, "You shouldn't be here. Really. Not as you've been."

"Excuse me?" I asked.

"No, really. Based on your past, you should be a prostitute, a drug dealer, an addict, or dead. You shouldn't be as you are: happy, at peace with yourself as I see you, well-balanced. You should be really messed up, but you're not."

"Okay. That is the most peculiar accolade I have heard, assuming you intend it as a compliment."

"Yes. I do. Think about it."

And that I did, fleetingly.

That afternoon I'd had a fun time presenting a talk on food regulations before about one hundred sixty-five attendees—CEOs, company presidents, food scientists, marketing executives, and lawyers—at a professional food industry conference. By this time, I had already spoken before numerous groups, including the World Congress on Food Science, by invitation, a decade before. Speaking before large groups was something I found that I enjoyed.

What was unique about today's experience was that I had allowed myself to be "me." In the past, I had spoken like most lawyers: from behind a podium, clicking through a PowerPoint, engaged, smiling from time to time, but static. I'd have many people coming up afterward remarking about how good the presentation was, but I had always felt I was a little stiff, pretty much glued to one place: behind the podium.

Today I had taken on a challenge. The presenter before me was a marketing guy. He didn't have slides; he talked. I watched him glide with ease, talking extemporaneously, though still informatively. Though his presentation felt like he was developing it as he went along, I loved the freedom expressed by his movement. He wasn't glued to the far side of a podium.

Momentarily, I thought, *Oh, gosh. I haven't done that before, outside of smaller meetings.* Part of me wanted to slide behind the podium and deliver my talk from the comfort of my established routine. Another part of me—a part I love—eagerly wanted to try and see what it felt like to stand before an audience, moving about freely, sans the security of a podium. Was this the time to try that out? This was a professional conference!

"Trying something out" is what you do in a beta run of your talk or in a Toastmasters meeting.

But within, I felt that urge to be brave. With a feeling of excitement balanced with wonderment, tempered with a slight, underlying hint of nervousness, I stepped up to the dais. The audio-visual staff already had the intro slide of my PowerPoint presentation reflecting on the wall behind me, stretching fifteen feet high and wide, dwarfing my petite frame. From my vantage point about four feet above everyone's head, I walked to the front of the stage, smiled, and took in the attendees' faces. I could feel their positive energy and interest in what I would say. Then I opened my mouth.

To my delighted surprise, the words tumbled out, not as I had fashioned them in my rehearsal. Better. It was almost as if someone were speaking through me. "Good morning. It is my pleasure to speak to you on 'Product Claims: Navigating FDA/FTC Regulations.' My name is Judie Dziezak, and I am the founder and managing director of the Dziezak Law Firm, PC." And off I went.

The audience was terrific. They were fully engaged with the content and laughed at the commentary I interjected about some of the details.

Afterward, as I made my way to the luncheon, I experienced a flood of compliments.

"Excellent presentation!"

"Congratulations! Your talk was great!"

"You did a great job up there!"

About twenty people congratulated me. The organizer took me aside and said, "That was excellent. You are such a good speaker. That was the best presentation we've had."

So, my husband and I decided to take in a lovely dinner that evening to celebrate the success of my talk. And he just now told me I "shouldn't be here," that I should be "messed up" and a drug dealer, a prostitute, or dead. I chuckled to myself at how it was a classic *non sequitur* to today's event.

"Look," he continued, "I know you're pleased with how things went today. But I never heard you gloat about what a great job you did. Not even today after your presentation."

"That's not true. I told you I was thrilled with how my talk went. I know it was good."

As if sitting before a Netflix screen, I flashed through highlights of my thirty-two-year career. Yes, I have been blessed. I have been successful in pretty much everything I attempted, including my work in three different careers—first as a scientist, then as a technology reports editor with a technology magazine, and finally, as a patent attorney working in litigation and other aspects of intellectual property law (for example, trademarks, copyrights, licensing) and FDA regulatory law.

"Okay. What am I supposed to say? 'For someone who's been bitten by rats, roomed with a stripper, and made bombs, I did an *amazing* job?' I have been blessed with all that matters—happiness, peace of mind, good health, and a funny, loving husband. And I am grateful for all I've achieved," I said. "But that is not who I am."

John persisted. "My point is, you have encountered so much adversity, so many obstacles in your path. Each one, you handled. You didn't just cave in from them."

He's right, I thought. *I didn't cave.* Instead, I taught myself how to reach deep within and mine my inner strength. I moved past my struggles.

So, if anything from my past can inspire, encourage, or offer an inkling of hope to help others continue reaching for the stars, I will step into my vulnerability and share with you, in naked truth, aspects of my life that imparted insight into my own inner strength. I don't have all the answers for overcoming adversity. I am far from being a guru. But from my struggles growing up with a mentally ill mother and an alcoholic father and having a proclivity for entering male-dominated professional fields, I have gleaned some elements of wisdom.

So here I share my story.

PART 1

SETTING ROOTS

My Family

Unraveling puzzles and finding solutions to enigmas color a large portion of my life since my earliest memories. I was quite content to be immersed in my own thoughts while engaged in a world of intellectual and creative activities. I loved tinkering with ideas and things. I savored details within the big picture.

My parents, younger sister, and I lived in a 945-square-foot, brown-shingled, two-bedroom bungalow in Hammond, Indiana. In three of its five rooms hung a crucifix or a picture of the Blessed Virgin or *Bozia*, my mother's term for Jesus. On the kitchen wall hung a framed picture of Leonardo da Vinci's *The Last Supper*.

My mother was a first-generation American whose parents were born in Poland. My father was born in Poland and came to the United States when he was three years old. Both my parents spoke fluent Polish when they didn't want their children to understand what they were saying. Their strong Polish heritage imbued every aspect of our lives, from holiday traditions to our daily fare.

My mother, Martha, was a homemaker. She was baby number thirteen out of fourteen children, twelve of whom lived. Before marrying, Mom worked in a factory packing laundry detergent and before that at a local hospital as a janitress. She met my father, Martin, at the same factory, where he was a machine operator in the margarine department. After she married, she never went back to work; she was a homemaker and stay-at-home mom.

Neither of my parents completed high school. Mom quit the tenth grade because, as she said, she didn't need an education: she was a girl and was going to marry someday. She did so at age thirty-nine. My father had a seventh-grade education. He was illiterate and because he couldn't read, he got his driver's license from connections at a local tavern. I always hoped he wouldn't be arrested.

Besides my biological mom, I was blessed with a string of *mothers of my heart*—four women from my mom's side of the family. They stepped up as mothers at different, but staggered, times in my life. They included a former actor who shared her love of theatre and the arts with me and of whom Mom was insanely jealous, a nurse who taught me table manners and how to wash my face and care for my complexion, a nun who loved deep discussions and music, and a former hairdresser who loved learning and begged me to let her do my hair in a "beehive" (never happened!).

Completing my parental complement were two uncles, Mom's brothers—Al, a bailiff at the Hammond federal court, and Lou, a fireman. They had a supportive presence in my life. In fact, Uncle Lou walked me down the aisle on my wedding day, and I had the honor of walking him down the aisle as a pallbearer when he continued his spiritual journey.

Streaming in and out of my life was a potpourri of other members of my family, seen mainly at family events. These included thirteen aunts, eleven uncles, and a myriad of cousins (ranging from eight years younger than me to thirty-nine years older than me) and their families.

From the outside looking in, my home appeared normal. Mom cooked huge holiday dinners, baked exquisite yeast goods, and looked after her relatives' children. To guests and people outside our immediate family, Mom presented as loud, strong-willed, and opinionated. You always knew where you stood with Mom. Dad's quiet nature complemented Mom's robust, outspoken presence. He had a strong moral compass and sound work ethic.

Inside, when it was only our immediate family, the dynamics of our home were a different story. Its normal state was akin to a war zone: domestic violence from Mom, abuse, belittlement, derision, name-calling, no support, and no discipline—though Mom was strict with other people's children and had outsiders believe she was strict with her own children. It often felt like I was holding myself up against a wall that was ready to topple over. No one outside knew what was going on inside our home. No one, that is, except for Mom's siblings and their spouses. Their children, my cousins, didn't even know.

Mom's siblings knew she was mentally ill. They knew she experienced unprovoked rage and mania, punctuated with depression. They knew my father was an alcoholic. They had their own families. Their hands were tied. Until I became an attorney, I never told a soul about my home life, except for my husband. In fact, it wasn't until we were married for thirteen years that I disclosed that my father was an alcoholic.

My dad was a kind, sensitive, artistic man. He accepted that he loved Mom more than she loved him. As a youngster,

I could see he understood her for who she was. When she got worked up and started shouting about something, he would dismiss it, saying, "That's the way she is."

Once, at age six, as I sat in the living room with Dad, I realized I felt comfortable with him, unlike the way I felt with Mom. He was like me energetically, though at that time I didn't think in terms of energy. We were cut from the same cloth. I even look like him. He cried at sad movies; Mom didn't. Mom would look at our teary eyes and say, "What? Why are you crying? It's only a movie. It's not true."

Dad and I shared the same gentle spirit and groundedness. His coworkers at the factory respected him. People sought advice from him. He was a thinker—smart, reasonable, to-the-point, and down-to-earth. Though he liked being with people, he tended to be reserved. Our home challenged his self-esteem and pushed his limits. The drama and noise scraped at his inner resolve. Alcohol became his escape. As time went on, his consumption increased as he needed more to achieve the same numbing effect.

Dad was my favorite parent. I love memories of him talking with me, drawing animals for me when I was young, making ice cream cones or his renowned cream cheese cake at Easter, taking my sister and me to his brother's farm where we'd barbecue hamburgers and play on the vast property, or racing with us in an aunt's long front yard (though I didn't like his letting me or my sister win). Or we would go for a walk where the turning point was an ice cream shop that we never failed to visit. Dad appreciated simple pleasures—sitting on the front porch after work and on the weekends, talking with neighbors, and enjoying the birds, squirrels, and even the bats that inhabited the parkway in front of our home.

My sister, Nita, arrived seventeen months after me. She was a surprise. Mom did not know she was pregnant. In my late teen years, Mom's siblings told me that about six weeks before my sister's arrival, the family gossip was, "Something is going on! Martha is as big as a house and is wearing Martin's shirts." When I learned about menstruation, I asked Mom how she could not have known. She averred she had no idea she was pregnant the second time around.

~⟲

After my sister's birth when she was still in a crib, I sat in the front room, taking in its silence. Silence was unusual. Through the air vent, I heard voices and sobbing coming from the basement. I had not been down those stairs before. I summoned the courage to fanny my way down the stairs.

Hanging from the steel risers was a rope. Daddy was sobbing.

Mom saw me coming up to them. "Daddy's going to kill himself. You're not going to have a daddy anymore," she said.

"I can't take it anymore. You treat me worse than a dog," Daddy cried.

Mom's response was, "Marts, how are me and the kids going to eat?"

As young as I was, I felt in my stomach that was not a good thing to say. I could feel my dad's energy slump even lower. I felt his deep sadness in my stomach.

"Daddy, don't kill yourself," I begged. "I want you to be my daddy. Don't kill yourself."

Sobbing, my dad looked at me as if he hadn't seen me standing there before. He dismantled the rope and scrunched down to my level. "I'm not leaving you, sweetheart," he said, wiping his eyes. Later in life, as Mom battered him, I wondered if I had made a mistake in selfishly pleading for him to stay for my sake.

~⌇

Holidays—Easter, Thanksgiving, Christmas, and New Year's—were huge family events, usually celebrated with Mom's side of the family.

Mom was a magician with her cooking and incredible baking. Though lauded for her cakes, she enjoyed making Polish food such as pierogi and sauerkraut with split peas (and salt pork, which stunk up the entire house when fried), various meat dishes as well as pig feet and pig tails (not at all my favorite; I was more of a vegetarian), and homemade kluski noodles. Also on the menu was czarnina, a duck blood soup made with prunes, its name derived from the word *czarny*, meaning "black." Gracing every holiday menu were homemade kolachki (Polish cookies) and Mom's poppyseed rolls. On Paczki (pronounced "pohnch-kee") Day, the day before Ash Wednesday, Mom always made delicious paczki, a Polish type of deep-fried doughnut filled with prune or apricot filling.

For about five years when I was young, around Easter, Dad ordered live ducks and geese that were delivered to our home and kept in the garage for one to two days before he butchered them. I didn't like the fact that they would be killed. I would appeal to Mom to unlock the garage door to let me see them. After a brief viewing, she'd quickly shoo me out. Dad used the duck and goose blood for czarnina. I assume we ate duck and goose meat, but I don't recall Mom saying she was serving duck or goose.

In the fall, the luscious aroma of apple slices greeted us when we came home from school. Mom was beyond generous with people. When a neighbor had cancer, Mom took her a hot lunch every day.

A practical woman, Mom didn't spend money needlessly. When she bought me a coat in the third grade, it was three sizes too large. "You'll grow into it," she said. It came down to my ankles. I had to wear the sleeves rolled up into six-inch cuffs. I did not dress like the rest of the kids in school. I wore the same clothes to school every day, prompting a fourth-grade classmate to ask why that is so.

When I was in the fourth grade, Mom bought one dress from the clearance rack at Goldblatt's. It was for me. I asked, "Where's Nita's dress?"

"She will wear this when you're done with it."

"By 'done,' you mean when I grow out of it, and it's worn out?"

"Yeah."

"You have two daughters," I told Mom. "You have to buy two dresses—one for each of us. I am not going to wear this unless you buy a dress for Nita too. Take this one back." She returned the dress but didn't buy anything for my sister or me. Later, I realized I didn't do the right thing. I should have told her to take back the dress and exchange it for one in my sister's size. I made a mental note to do that the next time. Years later when the school adopted uniforms, I was grateful because that meant we had to have clothes.

Santa Claus

December 1956

One of my earliest memories is of Christmas. I was fifteen months old. My sister had not been born yet.

Wearing a dress, I sat in the middle of the living room floor. A Christmas tree stood in one corner, its large, multi-colored lights illuminating the room. Beneath, in a crèche were baby Jesus, Mother Mary, and Joseph, showcased by a light bulb inserted into the back of the crèche. A few plastic camels and cows stood at one side. A ceramic angel guarded the other side. On each side of the crèche, encircling the tree, was a village of small houses the size of school milk cartons, light streaming from their colored windows as they sat nestled atop a cottony white "snow" around them. Christmas music played from the Victrola across the room.

Mom put a spinning top down in front of me. It was a gift. She bent down to show me how to work it. Holding its stem and flicking her wrist, she got it to spin. It wobbled briefly, then toppled because of the carpet.

My parents had been talking about Santa Claus the weeks before. I'd hear "Ho, ho, ho" and talk of Santa Claus on the WJOB radio station Dad listened to. I heard about Santa bringing presents. On Dad's radio, I heard a man talk about Christmas and giving Christmas gifts to your kids.

My parents didn't say the gift was from Santa Claus. So, I asked, "Who is this from?"

Mom answered, "Santa Claus."

"What did you get me?" I asked, thinking about WJOB talking about getting gifts for your kids.

"Daddy and I got you that," she said pointing to the top that she had just said was from Santa Claus.

Hmmm? "What did Santa Claus bring me?" I asked.

"That. Santa Claus gave you that," she said again pointing to the top that she had just said was from her and Daddy.

She keeps changing her answers. "What did you get me?" I asked. I knew what her answer would be.

"Daddy and I got you that," she repeated, pointing again to the same top.

I had to ask: "Did Santa Claus bring me anything?" I already knew what she would say.

"Yes, Santa Claus bought you that for Christmas," said Mom, pointing again to the top.

I stopped asking. From that exchange—five questions—I figured that there was no Santa Claus. I didn't know who he was, but I felt it was a lie. He didn't exist. I didn't understand why my parents and the radio and TV would talk about someone who didn't exist as if he did.

A few minutes later, Dad leaned toward Mom. Whispering, he said, "I didn't expect that. She pieced it together. She's really smart. She's going to keep us on our toes." Before marrying, Dad had helped raise his sister's four older boys, so he was familiar with toddlers.

Hearing him, I wondered what I had "pieced together." I didn't understand what he meant about me doing something with their toes.

People sometimes seem to think toddlers don't hear, don't see, and are not intelligent. They don't realize how much information toddlers can assimilate. Did my mom think that because I was young, my mind wouldn't hold what she had just told me?

The following year and the ones thereafter proved me right. Santa Claus never brought presents to our house, except once, when I was six years old.

That year, before Christmas, I let a neighbor girl in on a big secret: I told her there was no Santa Claus. He was made up. She told her mother. Her mother called our house and asked to speak with me. She was upset. "Never again tell my daughter that there is no Santa Claus," she demanded. If someone's mom was upset with me for saying that, it only confirmed that I was right. Santa did not exist. If he did, why would she care about what I had said to her daughter?

That Christmas, Santa visited our house. He showed up at the back door. No one used the back door, except to go into the backyard. On hearing commotion outside the door with bells ringing, my parents called to my sister and me to see who it was. When we got to the door, a man looking like Santa Claus with a white beard, a big belly, and a bag slung over his shoulder stood there laughing, "Ho, ho, ho!"

"Come on in, Uncle Al," I said. "Why are you dressed up like Santa Claus?" My parents and Nita tried to convince me that he was Santa, but I knew he was Uncle Al.

That was the second and last time I received a Christmas present from "Santa."

Blame

Early 1958

A loud crashing sound erupted from the kitchen, unleashing a stream of cussing.

"That goddamn Judie!" shouted Mom. "A plate broke. That goddamn Judie. This is all her fault!"

My sister and I were in the living room, sitting next to each other, watching *Bozo the Clown* on TV. From behind, with her silky black hair and me with my whitish-blond hair, we looked like we came from completely different sets of parents. She resembled Mom, and I resembled Dad. Dad was in his favorite chair near a bay window a few feet away at the front of the house where he had a full view of us, the TV, and the dining room. On the far side of the dining room was a doorway into the kitchen. Mom was in the kitchen at the back of the house.

When I heard Mom shouting, my stomach did a summersault. *She's blaming me for something I didn't do.* Emotion swelled up from my stomach to my throat. I began crying because Mom was blaming me. She didn't do that before.

Crying hard, I asked Dad, "Why is she yelling about me? I didn't do anything! I'm here. I'm not in the kitchen with her.

I'm HERE with you. Why is she blaming me for the broken plate?"

Another crashing sound: that's a second plate shattered on the linoleum floor. More loud cussing. "That goddamn Judie. It's all her fault that I broke this plate."

"You didn't do anything wrong, sweetheart. That's your mom. That's the way she is," answered Dad.

"Why is she yelling? I didn't do anything. I'm not even in the kitchen," I sobbed.

"I know, sweetheart. You didn't do anything wrong," he repeated.

His responses didn't soothe me. He might as well have not answered me. I wanted him to go into the kitchen and tell her to stop yelling and blaming me, but I didn't tell him that. I wanted him to do it on his own. He seemed to feel that his response was enough. It wasn't.

Crying hard, I felt my mom's icky anger directed toward me, entering my body, my stomach area like arrows.

Mom never talked like that about my sister. Nor did she treat her like that. *Why is she doing that to me?* I wondered. *Why? I want to know, why? Why is she acting like that?*

My pain started to dissipate. *It's not me. I didn't do anything wrong. This is not because of me. There's something wrong with Mommy.*

That summer, at around age three, I paid attention to how other moms in the neighborhood talked to their children. They were outside with other people when I observed them. So, maybe they were different inside their homes.

When we visited relatives, I observed how my aunts and uncles treated each other and their children. No one acted like Mom. But then Mom was different in other people's houses; there, she didn't treat me or Dad the way she did at home. She was two different people.

When my parents watched *I Love Lucy*, *The Donna Reed Show*, *Leave it to Beaver*, or *Make Room for Daddy*, I studied how the moms in those shows conducted themselves and how they treated their children. No one acted like Mom, with rage, shouting and calling their children or husbands names.

Yes, something was wrong with Mommy. She was crazy. When I came to realize that, it felt a bit shocking. I had to sit with it for a bit to let its reality sink in.

Later that summer, I needed to talk with my dad. I waited for the right moment. Mom was outside hanging clothes on the clothesline. Dad was on the front porch. He would sit on a card table chair looking out at the tree-lined parkway.

"Hi, Daddy," I chirped as the screen door closed behind me.

"Hi, sweetheart." He smiled on seeing me joining him.

On the top step a few feet away, I settled. Looking up at him, I shared with him what I had figured out. "I think Mommy is crazy. She is, isn't she?"

He didn't answer right away. For a moment, a look of surprise crossed his face, replaced by seriousness. His blue eyes turned sad like I wasn't supposed to know that. "Yes, she is."

"Can she be fixed?" I asked.

"I don't know. I don't think there's anything we can do," he responded. He sounded downhearted.

The Actress and the Nurse

1958

One warm, sunny day when I was three years old, our family packed into Dad's Studebaker coupe to visit Mom's brother, Uncle Lou. My sister and I were going to meet Auntie Virge, his wife of four years, for the first time.

Whenever we rode with Mom and Dad, I sat behind Dad and my sister, behind Mom.

Mom was agitated. She was in one of her moods. She complained for the entire ten-minute drive. This time, though, her complaints were not about Dad but about a "barfly."

"I don't want to see her. She's a barfly! She's a whore!" she shouted.

What's a barfly? I wondered. I had not yet heard that word.

"Martha, stop it. The kids are here," said Dad.

"It's true. She worked in her dad's bar. She's a barfly. She's a whore. I don't like her. I'm going to spit on her when I see her."

"Stop it! Martha. Stop talking like that. The kids are here. They hear what you're saying. Behave yourself when we're there." Dad had never told Mom to behave before.

"Okay. Okay. I don't like her. I'm going to spit on her," Mom sneered, pursing her lips. "She didn't even get married in church."

What was loud and clear was that Mom didn't like the lady we were going to visit. From the way Mom acted and what she said, I suspected that this lady was really nice. I supposed, too, that she was pretty. Maybe she was smart as well. Mom was jealous. Her voice, words, and actions broadcasted that like the WJOB radio station Dad listened to every day. How I hoped Mommy wouldn't spit on this lady like she did on Dad.

At Uncle Lou's house, I walked up each high concrete stair leading up to the door. It felt strange going there. The last time I was there, it was Busia's house (*Busia* is Polish for "grandmother"), but now it was Uncle Lou's because Busia left to go to heaven. Uncle Lou answered the door and invited us in. The adults talked. My sister and I stood near a desk in the living room.

From the back of the house, a tall, pretty lady with shoulder-length, curled, brunette hair strode into the living room. The first thing I noticed was her warmth and relaxed nature. She spoke for a short time with my parents and then turned her attention to my sister and me. She had a way of holding your attention. Later, I learned three words to describe her: elegant, dramatic, and outspoken. When she spoke to me and my sister, she looked us directly in the eye like adults do with one another. She said something that made us all laugh. I liked her. I was glad she was my auntie.

My new Auntie Virge was just as I had thought she would be: nice, kind, and pretty. Unlike my other aunts who were chubby with generous tummies, Auntie Virge looked like a movie star. She even had on red lipstick—what I saw as her signature as the years progressed.

What I didn't know at the time was that Auntie Virge was an actress. She attended college (which was part of the reason Mom didn't like her) and performed with a professional theater company, doing productions in the southeast before meeting Uncle Lou.

Boy, was I glad that Mommy didn't spit on Auntie Virge like she said she would. That would have spoiled the visit for everyone.

～⌒

Later that summer, I gained another auntie. This one was my Uncle Al's girlfriend. At the time I met her, they had been dating for fourteen years but had not married.

Mom came into the bedroom I shared with my sister. "My brother Al is here with his girlfriend. I don't know why he brought her here. He said he wants her to meet you kids." From the tone of her voice, I could tell Mom didn't like this lady, but she liked her more than she liked Auntie Virge.

"Come here. You need to change." She took us to the dining room.

"Where are they?" I asked.

"In the backyard. I didn't want her to come in." Mom didn't say why, but I figured that was because the house was a mess. It was always a mess unless she expected company.

"You're going to wear this." In her hand, she held our matching flowered short and top sets. The bottom trim on my shorts was blue and on my sister's, pink. I changed as Mom helped my sister into her outfit.

Outside, a lady with good posture and light pink lipstick stood next to Uncle Al, coming to a little higher than his shoulders. "Petite" is how Mom would later describe her. As we approached, I could feel that she was a gentle person. She seemed quiet. She didn't talk much. Her gray-white bouffant hairdo framed her face. Her hair color puzzled me. It didn't go with her young-looking face. Years later, I learned that she had been gray since she was twenty years old.

"This is my girlfriend, Mary Keefe," said Uncle Al as we walked down the porch steps.

"Hi," my sister and I greeted her.

"Is it okay if we call you Mary Keefe? We already have two Auntie Marys," I asked, aiming to keep family nomenclature as clear as possible.

"Yes. That's fine," she laughed. After that, any time I or my family spoke to her or of her, we used her full name.

Mom didn't offer them anything to eat or drink. That was odd.

Almost as soon as we met Mary Keefe, Uncle Al whisked her away. He said she had to go to work. She was a nurse at the hospital.

I liked this new auntie. *How lucky I am*, I thought, *to have two new aunties. And they both seem nice.*

The Seemingly Inconsequential Toothbrush

1958–1963

As a child, I longed for a toothbrush so badly. Though my immediate family had four people, there was only one toothbrush in the bathroom. It belonged to Dad. We were taught never to touch that toothbrush. "It's Daddy's," Mom would say.

Mom had no teeth. She had hers pulled when she was in her mid-forties and wore only a top bridge because we didn't have the money to get the bottom bridge.

When I was three, I looked at my teeth and Dad's teeth. He brushed his teeth, so I asked Mom for a toothbrush. She said, "No, you don't need that."

I didn't have brothers. Through the lens of a three-year-old, I initially thought that perhaps boys had to brush their teeth and girls didn't. But I reasoned that that didn't make sense because boys and girls both have hair, and my boy cousins brushed their hair just like my girl cousins did. (I didn't brush my hair. I combed it, as I didn't have a hairbrush until about the fifth or sixth grade.) *Maybe it's different with teeth*, I wondered. But that didn't make sense to me.

When I met Aunt Virge at age three, as she stooped down to speak with me, she studied my teeth. "Do you brush your teeth?

"No," I answered.

"They are so dark yellow, almost brownish. You should brush them. Take care of your teeth," she told me.

I felt uncomfortable being told I had dark yellow teeth, but inside I was ecstatic because that meant that I was right. *Girls do have to brush their teeth*, I told myself.

Feeling more confident with my newfound knowledge, I again asked Mom for a toothbrush. She gave the same response: "No. You don't need that."

That remark was disappointing. I wanted a toothbrush and didn't have a way to get one.

Over the next few years, I loved chatting with Aunt Virge but as soon as her eyes fixated on my teeth, that was my signal to scoot away.

Fast-forward to age seven when I was in the second grade. It was a cold holiday—Thanksgiving or Christmas—when my family went to Aunt Virge's house. A lot of relatives were there. I kept a lookout for Aunt Virge. I did not want her to corner me and talk about my teeth. I didn't want others to hear that I had dirty teeth. The time passed, and I thought, *So far, so good*. And just when I had that thought, a low, melodious voice sounded behind me.

"Hello, Judie. How are you?"

Turning around, I saw it was Aunt Virge. As we talked, the inevitable happened: she talked about my yellow-brown teeth. She asked why I don't brush.

I told her, "I just don't." I was too embarrassed to tell her I did not have a toothbrush, and I didn't want her to think my mom was bad for not getting me one.

That night I thought, *Now what? I can't brush my teeth and I can't bathe. So, I am a stinky kid with yellow-brown teeth.*

A few months later, a station wagon pulled up in front of our house. Aunt Virge emerged from the driver's side. At our front door, she handed Mom a small, brown paper bag. Before she dashed off, I caught her words, "for your children." It wasn't like her to not come in.

As Mom walked to the kitchen at the back of the house, I asked, "What did Aunt Virge want?"

Mom said, "She gave me something for you kids." Mom opened the bag and peeked in. She shook her head with disgust. "Oh, this is a bunch of crap." She tossed the bag into the kitchen trash bag. I knew it was toothbrushes!

After waiting until Mom was in the basement, I crept into the kitchen like a little ninja, stepping silently on my tippy-toes. I grabbed the bag out of the trash and tip-toed back into my shared bedroom.

There, I tore into the bag. In it were two toothbrushes, Pepsodent toothpaste, and red candies, which didn't make sense. I smelled the toothpaste. It was what Dad used. I squeezed it onto a toothbrush and brushed away. The bristles against my gums and teeth felt amazing, like they were shearing away heaps of wool from a sheep. Afterward, my teeth felt deliciously smooth. As I was too short to see into the bathroom mirror, I wondered if they had the dazzling star you'd see on toothpaste commercials. The red candies I found, looking into Mom's handheld mirror, turned some teeth red but not all. The *candies* I figured out were for checking your "toothbrushingship." When you chewed on them after brushing your teeth, they colored the parts of your teeth that you missed or could have done a better job at cleaning.

Afterward, I hid the toothbrushes, toothpaste, and bag, and shared that hiding spot with my sister. By then, Mom was back from the basement. She looked in the trash bag and discovered Virge's paper bag was missing. She knew I was the trash thief: I was the one who had been badgering her for a toothbrush. For what seemed like an hour, Mom unfurled a litany of curses against me and Aunt Virge.

That spring, like an angel interceding on my behalf, Virge convinced Mom to take my sister and me to a dentist. I had twenty-three cavities. For months afterward, Mom cursed Aunt Virge behind her back. She complained about the cost of the fillings as if that was Aunt Virge's fault. Though she declared that Virge was not welcome in our home, she did not enforce that proclamation.

~)

Fast-forward to 2010. My husband and I took Aunt Virge and Uncle Lou out for Easter dinner. My aunt leaned over to me and said, "You have such pretty teeth."

After thanking her, I told her, "Do you know what I tell people who compliment me on my teeth?"

"No. What do you tell them?"

I told her, "I say, 'I owe my teeth to my Aunt Virge.'" She looked perplexed.

I then shared with her my story, giving her an abridged version void of anything negative said about her. I expressed how much I appreciated her dropping off toothbrushes and toothpaste that spring of second grade. That saved my teeth, I told her, and allayed my concern that being brown, they were on track to fall out, rendering me toothless for life. Not only did her simple act lead to lifelong good dental hygiene habits, but it helped boost my confidence. My gratitude gushed as I treaded delicately to express how I understood her action that day took courage, particularly as I knew her relationship with my mom was tenuous and rocky at times.

Virge was eighty-seven at the time. She brightened, saying she was pleased to have helped me out. However, she looked at me blankly as she said she had no recollection of dropping off toothbrushes for my sister and me. Earlier that evening, her husband, who was ninety-one, said he did not remember walking me down the aisle for my wedding.

The seemingly inconsequential things we do or say can profoundly change someone's life, whether or not we are aware of that.

Meltdown

1960

Dad had a secret and let my sister and me in on it. Mom's birthday was coming up, and Dad wanted to take us to buy a present. "Shhh," he told us. "It's a surprise."

When he told Mom he was taking the kids out, Mom was right there at the door. "I'm coming too," she said. Despite his assurances that we'd be back soon, she was unrelenting. She left him no choice but to confess that we were going out to buy her a present. That made her even more determined to come along. And so, she did.

Dad drove us to Woodmar shopping center, whose stores Mom said were for rich people. We had fun going into several stores and letting Mom pick out her presents. Dad bought her a crystal beaded necklace, huge quarter-sized beaded earrings that she liked and that were in style at the time, a pair of nylons, and a bottle of cologne. She seemed happy in the stores.

On our way home, the wind shifted. Mom was beset with anger. She yelled and cursed because Dad didn't say or do something in the store that he was supposed to know to do. It was something like not giving her the bag to hold or not telling the clerk, "This is for my wife." Her yelling and cursing flowed into the house, into the afternoon, and into the evening. Mom's shouting intensified as she intermixed cursing with banging pots and pans in the kitchen.

Meanwhile, in my shared bedroom, with wrapping paper and ribbons and a bow from Dad, we wrapped her presents and arranged them atop the wrapped nylons to look like a bedroom: the necklace box, a bed; the earrings box, pillows; and the cologne box on its side with a tinfoil mirror glued to wrapping paper-backed cardboard, a dresser.

After she calmed down, Dad suggested we give her presents to her that evening so she could wear them to church the next day. Putting on happy faces, we gathered around her in the dining room and presented her with wrapped birthday gifts.

Our timing was off.

Mom eyed her gifts with tight lips. *Uh-oh.* Something was about to happen. In a split second, she hefted her wrapped package over her shoulder and spewing rage, thrust her gift against a wall. The sheer force of its impact split the individual boxes apart, sending them soaring to different parts of the room. With her anger now fully uncorked, she unfurled a fresh wave of yelling at Dad and me.

I picked up the individual boxes. Their wrapping was torn. My heart sank when I saw the damaged art arrangement now an abysmal mess. We could always count on Mom's anger and violence to disrupt our home. It was getting worse. In fact, it now seemed like it was an atypical moment of peace that interrupted the discordance.

In church the next day, she kneeled on the pew, rosary in hand, the light from a stained-glass window casting sparkles from her new necklace and earrings.

Mom's expression of unprovoked volatility had changed over the few years before this. She used to pretend to cry but had not done that for a while. The last time she did was when I was about to go into kindergarten. After shouting at Dad or me, Mom sat on the sofa, sounding like she was crying, with her head lowered into both hands covering her eyes. Her sadness made me feel sorry for her. Until she suddenly stopped making her crying sound. As I watched, she parted her ring finger from her middle finger. Sitting quietly, she peeked through the open "V" to see who was in the room. *Is she pretending to cry?* I asked myself. Seeing me, she quickly closed the V and resumed her crying sound.

"Are you pretending to cry?" I asked.

Dropping her hands, she quickly shot up straight, with no tears on her face, and glared at me. "Shoddop! You're so damn dumb."

That incident changed my reason for feeling sorry for her that day. Mom wasn't sad; that was part of her sickness. She was sick. Very sick.

That was the last time Mom pretended to cry.

My heart sank when I walked out of the room I shared with my sister to find Dad knocked out and sprawled on the living room floor. That was not typical. Nor was it typical for Dad to be drunk in the middle of the week, but he was on vacation.

I was five.

"Mom, what happened?" I asked, gravely concerned, as I kneeled next to Dad, touching his face. I already knew what happened.

"Ack, he's a goddamn drunk," she barked.

"Mom! You pushed him, didn't you?" Then I saw the blood. "He's bleeding. Why did you do that?" A trickle of blood flowed from his temple onto the carpet. Though it was not spurting, being young, I didn't know how serious it was.

"Mom, call the ambulance! Daddy's hurt," I pleaded.

"Ack, he's okay," she resisted.

"You have to call them," I begged.

Interrupting my pleas was an unexpected knock at the backdoor. Even though Mom had told me to stay put as she left to answer the door, I followed her into the kitchen at the back of the house. It was my godfather dropping off a bushel of tomatoes from Uncle Joe's farm. (Uncle Joe was Dad's brother.) Mom did not invite him in. That was unusual. As if noticing that, he asked, "Is Martin home? His car is out front."

Not missing a beat, Mom responded calmly and quickly, "No. He's at work. He car-pooled today."

I was torn about what to do. Intuitively, my gut was saying Daddy's wound was not serious. Fortunately, that was true. It turned out that it was a surface scratch from hitting the corner of the TV cabinet. No arteries or veins were torn.

Mom is like a powerful bull that doesn't think, I thought. *One of these days she could really hurt him.*

The Struggle to Stay Here

1961

In the first grade, at age six, I became aware of something happening to me. My class packed into the school gym for a Christmas show presented by the junior high classes. I took my seat. The lights were then turned down. I next remember standing up. It was time to leave. As I stood at the gym door leading into the school hallway, I wondered where my mind had gone. *Where was I for that entire time?* I was awake for the entire show, yet I didn't *watch* it. I was elsewhere in my thoughts, but I couldn't tell you what I had been thinking during that time. It felt gray and tumultuous like the inside of Mom's tub-wringer washing machine in action. That got me curious.

I noticed I didn't pay attention in class. A few times I caught myself gazing out the window. Some of those times I knew what I was thinking, but other times I was *gone*. I couldn't relate where I had been.

What got me to pay attention was my not knowing of a school event that spring. All the classes were putting on a singing performance for the monsignor at our Catholic grade school. On that day, I showed up to school in everyday school clothes: a navy cotton jumper, a white blouse—which

I assume was damp when donned that morning, as it always was because Mom would wash it the night before and we didn't have a dryer—old cotton socks more than likely with a hole at the heel, and worn brown shoes. My hair was poker-straight, perhaps a little dirty, with no ribbons, but combed through.

My girl classmates showed up in party attire: pastel taffeta dresses of lace with puffy multi-layered slips beneath, white socks with lace trim, dressy patent leather shoes, and huge colorful ribbons in their hair. In the bathroom, I scanned everyone's pretty dresses and felt out of place. *How did I not know I was supposed to dress up?* The teacher had obviously told the class. I thought too that given the prominence of the event, she must have repeated the date and instructions multiple times. I sucked it up and acted like I was dressed no differently than anyone else. They were only clothes. What we wear is not who we are. Deep down, though, I felt embarrassed for sticking out like a sore thumb by not being dressed up like my peers. Even if I had known to dress up, I couldn't because I didn't have a party dress at that time.

When it was our class's turn to sing, I marched onto the stage and took my spot. As I sang, I looked out into the audience. There in one of the front rows, behind the monsignor, sat a familiar face: Mom. She was with a classmate's mother who frequently came to our house with her daughter. *How did Mom know about this event when I didn't?* My mom often spoke with my classmate's mother. I wondered if they had talked about what their daughters would wear for this important event.

A few months after the school performance, Mom bought party dresses for my sister and me.

That event was a wake-up call for me. That's what alerted me to my drifting away in class. To counter this, I worked hard to be present. I would check in with myself to make sure I was *here* with my body.

My drifting continued into the second and third grades, though to a lesser extent. I don't recall what my grades were like at this time, but they couldn't have been good. Mom never talked to me about getting poor grades or good grades, as school was not important to her.

By the time I was in fourth grade, I had trained myself to stay in my body. I did that by engaging my senses. I paid attention to the scent of soap and the feel of my hands rubbing across each other when washing at the school's sink. I purposely sat up ultra-straight and lingered on the teacher's every word or listened to the inflection of her voice. Or I would press my knees together and feel their contact. Or I would run my fingers across the smooth, golden-brown desktops or the sharpened graphite tip of a pencil. By being attentive to how I experienced these things, I felt what it was like to be *here*.

By the fourth grade, I was present at all times in class. I could follow what we read; I knew what we had to do for homework. I became someone to whom classmates turned with questions such as, "What did the teacher say?" or "How are we supposed to do that?"

That remarkable shift in becoming attentive and present was attributable in part to having contact with Aunt Virge. She had me over to her home for lunch a few times per year and made a genuine effort to talk with me—a foreign concept in my house. Her interest in me as a person made me feel secure, seen, connected, and loved, though at the time I don't think I knew what love was. I felt safe in her presence and in her home. That played a huge role in helping me unfold my talents.

Birthday Presents

1960–1962

My parents did not celebrate birthdays or Christmas with presents. For birthdays and grade school or high school graduations, Mom would give a card. Sometimes it had a few dollars in it, or ten dollars when I was older. Christmas was a religious holiday, typically celebrated with one or two of Mom's siblings and their families. Some guests brought presents, but not always. For my First Communion, my parents gave me a delicate lady's gold watch that Dad bought at the local tavern, presumably from someone pawning it off. I think it was stolen.

My fifth and sixth birthdays were the exception to the "no gifts" pattern. For my fifth birthday, Mom threw a party and invited girls from my kindergarten class. I had been in school for only a few weeks and didn't know them well. Mom served sloppy Joes, coleslaw, potato salad, and cake and ice cream. A classmate's parent brought over a pin-the-tail-on-the-donkey game, popular at that time, that we played before the food. After the food, we didn't open presents.

Mom was in the kitchen cleaning, and we were free to play as we wanted. I took several girls through a scary passageway lined with spider webs, which is what made it scary. It was a narrow corridor formed between tall yew bushes in the front of the house and the recessed part of the house beneath a bay window. The girls wore party dresses with stiff, puffed-out skirts. One girl had torn her dress. A few got dirty after running around outside. One mother picking up her daughter asked, "How did you get dirty at a birthday party?" That was such a fun event!

A few months later when it was my sister's birthday, there was no party. I thought it was perhaps because she wasn't in kindergarten yet. However, even when she reached kindergarten, Mom didn't give her a party. I thought that unfair.

For my sixth birthday in the first grade, Mom and Dad surprised me with a gift. As Dad walked up the porch stairs from work a little later than usual, Mom shouted at me, "Get back! Get back! Daddy's carrying something heavy." It was a metal dollhouse with movable furniture. He picked it up at the hardware store. What a surprise!

They set it up in the dining room. I thanked them both profusely. But, I mulled, *What am I supposed to do with this? Move the furniture around? What made them think I wanted a dollhouse?* It was so incredibly thoughtful of them, but I didn't want or need a dollhouse. I didn't even play with dolls then. As I didn't want to seem ungrateful, I pretended to be fascinated with moving the furniture around, all the while thinking, *Kids actually enjoy this?* My preference was to be outside catching grasshoppers or weaving bracelets from the white-flowered clover plants that peppered our lawn.

Then, when my sister stood next to me to look at the dollhouse, Mom began yelling, "Leave that alone! That's Judie's. Let her play with it," as if my sister could possibly wreck its metal walls or interfere with my feigned captivation in moving a tiny plastic couch two inches to the right. I could feel my sister's sense of dejection. I told Mom we were playing, but she still shouted, "That's Judie's."

Didn't Mom think I would want my sister to join me in playing with this? That could have made it fun. After that, I associated the dollhouse with Mom's toxic behavior. I didn't play with it because of the yucky emotions it evoked when she yelled at my sister for coming up to me when I was near it. That convinced Mom that she was right: don't buy your kids presents because it costs money and they waste the gift.

Christmas that year is when it hit me: *Our house is different. It's not normal. Other kids get presents and we don't.* Our girlfriends down the block invited my sister and me over that Christmas day. Strewn across their living room floor was a sea of ribbons and torn wrapping paper, intersprinkled with gifts of all sorts. Our friends showed us the gifts they had received. On our walk home, I was concerned about how my sister was taking in the experience. She should have gotten a present. She was younger than me and deserved at least something from my parents. I told Mom that when I got home. Mom's response was, "Christmas is a religious holiday. No presents."

I didn't need presents and I still don't. In fact, much later, as I approached adulthood, I began to appreciate Mom's view as progressive. However, at the time, it wasn't *not getting presents* that was hard. It was not having been told, before seeing other children receive so much, that other families have a different perspective of Christmas. From that experience at our friends' home and my mom's comment afterward, I grasped that

Christmas had a different meaning in our home. My parents treated it solely as a religious holiday.

Later that year, when my sister's birthday was approaching, I was excited. I couldn't wait to see what my parents would get her. Her birthday came and went in a blink—no gift. On her birthday, I asked Mom, "Did you forget to give Nita her present?"

"I didn't get her nothing."

"You *have* to get her something," I urged. "You and Daddy gave me a dollhouse for my last birthday."

"I didn't get her nothing. Her godmother gives her birthday presents. She doesn't need another present."

"That's not right, Mom. That's not fair to her."

My heart sank feeling the inequity. Just a few months earlier, they had given me a birthday present that I had neither asked for nor wanted; but now, nothing for my sister. That was egregiously unfair. I thought back to the red tricycle I had to ride alone because they wouldn't get one for my sister. I knew Mom controlled what we had. *She acts like she has one daughter. It's not fair.*

When my sister's birthday rolled around after that, I didn't inquire about presents. I knew I couldn't change Mom, and I didn't want to hear that she didn't get her anything.

Twelve years later, I was surprised when Mom gave me a second birthday present: a hunter green, pull-on winter hat. How excited I was, as I really needed a hat for the winter. Wearing a puzzled expression, my college roommate commented, "That's what your mom got you for your birthday?"

"Yeah," I answered. "And it's perfect! It's just what I need."
How nice of Mom to think of me, I thought. Briefly, I hoped that
she would think of Nita for her upcoming birthday.

What was it about Mom's disparate behavior toward her
daughters when it came to buying us things? I don't believe
she loved either of us more than the other. In fact, I questioned
whether she was even *capable* of love, given her behavior.
I attributed her lopsided purchases to two assumptions:
1) her trying to be practical, though in a not-thought-out,
unbalanced way, perhaps thinking that anything she gave me
would eventually be handed down to my sister; and 2) her
possibly seeing herself as checking off a task as "done" on an
imaginary list of what mothers do—for example, buy your
child a present—without thinking to repeat that exact same
step for each child. She did the same with other events such as
birthdays, where she would celebrate her brother's birthday
that year but not her husband's or children's birthdays.

That Damn Nun! and Making Too Much Noise

1963

I had measles twice—first, standard measles from the rubeola virus, and later, German measles from the rubella virus, as I pieced together in my later years.

The first time was in April of the second grade. I showed Mom the dots on my stomach. I didn't feel sick, but I didn't know what to think about the dots. What are these? I'd already had chicken pox.

"Awk, you're not sick." Off to school I went.

As the morning progressed, I grew increasingly nervous with each new spot that appeared on my arms. I wished I had a mirror to look at the changes I was certain were taking place on my face. When I got home for lunch, red spots dusted my body from head to toe.

That, though, did not upset Mom. It was the phone call from school that did. The principal instructed Mom, "Keep your daughter home. Do not send a sick child to school."

That call ignited Mom's fury. "That damn nun! What's wrong with her? I did everyone a favor. That dumb, damn nun!" All afternoon she prayed her novena of curses.

Over the next two days, I became very ill. I was so sick that I was unaware I was moaning. I was sweating and rocking back and forth in bed. We didn't go to doctors. We didn't even own a thermometer. In fact, after Mom had my sister, she had not seen a doctor for fifteen years until she cut her hand on a glass and needed stitches. If my sister or I were sick, Mom would typically call our next-door neighbor, Emma, to look at us and tell her what to do. She didn't do that this time.

Instead, Mom invited Aunt Virge for a late lunch on a weekday. Virge was pregnant, expecting her third child in two months. She came with her two young children.

Before she arrived, Mom shooed me off my bed, threw on the bedspread, and told me to go to the other bedroom, Dad's bedroom. (Mom slept on the couch in the living room.)

"Don't come out!" she warned. "I'm not telling her you're home. I don't want her to know you're sick." At first, I didn't understand why I couldn't stay in my own bed when I was so sick. Then I realized the door to my shared bedroom was visible from the dining room. Mom must have thought that if that door were closed, it would be a dead giveaway that one of her kids was home. Aunt Virge might knock on it. But she wouldn't knock on Dad's bedroom door.

The problem was I was *too loud.* An air vent connected that bedroom to the living room that opened into the dining room where Mom's guests sat. With Aunt Virge at the dining room table, Mom opened the bedroom door. "Shoddop. Stop stinkasching! You're making too much noise! She can hear you, dammit. Shoddop." "Stinkasching" was Mom's term for "complaining." In Polish, it's *stękać.*

Because of my moaning, she burst in three times during Aunt Virge's visit to tell me to be quiet. From Mom's loud voice, Aunt Virge had to have known someone was home. Did she think Dad was home drunk and Mom was shushing him?

As I lay there, so sick, I thought about Aunt Virge and hoped neither she nor her children would get sick. When I was younger, I was at the house of a different aunt who was pregnant. When she sneezed so vigorously that we heard her from the other side of the house, and after her husband took her to the hospital, we learned she had lost her baby. Because I was so sick with what Mom said was measles, I wondered, *Could I cause Aunt Virge to lose her baby?* If I were in Mom's shoes, I would have canceled that lunch. I knew I would not have appreciated Aunt Virge inviting me to her home for a meal if she had a sick child at home. I wished Mom would not have invited her over. I asked myself, *Am I selfish for wanting her to have set aside a chance to entertain?*

You can't imagine my relief when Virge gave birth to a healthy third child.

Curiosity about Mom's Behavior

1963

What a strange experience it is to hear an adult checking up on your mom's behavior. That happened when I was age eight and visiting my Aunt Helen. As we sat on her back porch eating tuna fish salad sandwiches, she asked peculiar questions about her sister, like, "How does your mom act at home?" and "How does she treat your dad?" I thought that odd. I had never heard an adult ask such questions about another adult.

To all her questions, I was reluctant to say anything negative. I said things were okay. I didn't tell her about Mom's angry outbursts. For example, when Daddy gently told her in the car, "Sweetheart, don't toss the ice cream wrappers out the window," Mom forcefully tore the bodice of her dress down from her neckline to the waist, baring her slip and bra straps, and used a fistful of that fabric to try to wipe the outside window.

"Happy now?"

I did, however, tell Aunt Helen about how Mom would place washed silverware on the side of the kitchen table farthest from the silverware drawer and would throw the silverware across the table and across a narrow aisle between the table and drawer— a span of about three and a half feet—into the opened drawer, seeing how many landed.

To that, my aunt nodded her head knowingly, "Hmmm."

When I told Mom I had related that story to my aunt, let's just say she wasn't happy about it.

Mom usually didn't show her true self to people outside the home. One summer, she did. Neighborhood kids gathered regularly on our back porch. One day, Reggie, a neighbor boy, came over. He was three; I was around eight. Seeing him, Mom came outside and said in a digging tone toward me, "Reggie, watch Judie for me." She then went back indoors.

Reggie watched the door close. He then turned to me and commented, "Your mom is crazy."

I agreed, "I know."

Mesmerizing Immersion

1964

The bus dropped us off downtown on a summery day before the fourth grade. As Mom and I walked, the sunlight toasted our faces. Our destination was the Singer sewing store. *Why are we here? Mom doesn't sew,* I mused as we walked through the door.

Mom listened attentively to the lady showing her a sewing machine. "I'll take it," she said, and paid cash.

She bought a sewing machine? That puzzled me. *She doesn't know how to sew.*

Pointing at me, Mom then told the clerk, "I want to sign her up for sewing classes."

Flummoxed, I thought, *What? I didn't ask to take sewing classes. I don't even know if I want to learn to sew.*

The daughter of one of Mom's nieces was a few years older than me and sewed. After chatting with her niece, Mom often talked about what this girl made. I suspected that Mom wanted me to take classes so she could brag about what I made and would feel she was on the same footing as her niece.

"How old is she?" inquired the clerk.

"Eight years old."

Singer had an age requirement for their classes—nine or ten years old, I believe. I was too young.

But Mom had just bought one of Singer's more expensive models, so she persisted. The clerk excused herself and returned with the sewing instructor, Mrs. Hot.

"Are you the young lady who wants to learn to sew?" she inquired. I didn't know if I wanted to learn to sew. Mom and I had never discussed that before this lady's question, as we never talked about anything important.

Not wanting to make Mom look bad, I replied, "Yes."

"Okay, let's step over here," Mrs. Hot instructed, motioning to an empty spot near the front of the store. She asked me a few questions and paid close attention to my responses.

"All right, we can go back," she said motioning for me to return to where Mom and the store clerk were standing. To the clerk, she said, "It's okay. Sign her up."

The classes lasted six or eight weeks for a few hours each Saturday. Looking at me, Mrs. Hot said, "I will see you in class Saturday." I had no idea what I was getting into.

That Saturday, Dad and Mom drove me downtown, not saying where we were going. They didn't need to; I knew the sewing class was starting that day. As we pulled up in front of the Singer store, Mom said, "You're early." I hoped I would like it.

I loved the class. Sewing was a way for my sister and me to get clothes as Mom wouldn't buy them for us. A turquoise blue shift I made in class was a church dress, too nice to wear to school. That school year, Mom picked out a pattern for a jumper along with red plaid cotton fabric and selected which pattern version I would make for my sister and which for myself.

The next summer, Mom signed me up for another block of sewing classes.

That fall, the day after a parent-teacher conference, Mrs. Wade, my fifth-grade teacher, told the class that we would each give a short presentation on what we did that summer. "Judie," she continued, "is going to tell us how she made a three-piece suit, and she is going to wear that suit to class."

Well, that didn't take long, I thought. *Mom is already bragging about her daughter's sewing.*

From Mrs. Wade's inflection, it was obvious she didn't believe Mom. I could tell she didn't believe that suit even existed. The veiled tone of her voice resonated with "that is how you catch a rat."

Ah, she knew Mom from before this class, I figured. *She knows that Mom lies.*

Mrs. Wade's eyes widened in disbelief when I walked in on the due date wearing a green, three-piece suit of a skirt with a zipper, a sleeveless top with a back zipper, and a long-sleeve jacket. During my presentation, she nodded as I spoke, convinced that I had made the outfit.

My mother was indifferent to the end products of my craft. She never commented, favorably or negatively, on anything I made.

Surprisingly, my biggest critic was Aunt Virge. Whatever I made she examined meticulously, looking at the seams, examining the facings, and prying the hem away from the body of the item to judge the stitching. She was awe-struck when she saw I used one particular advanced technique. "What is this? Oh, it's an invisible zipper!" she exclaimed excitedly.

Aside from that, her comments were consistently harsh. I didn't agree with her assessments at all. On a few items, she remarked that the stitching on the seams was uneven. Thinking I had messed up, I checked the same piece and would find the stitching to be straight. My seams were always straight because I used a seam guide affixed to the machine, set to yield a perfect, standard, five-eighth-inch seam, and I checked each seam after working it before considering the item completed. I was my own critic and an unmerciful one, at that.

Aunt Virge's brutal critiques made me curious about her work. One day, I had the opportunity to examine a top she had made that she dropped off for her daughter who was at our house for the day. I ventured into my own critique. I looked at one side seam and oh, my goodness, did it swerve to the right and left! I looked at the other side seam and saw the same. I caught myself giggling. I couldn't believe the poor workmanship. She did not use a seam guide. It was the worst-made item I had ever seen. She had no facings on the neck, and her stitching around the neckline and armholes was atrocious. The stitching wavered back and forth from the edge like a squirrel had charted the course of the needle. From that, I learned that when people criticize your work, it doesn't mean they themselves are masters of that art.

Long before sewing, because neither parent commented about anything I did—when I brought home my report card, when my clown artwork appeared on the 1960s children's TV show *The Land of Ziggy Zoggo,* when I cleaned my shared room, when I won an award or received other recognition—I never felt that I had to meet anyone's expectation of me. It was natural for Mom to criticize my hair or how I looked, and so I never felt a need to try to please her.

That absence of expectations from others was invaluable. It bestowed on me a sense that I set my own expectations of myself and was accountable solely to myself. It relieved me of any need to seek validation from others. As a result, any project I undertook, I pursued with a sense of wanting to do the best I could, of mastering whatever I took on. I became intrinsically motivated. Decades before this writing, I cast it as perfectionism. But in looking back, I see it was not about getting it "perfect." It was about doing my very best. In the business world, when I was older, if I playfully put together a corporate presentation to be given to executive management, rehearsed it only once, and felt I had achieved what I wanted, that was it for the project. I wouldn't gnaw it over and over.

In addition to being an outlet for creativity, what I loved about sewing was how it diverted my attention away from the everyday discordance in my house. It opened a world of creativity for me where I felt like my physical self, my soul, and a creative aspect of me all melded together into a giant ripple of lusciously vibrant color riding on a magnificent, invisible wave of energy. Working on an art project, delving into schoolwork, or untangling a math problem immersed me in the same experience. For others, it may be competing on the school swim team, playing basketball, or mastering a piano concerto.

Over the years, I honed this sewing skill to professional status, though I never worked in the tailoring art. As a child, I explored ways to change up patterns to make them more challenging and interesting. Up through grade eight, Mom restricted what I could make for my sister and me. In grade eight, thanks to Aunt Virge's provision of gray wool fabric, I made a jumper from a pattern Mom gave me. It was a women's size twelve that I adjusted to fit my petite, skinny, adolescent body of less than eighty-five pounds.

In high school, I reveled in the challenge of shortening a cousin's communion dress by separating the bodice from the skirt at the waistband, so its ornate lace bottom edge and the hem of the underskirt remained untouched. In my junior year of high school, I crafted a floor-length winter cape from a *Vogue* pattern. I also made my high school graduation dress, and in grad school, almost all my clothes.

My love of this immersion into creativity unfolded into the making of my wedding dress from two designer patterns—a long evening gown topped with a short, cropped jacket with mitered sleeves, a shawl collar, and pearl buttons—and later a few business suits, drapes for the living room and several bedrooms, and a self-designed duvet with flange pillows, all of designer fabric. Though I had to shelve this interest once my professional career took off, for the few suits I made, I spent much more on fabric than I would have had I simply purchased high-end business attire.

I feel gratitude for my mom persisting in getting me into that six- or eight-week course when I didn't meet the age requirement. That was a gift I treasured throughout my life. And it was this gift that helped me channel my focus and attention into a creative, productive stream, away from the rein of toxic drama that permeated my childhood home.

The Circus

1965

An entirely different experience colored the second time I had measles.

It was late spring of the fourth grade. I was age nine. This time, I did not feel systemically ill, though I was speckled in dots. Mom, however, summoned our neighbor Emma, who brought her thermometer. She told Mom I needed to go to the doctor right away. She offered to drive us. Mom phoned the office to say we were on our way.

Because Emma was waiting for us, Mom wouldn't let me change. I didn't have pajamas or a robe. So, to the doctor's office, I wore the mismatched clothing I had slept in. Emma parked her car and went in with us.

The elevator to the doctor's office was inside a bank building. We walked into the bank, Mom in worn-down loafers and an old, flowered, cotton housedress contrasting against her olive skin and her pitch black, naturally tight-curled hair framing her dark brown eyes; me—fair-skinned, blond, and very skinny—painted head to toe with red dots, wearing mismatched bedclothes; and Emma, in a shirt and slacks, blending in with everyone else.

Mom loved any opportunity to project her voice—a true gift that ensured she could be heard a hundred feet away without over-exerting her larynx. Her big-boned frame with perfect posture confidently commandeered the lobby. Mom's thunderous voice shattered the silence: "Stay back! Stay back! Measles! Measles! Coming through! Stay back!" Her words synced with exaggerated hand movements as she gestured like a wild orchestra conductor. People glanced from her to me to Emma. If she did that today, she would likely be arrested after the first two syllables, taken as a bank robber.

A sparse group of people near the elevator dispersed quickly, eyeing Mom. I questioned why Mom was heedlessly drawing attention to us. At the elevator bank, Emma looked at her as if she were a caveman unleashed into the twentieth century.

The doctor diagnosed me with German measles. Mom told him I had already had measles. He explained that German measles is caused by the rubella virus, which is different from the rubeola virus that is responsible for standard measles. He said people rarely get measles twice, but it is possible because they are caused by two different bugs.

Afterward, I wrestled with why we treated the situation as an emergency. It was only measles. I had been sicker in the past and each time I had come through okay without medical intervention. I realized, too, we could have walked in and discreetly asked people near the elevator to clear away. That would have been as effective in promoting the same level of safety for those inside the bank. Mom's approach, however, guaranteed we did not go unnoticed.

In the days following that scenario, I asked myself which was worse: the measles or the circus we put on in the bank lobby. My conclusion: the circus. I didn't like the expressions on people's faces as they gawped at Mom that day.

Later that fall or the next, my sister had extreme pain on her right side. A few years earlier, a classmate of hers had landed in the hospital for months following a ruptured appendix. I was concerned. I told Mom she needed to call the doctor.

"No," she said.

When she went outdoors to hang clothes, I called the doctor's number listed on a cardboard sheet kept by our rotary-dial phone. Explaining the situation to the nurse, I described the pain and its location and expressed my concern. The doctor—keep in mind this was decades ago—called me back and said to monitor the pain. If it got worse, I was to tell my mom to take action.

It turned out my sister was okay, but the incongruence of Mom's actions was disconcerting. She had ignored my serious sickness, jumped at a neighbor's instructions when I was not lethargic with illness, and ignored what could have been a ruptured appendix. I wished Aunt Virge had a say when we were not feeling well. She would know what to do.

Strategically Folded Arms

1965

"I'm going to my sister's. I need peace," said Dad, trying to calm down from Mom's belligerence and fusillades of name-calling. Dad was upset; it was viscerally palpable.

"I'll go with you, Daddy," I piped up, climbing into the Studebaker.

Interrupting the car door from closing, Mom yelled at me. "Get out of the car." She then softened. "Come here. I want to show you something," she said, curling her index finger for me to step out of the car.

As I stood before her, she tore off my summer top, ripping it. Holding the crumpled mass in her hand, she uttered with glee, "Okay. Now you can go. I hope Faye's boys are home!"

I was bare-chested and nine years old. And we were going to see my aunt who had five boys, all a few years older than me.

On our way there, Dad drove most of the way in silence. Finally, he said, "Mom's crazy. She's really crazy." That was the term we used. We were not educated to know otherwise.

"Daddy, I wish you would leave her. I will go with you," I said.

"I can't, sweetheart," he responded.

Because Dad was visibly upset, I didn't probe and didn't ask for his shirt.

At my aunt's house, we walked in through the unlocked backdoor, then up the steps to the kitchen. That's what everyone did when visiting Aunt Faye.

Wiping off the kitchen table, she smiled when she saw us. "Hi, Martin and Judie. Come in. Have a seat," she said, motioning to the kitchen table. Her eyes lingered a few seconds on my bare chest as if she were wondering why I wasn't wearing a top. I always wore a top, and it wasn't that hot outside. From the inquiring expression on her face, it felt like she sensed something was amiss but didn't ask.

My aunt didn't offer me something to wear. Nor did I ask for a top. I didn't have it in me to ask for something to cover myself.

We took a seat at the kitchen table. Not too long into our visit, one of her sons entered the kitchen. Seeing us, he joined us. I strategically folded my arms across my chest to cover myself. I was on pins and needles. He was a teenager. Engrossed in their conversation, the adults were oblivious to his eyes ogling my hands.

I then thought, *Why should I be embarrassed that he will see something? He has what I have. I have nothing to be ashamed of. I look like a boy.* At that, I dropped my hands, sat up straight, and held my head high, mustering every iota of confidence I could, as I infiltrated the adults' conversation with a question. *Let him look*, I thought. *There's nothing here he hasn't seen.*

Baring me of my clothes and thrusting me to be seen, partially naked, by others seemed to infuse Mom with a sense of superiority. It was the same sense of power she emanated when she told bald lies about someone, sometimes right in front of that individual. The kind of lies that were constructed so that if the person tried to defend themself, they—not she—would come across as lying. She seemed to equate her words and actions that compromised the reputation of others with bringing shame to that person. That was how she wielded power. To Mom, diminishing others was gamesmanship, and she was the master.

The following summer, I confronted Mom about her behavior. "Sometimes you do and say hurtful things to me. For example, you call me dumb or ugly or lie to others about me or tear off my clothes. Why do you do that?"

"Awk. You're too sensitive. Laugh it off," she fended off my question.

"I don't want you to treat me like that anymore. See me as Aunt Katy or as one of your nieces. I want you to treat me like you treat them, with respect."

"Oh, just laugh it off."

I realized she was not going to change.

Annoying, but Effective

1965

Although Mom usually didn't take me to see doctors when I was sick, I did see an ophthalmologist. My fourth-grade teacher, Mrs. James, told Mom she thought I couldn't see the blackboard. "You need to get Judie's eyes checked."

Getting that directive from a teacher was like an order to my mom. She followed through without question. She got a doctor's name from Aunt Virge, whom she secretly respected for her wisdom, and took me for what became a yearly exam.

Mom and I took taxis to and from the eye doctor. One wintry day after a late afternoon visit, we could not get a taxi. Not one taxi had come by. We started walking with hopes of flagging one down as it was already dark outside besides being freezing cold. Snow packed into the holes in my boots, melting into icy pools of water.

We made it to a furniture store that was still open and stepped inside to warm up. Instead of standing by the door, Mom and I meandered through the store. This was a fine furniture store, one we would typically not enter, where everything was expensive. By age nine, I understood the value of money and the cost of things. Seeing how the few customers there were dressed, I saw we clearly did not fit in.

Near the back of the store, a Queen Anne sofa caught Mom's eye, with its intricate wood surrounding a floral tapestry fabric. She stood before it for a while, prompting the attention of a salesman dressed in a suit. He started a conversation with Mom about sofas.

Mom had a perception of how wealthy society women conducted themselves, and that day she enacted that persona. When she wanted to be perceived as a society lady—someone smart and wealthy whom she termed a *pani* (Polish for "lady")—she would hold her lips pursed as if she were about to kiss someone. Yes, it looked strange, and I told her that many times. I told her it looks like she had just sucked on a sour lemon, but that did not convince her to relinquish the behavior. What does a little kid know?

Another element of her impression of a society lady included answering yes to questions with a long, drawn-out "ahhh-hhaaa," followed by quickly reshaping her lips into their pursed formation.

With the salesman, she combined the pursed lips with the "ahhh-hhaaa" to his questions.

When he walked away, she commented on the high cost of that sofa. I told her, "He thinks you're going to buy it." I don't recall the price, but I do know it was very expensive, something we could not afford. "No, he doesn't think that," she remarked.

Sure enough, he showed up with a paper and pen and wanted her signature to lock in a sale. I could feel Mom's anxiety. She didn't know what to do. Beneath her furrowed brow, her eyes darted back and forth between the salesman and the sofa. I felt I had to do something.

"Mom, that's not going to go with the drapes. It will look out of place," I said.

Mom was silent.

"It goes with everything," countered the salesman. I could tell he was eager for this sale, if only he could get this kid to be quiet.

"No, it's not going to go with the drapes. The sofa has large flowers, and that will clash with the pattern in the drapes. It's not going to look good." I was proud of what I had learned about fabric since I started sewing the year before.

Mom was silent.

"No, the sofa will look great. It goes with everything," he reiterated, this time more adamantly.

"No, it's not. How do you know? You haven't seen the drapes or the colors in the room. Mom, why don't we go, and you can look at the drapes and come back if you think it'll go."

The salesman was ready to whomp me. I could see it on his face and feel it in my stomach.

"Yeah. Let's go," said Mom, pursing her lips.

Outside, she was silent. I could feel her disappointment about the sofa. She liked it. It was unusual for her to be quiet. Loud and brazen were her signature.

"Mom, did you want the sofa? Did I do anything wrong in there?"

"No," she said. "Let's find a taxi. It's cold."

She seemed relieved that I had intervened. I could tell she didn't know how to extricate herself from the well-dressed, glib salesman without calling attention to her status as a blue-collar wife without money. I could feel her relax from being pressed into a purchase she wanted but could not afford.

Mom did not spend outside her means. My parents lived paycheck to paycheck. Until a decade later, they had neither a savings nor a checking account. So, if she didn't have the money available at the time, that purchase was not going to happen.

That late afternoon, I felt I had done a good thing: I had rescued Mom.

Bunnies

1965

It was a surprise from Dad and Uncle Joe: A large metal cage sat beneath the magnolia tree in our backyard. It was there when I returned from a friend's house. The cage was on the side of the tree that faced the alley, opposite the trench Mom had dug around the front of the tree for decomposing watermelon rinds, cantaloupe seeds and shells, and coffee grounds that sat atop grass clipping, from time to time prompting Rick next door to admonish Mom that the foodstuff would draw rats into the neighborhood, only to nettle him because Mom ignored him.

Peering through the cage's wired walls were the inquisitive eyes of two rabbits: one for my sister, and the other for me.

Earlier that summer, Dad and Uncle Joe had watched my sister and me holding Uncle Joe's rabbits at his farm. While that was kind of them to think of us, no one asked if I wanted a pet rabbit. When I saw the cage, I immediately knew I would be the one taking care of the rabbits and cleaning out their cage, not Dad or my sister. I know it sounds ungrateful, but I didn't want pet rabbits or the responsibility for their care. Holding one was quite different from being responsible for one.

My dad and uncle looked so happy. I couldn't tell them I didn't appreciate their gift. So, I went with the flow and named my bunny Regina, which means "queen."

These were outdoor rabbits. In their cage, they endured several brutal rainstorms, brilliant flashes of lightning, and the piercing roar of thunder. They had to be frightened. The wicked storms reminded me of the potential peril posed by being beneath a tree or in contact with metal during lightning. Fortunately, none of my concerns materialized.

About once a week, my parents allowed Regina and her sibling to romp freely in the yard as long as they did not veer onto our neighbors' property. Mom wanted the rabbits caged at all times, though Dad took a more liberal view and said it was good for us kids to interact with these beautiful furry creatures. However, because my contact with Regina was in infrequent holding or in talking to her, separated by metal caging, I never experienced her as a pet. I suspected she wouldn't be with us long. She was a responsibility that I cared about. I found I didn't mind cleaning the cage, which I did with meticulous care, removing every speck of poop and debris. After reading that rabbits eat their droppings, called cecotropes, I made sure to clean the cage more frequently as I didn't favor the idea of them consuming their own poop.

By late summer, after an unanticipated litter, we had a fluffle.

Several times I asked, "What will we do with the rabbits when the weather turns cold?" No one would answer my question.

An answer came in late summer before school started. It was midweek when I came home from playing at a friend's house. The cage was dismantled, and the rabbits were gone. *Where did they go?*

Bizarrely, Uncle Joe was also over in the middle of the week. Something was up.

No sooner had I gotten home than we sat down to dinner. Another strange occurrence: when we had Uncle Joe over for dinner, Dad always fried T-bone steaks in butter with onions. But that was not on tonight's menu. Instead, it was peculiar-looking meat mounded on two platters in the middle of the table.

Mom never sat down during meals. I recall her sitting only three times for a family meal. She'd hover around the table, gliding from one person to the next, pointing to heaping dishes of food atop the table. This meal was no different.

Mom pointed to the mysterious meat, saying, "Take a nice piece."

I looked at her, "Are these our rabbits?"

"Be quiet and eat your food."

"Are they?"

"Shoddop and eat your food."

Her response was telling. Yes, for dinner, Mom was serving us Regina and her family. I skipped the meat that evening and the next few nights. From the beginning, I knew the bunnies were not going to be our pets forever. Dinner proved my instinct correct.

You Stink!

1962–1967

When I was still little, I asked neighborhood girlfriends, who visited on Saturday evenings before going out with their parents, if their pretty scent was perfume. They said it was soap; they had just taken a bath. I begged Mom to let me take a bath. Each time, she responded, "No." Mom never took a bath or shower. She must have washed herself in the sink. Dad showered at work.

"You stink!" Arlene Roba told me. I was in the second grade. "You have to change your underpants." No one taught me to change my underpants regularly. Hearing this, Mom was angry. Not at Arlene, nor at me. Now she had to buy more underpants and wash them. After that, I changed my underpants but was still not allowed to bathe.

When we went to a wedding, dinner with Mom's brother, or a family event at an aunt's house, our luxury was soaking our feet in a dish pan filled with hot, soapy water. I would carefully carry the filled plastic pan into my shared bedroom and soak my feet for ten to fifteen minutes. For social events, Mom always said, "Never go out with dirty feet." But that was where hygiene stopped.

How I yearned for a bath.

In the sixth grade, safely ensconced in a locked bathroom, my turning on the tub water prompted Mom to pound on the door.

"Shut that water off! You can't take a bath! That's *my* water! I need it to wash clothes tomorrow. I'm shutting the water off to the house."

In the summers leading into grades six through eight, when Uncle Al and Mary Keefe took my sister and me to a nice restaurant for dinner, besides soaking my feet, I cleaned myself on the back porch. My system involved rubbing dirt off my forearms and upper arms with my hands, and then using Mom's handheld mirror to check for any remaining dirt, or asking Mom to spot-check me.

My wish for a bath came true one summer when Mary Keefe took my sister and me overnight to a Howard Johnson hotel to use the pool. That night, Mary told me to take a bath before going to bed. I was thrilled. Submerged in the warm water, I realized I didn't know what to do. *How do you take a bath? What do you do first?* Here I was, eleven years old, and I didn't know how to take a bath. I figured it out, but that didn't change things at home.

In the seventh grade, my teacher, Mrs. Comfort, stood next to me one day in history class. She paused and stood there quietly for what seemed like an inordinately long time. She then returned to the front of the room and stopped history class. She began talking about teenagers' bodies: "When you become a teenager, your body changes and starts to smell. You need to bathe." I knew she was referring to me. I had not told anyone that I was not allowed to bathe.

After Mrs. Comfort's talk on hygiene, I started washing myself in the bathroom sink.

When I reached high school, I did not want to stink. One day before the semester started, I proclaimed to Mom that I would be taking showers. Over her protests, Dad supported me. He related that his coworkers said their girls take showers. After that, Mom was all right with me bathing. She stopped yelling and didn't turn off the water to the house.

The Hairdresser

1965

Before the fourth grade, though I knew who my relatives were and saw them occasionally at family events, I didn't know them personally to any great extent, except for Aunt Virge. The fourth grade and up was when my aunts and uncles stepped into my life in a bigger way, taking my sister and me out for day trips, to local events, or for lunch or dinner.

The summer before the fifth grade I started spending an occasional weekend with Aunt Mary, Mom's sister, who lived in Chicago. Others in Mom's family called her Marie—her name—but in our house, she was known as Mary. She was tall and willowy like a bamboo plant, her subtle sway foretelling her relaxed, easy-going, peaceful nature. A former hairdresser, Aunt Mary had wavy black hair that swooped down across one side of her forehead, feckly caressing her eyebrow before curling back to the side of her high cheekbone. As she spoke with me, she would tilt her head to one side. Mom's sisters called her eccentric.

At age nine, I would take the South Shore train to Chicago by myself, and Aunt Mary would meet me on the ramp of the Randolph Street train station. She always wore a stylishly angled hat, the kind that hugged the head. After navigating through the mélange of smells wafting through the station—fried foods, baked chicken, hotdogs, bakery scents—we would take a bus to her home where we talked and read and laughed until she would realize it was 11:30 p.m. and we still had not had dinner.

Then, using a pressure cooker, within a matter of twenty minutes, she would magically cobble together the most mouth-watering *golabki*—Polish stuffed green peppers with tomato sauce. They were as good as Mom's, but I would never dream of telling Mom that. During those visits, because my aunt was a wellspring of knowledge, I learned so much about nutrition and health.

I memorized Aunt Mary's phone number and sneaked a phone call to her when Mom was outdoors. They were short chats. I loved hearing her voice. What I didn't foresee was that these calls would appear on a phone bill, where Mom discovered them. After that, I waited until Aunt Mary called our home. That was infrequent. Sometimes when an aunt called, I would hear Mom say, "They're not home," referring to my sister and me. She blocked my contact with certain aunts and later with Mary Keefe.

As I got older, if someone telephoned me or if I called anyone from home, Mom stood four to five feet from the phone, watching and listening in to my calls. She listened to my end of the conversation with *everyone*. No privacy. If I went out and came back in the afternoon, she would inquire, "Did you see Mary Keefe?" Anger would consume her if I truthfully answered yes. I had to hide my visits with Mary Keefe from Mom, along with my joy in talking with Aunt Mary.

Math, Butterflies, and Bees

1967–1968

I loved math. In the summers leading into the seventh and eighth grades, I loved going through the math books for the oncoming year. I prepared a schedule and worked out the problems at the end of each chapter, leaving the periodic *challengers* to savor during class. I would figure out the answers on old newspapers but didn't save them so I could enjoy doing the math problems during the year.

In those summers, I also combed through Dad's parsley plants. They grew in a flower bed at the back of our property in front of our one-car garage, beneath spectacular, bright-colored blossoms of Dad's three-foot-tall dahlia plants.

On checking the parsley plants' stems and leaves, I noticed tiny, almost imperceptible dots. The first time I saw them, I was convinced they were eggs of an insect. I didn't know which insect, but I was determined to find out. I watched and wrote up what I saw happening with the black dots within large pickle jars Mom gave me to house the leaves and stems that I broke off. With fascination, I watched as larvae sprung from the eggs and grew into caterpillars, each of which, when done growing, structured a chrysalis about itself. When a chrysalis began throttling and breaking down, I marveled at the mysterious, beautiful black butterfly that emerged. Some had a blue iridescence. From my visits to the library, I found they were eastern black swallowtail butterflies. I always released these graceful, ethereal beings to fly away freely into the world.

In those summers, also using a large pickle jar, I captured huge, furry, black and yellow bumblebees that hovered over Mom's succulent stonecrop plants along the north side of the house. I wanted to observe them up close. After examining them briefly, I let them fly away, free and unharmed. They never stung me. Had I the respect back then that I have today for bees, I would never have dreamed of capturing any, even for observation.

Immersion in Tranquility

1967

The scientific literature abounds about the positive effect of tranquility on our bodies and minds. I experienced its effects firsthand the summer before seventh grade. My spa-like experience was a two-week driving vacation with Uncle Al, Mary Keefe, and my sister to Georgia, Florida, and Louisiana. Much of our trip was spent in silence, which was normal, as we tended not to chat. The quiet, relaxed vibe suffused through the car and our interactions, flowing into my being, relaxing my mind and body, and feeding it with intangible nutrients that were absent from my home but that I unknowingly craved.

But before the trip was anything but tranquil. To help ready us for the trip, Aunt Virge paid for swimming classes at a local high school for my sister and me.

I was eleven. I had outgrown my swimsuit and kept asking Mom for a new swimsuit. Although class was starting the next day, I still didn't have a swimsuit that fit. That afternoon, Mom tasked her bachelor brother, Uncle Al, to take me downtown to Minus department store to buy me a swimsuit on his lunch hour. She gave him money for it.

Only one swimsuit in my size hung on the rack. It was pink and thin across the front. I was a preteen with tiny pubescent breasts. With alarm, I examined the thin fabric and knew my nipples would show through. The clerk asked, "Why don't you try this on?"

I didn't want to because I knew how the front would look. I didn't know how to decline as I needed a swimsuit and that was the only one close to my size. *How do I say no?* When I wiggled my arms into the straps, sure enough, there they were. Staring back at me in the mirror were a pair of huge reddish rings, each ring surrounding a tiny bump, each looking markedly like a flying saucer.

"Do you like the swimsuit?" the clerk asked through the curtain.

"No."

"Why not? I think you look nice in it," she said, stepping into the room. "Why don't you go show your uncle and see what he says?"

Could she not see my nipples showing through the thin fabric? I couldn't let my uncle see my nipples! "No, I will take it." I gave in because I needed a swimsuit and this was my only opportunity to get one. More importantly, I did not want to make a fuss and have my uncle see my nipples.

I knew I would be mortified when the suit got wet and my nipples looked bare through the thin fabric. *That, I will deal with when the time comes,* I told myself.

Who picked out this fabric for a swimsuit pattern? I wondered. I had been sewing since age eight and even I knew that was the wrong fabric to use.

I wished Mom would have gone with me. For a few weeks, I had been telling her I needed a new swimsuit. This did not just spring up on her. If she had been with me, I would have shown her how the nipples showed through. I would have asked if we could go to another store.

As far as Mom was concerned, the gradual molding of a girl's body into a preteen contour was unremarkable. Wrapped in her own thoughts, she was oblivious to how self-conscious preteen girls could be about changes in their bodies. As the clothes she bought for my sister and me were always in much larger sizes so we could grow into them, it's no surprise my first bra was three band sizes and three cup sizes too large. At age fourteen, I was a stick-skinny kid weighing less than eighty-five pounds, and Mom gave me a 36C bra. Even decades later, I never did grow into that size. For Mom to anticipate any connection in a preteen girl's mind between swimsuits and nipples would have required an unfathomable shift in thinking.

In swim class, I was mortified each time I had to get out of the water. Yep! When I looked down, those two flying saucers were beaming out for everyone to see. I would drop down so the water line hovered just above them. Out of the water, I'd walk around with my arms strategically folded across my chest and move my hands up and down the opposite upper arm, making it look like I was trying to keep warm.

On that two-week vacation with Uncle Al and Mary Keefe, I took my old, tight, too-small swimsuit. At least I didn't look risqué, or so I thought. No tiny spaceships on my chest!

We had a glorious time. We strolled through greenery, saw monkeys and birds in Florida's Monkey Island and Busch

Gardens, took a glass-bottomed boat ride, watched crocodiles near the Keys, strolled down Bourbon Street in New Orleans during its active hours, and had our first taste of oysters. We wasted no time on the road; my uncle clipped along at ninety miles an hour on the expressway.

When we arrived in Miami, Mary Keefe assessed the dresses we had brought for going out to nice dinners. Mine was a hand-me-down from a cousin. It was too big, hanging on my skinny frame to dangle a few inches above my ankles. I don't recall what my sister's dress looked like, but it was most likely a hand-me-down from me.

Seeing our dresses, Mary took us both to a department store and bought us dresses that fit.

In New Orleans, before taking us to a fine dining restaurant for a *prix fixe* dinner, Mary Keefe gave us lessons on how to eat soup: "You scoop the spoon away from you." This classy way of eating soup was much slower than drinking the last spoonfuls from the bowl as we did at home. I assumed she didn't want to be embarrassed by us.

In Atlanta, Mary Keefe showed me how to wash my face and care for my skin. Acne had started developing on the sides of my face near my ears, perhaps from dirty hair. To counteract that, on the trip and most times that Mary Keefe saw me, she dabbed cologne on my cheeks so the alcohol could help dry up the pimples.

The two weeks flew by in a blink. Before closing the trunk on our return trip home, I packed up a collection of shells that I had carefully curated from the beach.

When my uncle pulled up in front of my parents' home, I felt like a new person—relaxed and changed, with a new dress, updated table manners, and skin care instructions. Being immersed for two weeks in a calm environment replenished my body inside and out. Its effect was palpable, especially on my nervous system. I wondered if that was how it felt to live in a tranquil environment.

Snowball Cookies: A Trigger

1968

Sophisticated and polished with a touch of bohemian, Aunt Virge introduced me to an entirely new world: theatre and the arts. When acting at the community theater, she would ask my sister and me in our preteen years to run the refreshment table and greet attendees upon their arrival. How I enjoyed watching the plays, particularly those where Virge had the lead role—this tall, dramatic, confident woman with her strong, low voice captivating the audience. She also introduced me to the Art Institute of Chicago, one of my favorite places that I also visited with Uncle Al and Mary Keefe, who further expanded our world by taking us to the ballet to see *The Nutcracker* at Christmastime.

In the wintry months, I loved spending a day with Aunt Virge and her family. I saw them a few times a year, and each time was a splash of positive, revitalizing energy into my system. Aunt Virge made the experience so much fun. We talked, played games, did artwork, or made cookies. It was at her home that I first tasted radishes, broccoli, cauliflower, olives, lettuce, and green leafy salads. In our home, we enjoyed the Polish version of salads—cucumbers with onions and sour cream. At Aunt Virge's, one Sunday afternoon when I was twelve, we made pecan snowball cookies from hand-shelled pecans. I memorialized my newly discovered love for these treats in a recipe that I took home.

Aunt Virge's home had the ingredients that were missing from my house: peace and harmony permeated the atmosphere at her home, along with a noticeable respect she held for her husband. The ambience was like a cocoon that enveloped me in its folds, letting me be me and welcoming everyone present to be who they truly were within. This was not a place of war-zone mentality. Even when Virge expressed an opinion, she did so with dignity and respect for the listener. No derision. No shouting. No swords of contempt slashing open the spirit of another. Solely an expression of a thought. I took that in.

My home was like that only when we had people over. Otherwise, its essence was bereft of peace.

To surprise Mom, one Sunday that spring when she was at a church function, I made pecan snowball cookies. I was twelve. I timed it so the cookies were cooling and our small kitchen was cleaned when Mom got home, except for a baking sheet and wire racks adorned with the yummy treats. I thought she'd be delighted. Instead, rage colored her face as she entered the kitchen. Too late, I recalled that she had heard me talk about these cookies and knew I got the recipe from Aunt Virge. *Ugh!*

Grabbing a cup (we didn't use glasses at home), she smashed the cookies with ferocity, working quickly, forcing the cup's bottom against the cookie sheet, and cursing along the way. Midway through, she tossed the cup aside and used her fist, smashing the cookies on the cookie sheet into a heap of crumbles after discovering that was faster. Pounding on the wire racks, she sent crumbled cookies flying around the kitchen. After switching to her fist, not one word did she utter as she worked through the cookies.

"What are you doing?" I implored. "I made these for you and our family!" I raised my voice to grab her attention. I was in tears, shaken by her violent reaction to my making cookies. But she was so entranced in destroying the cookies that she didn't hear me. Whatever was going on in her mind muted my appeals.

For a moment I stood there, watching her furiously smashing my handiwork. I felt so sorry for her. She was really sick. What had set her off? Was it that I used her kitchen? Did she feel threatened? Did she now feel that she had to worry about competition in baking, an area where she deemed herself a master? Was it that she knew I had used Virge's snowball cookie recipe? Or did she just have a fit where, from time to time, she got violent for no reason? Whatever was going through her mind was not healthy for her or anyone in our family.

Later that week, I approached her privately and delicately suggested she talk with someone. She needed help. That did not go well. It turned into her shouting and condemning me.

Next, I talked with my dad. He agreed, "Yes, Mom's crazy."

"It's not right how she treats you, Daddy. She's always shouting at you and shoving you. That's not right. I worry about you each time your head smacks against the wall. She could kill you!"

Dad now drank on the weekends. Mom controlled the money in the house. Dad cashed his check and gave her the money to run the house. Mom would now agitate Dad to the point that he would ask her for money for booze. After she gave it to him, as he approached the front door to leave, Mom, with her robust strength, would shove him, throwing him off balance as he struggled, toppling backwards, landing on the sofa across the room with a loud crack as the back of his head smacked the plaster wall.

"You should leave her. I wish you would. I'll go with you. You will be happier. We will both be happier without her," I pleaded. "She doesn't want help. We can't go on like this."

He didn't want to do that: "She is my wife. I promised to take care of her. I am going to stay with her. When I married, I married 'for better or for worse.' I promised her that."

I felt sad. What I saw was him experiencing only the "for worse" part of his promise. I could feel that he knew that too but accepted it stoically. He was a man who did what he believed was the right thing even when, deep down, he knew it was the wrong thing for himself. The next five years took an egregious toll on Dad.

From Dad's decision, I knew I had to accept the violence and craziness within our home. No one outside our home knew what was going on, or so I thought at that point. I didn't share that with anyone. In retrospect, I wish I would have told someone—a school counselor, a teacher, anyone outside the family. If I could turn back the clock, I would.

What, then, to make of my newly discovered joy of baking? Mom's cookie-smashing fit was not going to quash that. That summer, Mom always had a collection of cake mixes around, along with a few cans of icing, a new entry into the marketplace. When she would be out for the afternoon, I would make a two-layered cake from a box of cake mix and frost it as nicely as I could with canned icing. Without cutting into the cake, I would gift it to our next-door neighbors, Rick and Irma, and ask them to please not say anything to Mom about it. I believe they understood why. Over that summer, three cakes sailed over to Rick and Irma's house. After each creative venture, I extinguished all traces of my even having been in the kitchen: I'd scour the kitchen, open the windows, run the fan, and race around the house with a can of Lysol spray to dissipate the baking aroma. Those extra steps ended Mom's apoplectic fits of rage over my baking indulgence.

Shhh . . . Siblings' Secret

1968

On weekdays, our phone got a workout. A lifeline to the outside world, it was in near-constant use, by either Mom calling her family or them calling her. What I loved was answering and feeling that connection with people outside my home. One call stands out. I was twelve years old.

The caller was Mom's best and closest friend, her sister Katy. "Hi. Is this Judie?"

"Yes. Hi, Auntie Katy," I answered, recognizing her voice. "How are you?"

"I'm fine. Is your mom home?" she asked, as she always did when I answered.

"No, she's outside hanging clothes."

"Good. I was hoping you would be the one to answer. I want to talk to you," she said.

She wants to have a conversation with me? That was odd. I seldom saw Katy or most of Mom's other five sisters as they either had their own large families and I was the age of their grandchildren, which was the case with Katy, or they weren't friends with Mom. When I did see Katy, she never showed an interest in speaking with me one-on-one. In my few visits to her home, she and Mom chatted in the kitchen as she treated me to a slice of her delicious carrot cake, and then they would send me out to her front porch swing so they could talk more.

"It's about your mom," she continued. "You're getting older. You should know that your mom is crazy. I want you to know that. You should go out with your dad from time to time. Get him out of the house, away from her. It's not good that he's with her all the time."

Wow! Because of her close bond with Mom, her comment felt like a breach of their friendship. My unspoken response was, *You're just now discovering that? I knew that when I was two.* That was the only meaningful conversation I had with Aunt Katy. We never again discussed Mom's mental state.

That same summer, another time I answered the phone, it was Mom's sister Bertha, who also had grandchildren my age. "I'm glad your mom is not home," she said. "I called to talk with you."

Outside of exchanging pleasantries, Aunt Bertha had not talked with me, one-on-one, for more than ten years, since the day my sister was born. I was almost seventeen months old then. That morning Auntie Bertha was the only one at our house when I woke up. The phone rang and after that call, she told me the good news that I had a baby sister. She also taught me about hygiene: when I was going to use the potty-pot, she said, "Today you can use the big toilet" and sat me on the toilet in the bathroom, holding me securely. She then taught me good bathroom hygiene habits. I always credited her with teaching me that.

Now, after all these years and all our ultra-brief chats when I'd answer the phone, Aunt Bertha wanted to *talk* with me? It felt important.

"I've been wanting to talk to you, but your mom is always home." She went on, "There's something I want to tell you: your mom is crazy. You need to know that. Okay?"

Over the next four years, until I was age sixteen, three more of my mom's siblings and two of their spouses sought me out, privately, to inform me about Mom's mental state.

Uncle Al and Mary Keefe were both direct: "Your mom is crazy."

Uncle Lou expressed the same sentiment: "Your mom is sick. She's not all there."

Aunt Virge was the most sensitive: "Your mother is mentally not well" with an emphasis on the "not well."

The last to come forward was Sister Ann, my mom's sister who was a nun. She was discreet: "Your mom needs help; she's not well."

Uncle Lou was the only one who mentioned Mom's mental illness more than once after she reached eighty. Apart from him, none of these seven relatives ever again openly discussed Mom's mental state, asked me about it, or even referred to it. It was a secret, shared and protected among her siblings. I shared it with no one.

Knowing that others knew Mom was *off*—even though they kept that information hushed and tightly under wraps, solely amongst themselves—helped me enormously to cope with Mom's behavior. It brought me comfort, support, and a sense of connection to a small band of family, the guardians of a secret.

Unfortunately, back then, around the late '60s to early '70s, mental illness was a societal taboo. People did not discuss any aspect of it, and treatment options were limited or reserved for those wealthy and open-minded enough to seek help.

Boob Time

1968–1970

As a child, I was prone to respiratory infections.

In May of the eighth grade, at the age of thirteen, I got really sick. On a Sunday, my parents and sister went to a party at a relative's house with Mom taking her homemade baked goods. Before leaving, Mom instructed me, "Don't answer the phone." I couldn't even if I had wanted to. I was so sick. I lay in bed, sweating with a fever.

That week she took me to our pediatrician. After diagnosing my condition as the flu, he announced he was going to do a breast exam. Against my protest, Mom told me to be quiet and let him examine me. "Self-conscious" pales with how violated I felt by this gray-haired man rubbing his hands all over my little boobs, staring at them with an inapt, closed-mouth smile plastered on his face and squeezing them as if he were trying to extract honey from the nipples. I did not understand the need for that. I had a bronchial cough. That came from my lungs, not my boobs.

A year later, I ended up in the hospital with another bronchial infection. Over my short time there, this same pediatrician came in nearly every day and examined my little breasts on my skinny frame. The second day I told him, "You just examined my breasts yesterday. They haven't changed since then."

He replied, "You can't have enough breast exams."

What? That did not feel right to me. Something was off. I was there for a respiratory issue. But who would I tell? Mom? Each time, Mom was right there in a chair next to the bed, rummaging through her purse, looking straight ahead, popping a lemon drop into her mouth. Her response was silence. She did not question his conduct.

Years later, I wondered whether Mom would have intervened had the doctor inserted his finger into my vagina. Or would she have responded as she typically did, with silence and inaction?

Phone Marathon: "She's crazy!"

1970

By age fifteen, my sophomore year in high school, pimples were taking up residence on my face. I washed my face as Mary Keefe had taught me, but that didn't help.

"Please take me to a dermatologist," I begged Mom.

Her answer was always the same. "No, you don't need that."

I didn't want to have an acne-riddled complexion. So, I moved on to the next phase of Mary Keefe's instructions: use a hot compress, then gently poke the pimples that have come to a head with a pin to release the junk within.

"Don't squeeze," Mary taught. "The contents of a pimple contain bacteria." Then "gently dab the popped pimple with alcohol to help it dry up." As she was a nurse, I trusted her guidance.

Following her advice, I used a hot compress. But I didn't lock the bathroom door. That was my mistake. Mom shoved open the door and watched silently as I gently poked at a pimple head with a needle I had disinfected with alcohol. I explained that Mary Keefe said to use alcohol and a needle to gently pop pimples when they come to a head. Mom said nothing in response. Unobtrusively, she left.

A few seconds later, I heard her on the phone in the dining room, calling one person after another, zealously shouting into the receiver, "Judie is sticking pins into her face. She's crazy. She's gone crazy!" As soon as she hung up, she immediately moved on to the next person, as if on a mission.

That's Mom, I thought.

None of my friends had a pockmarked face. When Mom finished her calls and went outdoors, I phoned Aunt Virge who was knowledgeable about nutrition and self-care. I did not relate what had just happened. Instead, I talked with her about dermatologists. A few days later, she called Mom, and Mom started taking my sister and me to a dermatologist.

Dr. Stein's in-office treatment consisted of shining UV light on my face as I wore eye-protective goggles, then taking a sterilized needle and gently popping the pimples. Mom watched quietly as he worked systematically across my face.

I was curious if she still equated the use of a needle with a "crazy" state of mind. I concluded that she never really regarded my using a needle to pop pimples as "crazy." Otherwise, she would have shouted that flat-out, with volume, as she watched me in the bathroom. And she would be calling me crazy several times a day. No, she didn't believe that. I reasoned that she couldn't help herself using my pimple-popping effort to malign me. She was sick.

Putting myself in her shoes, I concluded that, in her eyes, her phone-a-thon achieved her intended purpose: to sculpt others' opinions of me in a negative light. *Does Mom feel like a societal misfit?* I wondered. *Is that why she does that?*

I questioned why when talking with her family, she characterized her own daughter as "crazy." I tend to be harsh in my self-assessments, but I have always perceived myself as thoughtful, sensitive, introspective, kind, smart (post-seventh grade), wanting to do the right thing, and willing to help those in need. If I had a daughter who I thought was mentally ill, I would not call ten to twelve people, one immediately after the other, and shout with bravado, "She's crazy!" Mom's behavior was entirely devoid of reason.

By this point, however, I expected her to exploit my facial acne or menstrual cycle (announcing when Dad came home from work, "Judie's on the rag today") or whatever she could to channel embarrassment my way and garner attention for herself.

I was not ashamed of how Mom portrayed me on those calls, labeling me "crazy." It didn't matter what she said about me because I knew she wasn't all there. What I didn't appreciate was her consistently exploiting any opportunity she could to denigrate me before others. That was wrong, and her targeting me was hurtful. When I thought about her mental state, I didn't feel any anger toward her. I didn't feel any desire for revenge; that was not like me. Instead, consistent with the past, I felt sorry for her. I wished she would get help. Yet I told no one.

Running on Empty

1970–1971

In high school, it was not unusual for me to come home late because of extracurricular activities: choir practice (only for one year as singing was not my thing), orchestra practice, or the school newspaper.

In my sophomore year, some days I got off the city bus at 8:20 p.m. and walked the half mile home, over ice, carrying a few books. One time when I got home, the kitchen was dark and cleaned up.

"We don't have any food left," Mom said. She had served the last of it at dinner. "I didn't have a chance to go to the store. Daddy had to take a grape jelly sandwich for lunch. That's all we had," she said, aside from food at dinner.

I was famished. I hadn't eaten since lunch. I had a test the next day but was not going to disclose that.

"There's a bowl of candy on the dining room table. Have some of that." Candy was always readily accessible, with no restrictions. I was not into candy then.

This was not the mom I knew growing up. We always had a well-stocked refrigerator and downstairs pantry. This was disturbing. Something was going on with Mom. After her brother Al had passed away that October, her behavior changed. He and their sister Katy were Mom's closest friends. It was as if the emptiness of the fridge and pantry metaphorically reflected the void she felt within. I tried to step into her mind to experience how she must have felt. I can only assume that she kept up her stoic front because she didn't want to be seen as weak, crying over the loss of her brother. She needed to grieve but fought that. I know she had to be in her own internal hell as the "no food left; have some candy" script replicated itself several times that year.

She needed to talk about how she felt.

However, our household did not have the tools for dialogue. We did not speak with each other about anything other than practicalities—not our feelings, thoughts, or concerns. Dad was the exception; he'd say he loves me. Also, for a few years, he and I spoke openly about Mom's behavior. But outside of that, our family did not communicate. Conversation is not an art I learned at home.

That pattern percolated to our contact with family outside our home. When Uncle Al picked me up from grade school at lunchtime for what we called "dinner" (our house operated on the European convention of eating the large meal at midday; my classmates called that meal "lunch"), as I got into the car, he would greet me. But he didn't inquire about what I did in school, who my friends were, or how I saw the world. Though I know he cared about me, he didn't try to chat. Nor did I. Perhaps it was because I was a kid. On our two-week vacation with him and Mary Keefe, we did not speak much. That was a pattern with both immediate family and most adult family on Mom's side. Aunt Virge was the exception at that time; she seemed genuinely curious and open to my thoughts.

Even at our holiday dinners with company at our home, conversation lagged. Mom glided around the table, not sitting down to join us. Her focus was on ensuring everyone had enough food, versus conversation. Dad socialized and talked when he joined us. However, that was infrequent. On most holidays, like any day when he was home, he lay in bed for the day, even if he was sober, quietly surfacing to use the bathroom and saying hello but quickly retreating back to bed. When his family visited—an infrequent occurrence—it was different: he was always sober then, and he socialized, laughed, and ate at the table. But with Mom's family, he rarely did that. I attributed that to how they treated him. From my observations, all the aunts treated Dad as family, but the men seemed to dismiss him as a peer. Though cordial, they would say hello but that was it. I assumed Mom's hyperbolic portrayal of Dad's alcoholism, long before it got serious, tainted their view of him.

My immediate family's pattern of noncommunication stemmed from us being so wholly independent of each other and from Mom being ill-equipped to provide emotional support, with herself needing that to such a great extent from others. Within our home, in terms of communication and emotional support, we were like widgets in a shoe box, each complete and integral in ourselves but isolated from and noninteractive with each other. Here, I speak solely of my perception of my experience with my family.

I was hungry for conversation with adults. As a young kid, in the summer, I would try to sense if a neighbor sitting on her porch steps would be open to me joining her. If so, I would sit down and chat—something missing at home. What drew me to my four "mothers of the heart" was their openness, which I saw as an invitation to connect. Though I saw each only a few times per year, more so with Virge and Mary Keefe, they filled a void within me, and I felt seen.

An Ice Cream Cone

1972–1973

I was thrilled to practice for my driver's license and wanted to learn to drive well. I asked Aunt Virge to sit with me as I practiced driving. It was also an excuse to visit with her.

My parents said goodbye to us as we drove off in Dad's 1969 Skylark one Sunday afternoon. Our driving-chat visit included a stop at Dairy Queen for an ice cream cone. On our return, as we approached the house, Mom was outside waiting for us. She ran to the car before I even finished parking. She was shouting. I got out of the car and could feel a tsunami of her anger washing over me.

"Where have you been? Did you go to a bar? Where did you go? You were gone for more than an hour! Where have you been? I was so worried about you. Were you at a bar?"

"I was with Aunt Virge. You know that. You said goodbye to us," I answered calmly, hoping my tone would induce her to calm down.

The shouting drew Dad outside. Unraveled by the commotion and drama, he said to Mom, "Give me money for booze."

Her belligerence continued. She flung her anger at me, not Virge. Virge's eyes were wet. She was crying. Bathed in

Mom's wrath, she kept saying to me, "I'm sorry. I'm so sorry." Pausing, she stammered, "I . . . I . . . I am going to go." Virge was not someone who hugged. This time, though, she wrapped her arms around me and embraced me tightly for more than a few seconds as if I were going off to war. In a metaphorical sense, I was already in a war.

After Aunt Virge left, I went indoors with Mom trailing behind, still shouting.

Dad then became her target. "Give me money for booze. Ple-e-ase," he begged. They had a routine where Mom would require Dad to plead his request several times. When she finally gave in, she would throw money on the floor and spit on him as he picked up the bills. My heart went out to him. Never did I hear him curse at her or call her names as she did with him. It was like watching an out-of-control orangutan flinging its feces at the sane zookeeper. Dad went to the tavern for whiskey.

What was this outburst about? I wondered. *How could Mom even imagine Aunt Virge and me going to a bar?* I was seventeen and a reserved, nerdy goody-two-shoes who didn't drink. Mom knew that. Virge was a responsible adult. Mom knew that too. She also knew it was vastly out of character for me to waste an opportunity to practice driving with anyone.

That was when the word "barfly" popped into mind—a word Mom had used eons ago to describe Virge. That mental utterance revealed the answer: Mom's behavior today was a strike at Virge, not me.

I recalled Virge saying that she had helped her dad at his tavern in her late twenties or early thirties. That fact—coupled with Mom's unflattering language about Virge within our home, which told me she felt inferior to Virge—presented a delicious opportunity, I contextualized, for Mom to turn the tables and make it look like she regarded Virge as irresponsible, though that was not true. Mom's comment of being worried about me was also not true, I believed. The previous winter or two when school was closing midday because of blizzard conditions and I missed the last bus and used the phone in the principal's office, before they closed, to call Mom so she wouldn't worry, her response was, "Find your own way home." How could she not be concerned then but worried now that I was with Virge?

No, today was Mom showing Virge one-upmanship. It was a tactic of diminishment.

In my shared bedroom, I pulled out a psychology textbook that my aunt, the nun, had given me and that I had previously scoured cover-to-cover while in the seventh grade, trying to diagnose my mom's condition. In college, my Abnormal Psychology class used a later edition of the same textbook. Back then, the book had a discussion of histrionic behavior and schizophrenia but nothing on other forms of psychopathy or sociopathy. Mom had a desire—if not a need—to hurt people. When successful, that brought a sense of triumphant jubilation. I never saw her experience guilt or remorse. Instead, inflicting pain on others seemed to fulfill her on the same level as discrediting or lying about women whom, I reasoned, she esteemed as more evolved than herself.

If today's incident was intended to push Virge back from interacting with her girls, it failed, thankfully. The following summer, after high school, Aunt Virge told me about auditions at a community theatre for Thornton Wilder's play *The Matchmaker* and suggested that my sister and I try out. *How fun!* We did, and I got a small part; I played an eighty-year-old, deaf, half-blind housekeeper. My sister exquisitely played Ermengarde in the lead role. Our parents didn't come to see her, though the production ran over two or three weekends. I told Mom, "Nita has *the* lead role. You *have* to see her. She's incredible!" That didn't nudge them to the theater. They missed an opportunity to experience a facet of their daughter as a naturally gifted actor.

Guests Unwanted

1972

Seldom did I invite people to my home for fear of Mom's behavior. The few times I did, though, Mom surprised me: she acted *normal*. She was kind and adopted a veneer foreign to me. For example, one summer during high school, two friends—Bev Mollak and Clair Lanvich—called and said they were on their way over. They hung up quickly so I couldn't avert their visit, as I usually did.

Seeing me straightening up the house, Mom caught on. From the garage, she brought in two shovels, two rakes, and various garden tools, and laid them across the junk already on the dining room table. "When they see this, you'll be so embarrassed! I'm going to tell them *you* brought these in. You'll be so embarrassed!" she threatened.

I regretted not telling my friends earlier about how Mom was at home. I didn't want them or any of my peers to know that about my mom. I felt that information was somehow a reflection on me. Everyone else's mom was modulated. My mom was crazy.

I picked up a shovel to return it to the garage. Mom yanked it out of my hands, shouting, "Leave that there!"

Both of my friends' homes were organized and neat. I didn't want them to see shovels and garden tools on our dining room table. I knew Mom would not hesitate to lie about how they got there. I had already witnessed her lying with ease countless times about my dad to his sister and her family. I pleaded with her. She stood guard over her artful tabletop arrangement, giddily laughing, "I can't wait for them to get here!"

I continued straightening up the living and dining rooms.

At the doorbell, I scurried outdoors. I suggested we walk downtown, but my friends wanted to stay. We sat on the front porch stairs, visiting. Mom brought out strawberry ice cream cones for each of us and joined us. She was nice as pie. The whole while, though, I fretted within about whether either friend would have to use the bathroom. Thankfully, that need did not arise.

An Alter Ego

1960 | 1968 | 1972

When I went out with Mom, she was a totally different person outside the household. She could be pleasant, especially if strangers were around. I enjoyed that side of her. She would quip about quotidian matters—who she saw that day, who called that morning, or what happened in the neighborhood. A few times, she shared advice, such as "Never ride a bicycle. It will give you a big ass," or "When you bake, add salt to egg yolks. That turns them bright yellow," or "Have at least one baby so people don't think there's something wrong with you." Mom's being relaxed helped me relax when I was out with her. Plus, after we'd ventured out, she always seemed a little kinder.

Like many women in our neighborhood, Mom didn't drive. To go downtown, we took the bus. One bus ride stands out to me. When I was around five years old, we were on the bus, returning home. Mom sat with my sister and told me to take the seat behind her. In the window seat sat a large-framed, chocolate-colored woman who gave me a beautiful smile. Holding out a small white sack, she asked, "Would you like a bonbon?" Hearing her invitation, Mom turned around and in her typical loud, resonating voice, barked, "Don't take that. She's a n****."

The contempt in her voice prompted a summersault in my stomach. Mom used that word at home and always with contempt. I was embarrassed for Mom, for myself, and for the lady. The lady appeared nonplussed, as if she had heard that word so many times before that it had lost its sting.

She smiled sweetly back at me. "That's okay, honey," she said. Winking at me, the lady tilted the bag toward me and mouthed "It's okay. Take one," and smiled.

I mouthed back "Thank you" and bit into a bubble of luscious sweetness. I never had a bonbon before. When Mom pulled the buzzer cord and stood up, I knew it was time to leave. I thanked the lady again and waved goodbye. On our short walk home, I wondered why Mom had called that lady a name. She looked like Mom—two arms, two legs, large boned. She was a person, just like us, but with one big difference from Mom: the lady was kind.

When I started driving, our going out expanded to trips to the bakery, downtown, or to a mall. We always got a bite to eat, whether it was pie and ice cream at Walgreens, a hot dog at Sears, or a sandwich at Kresge's. I wished we would go out as a family. We never did. We never went to a restaurant with Dad.

When I needed a winter coat in the eighth grade, Mom took me to an expensive ladies' store that was having a clearance sale. There, I saw two coats that were possibilities and was deciding which to get. When Mom learned the sales clerk had a son in my class, she surprisingly uttered with striking self-assurance, "I will take both coats."

I was shocked. I didn't need two coats. I told the clerk and Mom which one I wanted and explained what I didn't like about the other one.

Shushing me, Mom said, "No, Judie, you'll wear them both," in a tone suggesting money was not an issue. By that time, I was aware of the cost of things. We didn't have that kind of money. On the bus ride home, I felt guilty for getting two coats and concerned about how I would explain this to my sister.

Mom never bought anything for my sister when she was with me. I found that curious. I would ask her, "Why don't you get that for Nita?"

"No," she'd say, and we would move on.

I didn't like Mom buying me things, even necessities, because when she did, she would go on and on about how much that item cost: "Oh, those tampons were high," or "That desk lamp was seventeen dollars. That's so much money." I'd feel guilty costing her money.

The Nun and a Sliver of Insight

1972 | 1974

On a South Shore train ride home from Chicago, one of my *other* mothers, Sister Ann, filled in a gap about my mom. I had always felt Mom had experienced something unspeakable growing up. I felt that she detested herself, but I didn't know why.

On the train, Sister Ann leaned toward me, her demeanor serious. She said, "You're seventeen now and very mature for your age. I think it's time that you know what happened to your mom." I listened intently. Speaking softly, Sister told me that Busia ran a boarding house for out-of-town men who found work locally. She then shared a secret known to only a handful of Mom's siblings: "A man staying there raped your mom when she was five years old."

She paused for me to take that in. The expression etched on her face suggested horror. I could feel her pain in my stomach.

Continuing, she said, "Busia called the doctor. That was highly, highly unusual in our house. I watched him close the door behind him after examining your mom. He stood there, his head hanging down, shaking it as if in disbelief. When he looked up, he said, 'Her nerves are shot.'"

I interpreted that to mean that my mom had had a nervous breakdown. Sister was a few years older than Mom. She observed her sister, highly traumatized, and the aftermath in their home. That was in 1919, well before counseling was mainstream.

The train conductor was walking by. I didn't ask questions. I felt that Mom's family had swept that experience under the rug. Was that why she was mentally ill?

I let a few months elapse before broaching the topic with my mom. Though I didn't know anything about counseling, deep within I felt she needed to talk about what had happened. She needed to let it out. I waited until she and I were the only ones home. Delicately, I asked what happened when she was five years old.

Immediately, the veins on Mom's neck protruded, her face turned a brilliant fiery red and in apoplectic rage, she unfurled a litany of swearing. Mom could out-cuss anyone. She was infuriated, not with me but with my aunt. "That goddamn nun! She should have kept her mouth shut. That's secret. Nobody is supposed to know! Nobody is supposed to know!" That's when I knew my instinct was correct all along.

Years later, I learned that Mom's wounds ran far deeper than I could imagine. One evening after coming home from my summer office job, I must have been more contemplative than usual because Mom asked me what happened at work. That was a first. She had never asked me anything about anything in my life before, such as how my day went, what I did with friends, or what I liked or didn't like about anything. However, that evening, with a voice that hinted of concern, Mom opened a dialogue we'd never had before. In response, I gave a synopsis of the bare facts.

At lunchtime, a male coworker in his fifties waited for me in the backroom at the office. When I went to get my lunch, he grabbed me. It was hands all over and a forced tongue trying to get down my throat. I fought and pushed him away. I came out, ashamed.

Rose, a secretary in her fifties, noticed and said, "Oh my god! Bob did something to you. What did he do?"

Apparently, Bob Higgens had a reputation. Rose advised me to speak to the head manager. Before doing that, I had to process what happened. At home, I pondered what to say. That's when Mom noticed my reflective state and inquired about what had happened.

Her response did not surprise me. I should have anticipated it. "Good for you! Good for you!" she shouted exuberantly. "He should have raped you! I wish he would have raped you!" She repeatedly roared that, zestfully, for the next hour.

I realized my mistake: I had allowed myself to fall for her chicanery of feigning concern. Those hollered ill wishes were genuine. They were from the mom I knew. They spoke her truth and were utterances from the dark chasms of her psyche.

Unexplainably, I understood how bad she must have felt deep down inside from having been raped as a child. I had not yet learned about projection. But I felt she truly hoped I would have suffered what she had experienced so she would not feel alone. I reasoned that in her eyes, she then would not be the only one who was *damaged*. She would have an equal. That is how she had to have perceived herself, I believed. At that moment, I felt sorry for her. She was living in her own fabricated hell.

The next morning, I spoke with the head manager. He said he would talk with Bob. He didn't have to wait long. Bob was outside the closed door when I exited. Bob entered and shut the door. A few minutes later, robust laughter erupted between them.

That evening, Mom had "news." Bob was well-respected in his community and played tennis with Aunt Virge. Mom didn't ask if I did anything to address the situation. Nor did she advise on how to handle it. She did not express concern or compassion, but she shared this incident with her family. I didn't want to hear what she said about it.

College, Not a Question Mark

1972–1973

In both my junior and senior years in high school, the Kiwanis club invited my parents to an honors dinner they hosted for the top ten students of local high schools. Mom refused for both parents to attend. In my junior year, Virge and Lou took me. My senior year, my best friend's parents took me, though Mom tried in vain then to rattle me into not going. I waited for them on the front porch.

College was never a question mark for me. I had planned on college since the fifth grade when I wanted to study paleontology and then later, physics and math. I loved school. I loved, and still love, learning new things. What I don't know fascinates me, as does what I can learn and use to help others.

At age sixteen, I started looking into colleges. Concerned about where my interest was taking me—and possibly worried it would lead me to leave home—Mom insisted I quit school. I was at the top of my class and the following year was voted Most Likely to Succeed. She'd say, "You don't need that" or "You're always doing homework." To her, reading was "doing homework."

Intellectual engagement was my escape from the insanity at home. Burying myself in intellectual pursuits and creative efforts was how I escaped the chaos around me. I luxuriated in that. I still love learning.

As I typed out letters to colleges within the state (yep, with a typewriter), Mom put down the law: "You are not going to college. You can't go. I'm not going to let you." She later included Dad in her fiat, saying they both banned me from going, but I knew it was exclusively Mom's decision. She told me, "College girls are whores. They go to college to get knocked up." She would follow that with "We don't have the money for college, and you're a girl. You don't need school. Get married (I was a late bloomer who wasn't even dating), drive a big car, and have a lot of kids. Oh, you'll be so happy."

Well, that was not in my DNA. Though banned from going to college, I went anyway. And I was the black sheep for doing so.

In selecting a college, I had to be pragmatic as I was the one paying for my education. When I told Mom I would get scholarships, she retorted, "Ack, you're so goddamn dumb. No one is going to give you a scholarship."

Fortunately, I was offered several scholarships. I selected a school based on my ability to meet my fiscal obligations: a small liberal arts school in Indianapolis called Marian College, now known as Marian University, which opened the second medical school in Indiana.

Sister Ann had been in my life in a profound way for the past few years. A gentle soul with a soft voice, a quick smile, a muted ebullience, and a heart infused with humanity, she tended to look for the good in people.

Sister Ann, my dad, and Nita attended my high school graduation. At dinner at our home, Sister Ann inquired about my plans. A few weeks later, she surprised me. She called to say that she had seen an article in a local paper about a high school salutatorian who was going to attend the same college. She had already contacted the girl's parents about us meeting, and they invited Sister and me to their home for a Sunday lunch. I was touched by Sister remembering the name of the college and making the extra effort without being asked. That was the first time anyone, aside from teachers, showed an interest in my formal education.

I had never known Sister Ann to drive. In fact, I didn't even know she knew how. But that Sunday, she picked me up with the convent's car and expertly navigated the expressway for me to meet a potential friend. By the end of the day, I had a new friend and roommate. Sister contacted the school to make the requisite arrangements.

"Brainwashed"

1973

A few weeks before starting college, I observed Dad walking through the living room toward the front door, his gait slower than what I recalled. His energy was depressed, and his posture was slumped. The bounce and groundedness of his presence had long since expired. Gray stubble peppered his face. That was not like Dad. He was in his eighth month of retirement.

As he turned the knob of the screen door to the front porch, he paused. He turned his face to mine. I was seated on the sofa about twelve feet away. Pain, sorrow, and despair streamed from his eyes. With his head hanging down, in a cringy voice unlike any I had heard from him, he groaned, "Nobody likes you"—exactly what Mom always told him. Turning the knob, he stepped outdoors.

Oh my gosh, I thought, *Dad has been brainwashed! Mom brainwashed him with her name-calling and brutal shoving.* That was my first thought. By now I had learned that sometimes people say to others what they think about themselves. It pained me to see how he had changed, how he had adopted Mom's mantra as a self-belief that no one liked him.

I was involved in my own life and in trying to stay under Mom's radar. I was not monitoring Dad for behavioral changes; I didn't feel I needed to. Undoubtedly, they had to be tiny, one after the other, like grains of sand rolling down a hill, each almost imperceptible from the one before, but all collectively and powerfully breaking Dad's spirit and diminishing his perception of himself.

I took in the breadth of what I had just witnessed. It was overwhelming. That was not the man I knew as Dad. How did he let that happen to himself? Dad always loved Mom more than she loved him. He stayed with her despite all the discord she wrought in our home. He absorbed her wrath and believed her venom. It shaped him into whom he had now become— visibly broken, a shell of the man I knew as a youngster.

As I looked back to a few months earlier, one tell-tale sign of Dad's shifted self-belief was that he stopped washing himself. An uncle had to talk with him about hygiene, which was most unusual for my normally clean-shaven, Old Spice aftershave-wearing dad. Only in retrospect did I view this as an expression of his manipulated self-beliefs, as presumably severe depression. Never did I feel that his one-time comment reflected how he genuinely felt about me.

You would never have known this was a man who, fourteen years earlier, had been so strong-willed that when he decided to quit smoking, he never again touched a cigarette. With alcohol, he never made the effort because it assuaged his pain, even after I had talked to him a few times about getting help. Over the past couple of years, his drinking had intensified. The year before he retired, his employer sent him home once because he went to work intoxicated, as by then he drank daily with Mom churning his soul relentlessly. He was now at one quart of whiskey a day.

My thoughts next turned to me. Gratitude. That's what I felt for having the wherewithal to attend to myself. For immersing myself in school, books, math, art, extracurricular activities, and sewing. For being blessed with *other* mothers who truly cared about me. I looked back at my self-image when in the seventh grade. At that time, I perceived myself as the ugliest and dumbest one in the class. After each history test, Mrs. Comfort off-handedly remarked, "Judie had the highest grade." Finally, after the fourth test, I grasped reality and shifted my self-belief. I felt blessed that I didn't let Mom plummet my belief in myself.

I would love to say that after Dad's comment, I went outside to sit on the steps and talked with him, or tried to get him to see the fallacy of his self-beliefs, or coaxed him to get help. But I would be lying if I said I did that. That is what I would do today. But at that time in my life—at age seventeen—given the dynamics in our home, that did not cross my mind. We truly were like wholly independent widgets in a shoebox.

Hermitage. That's how I experienced my home during my growing-up years. There, my survival depended upon cloaking myself with invisibility to attenuate its abrasive ambience. I was sensitive. Outside my shared room, I would feel into the environment to gauge Mom's mood; I'd feel its energy. In that home, invisibility was my protection. I wished my dad would have discovered that cloak, too.

PART 2

SPROUTING

College: Freshman Year

1973–1974

At the start of my freshman year, my parents refused to drive me the three-and-a-quarter hours to campus. It was actually Mom's decision. I wasn't surprised. Aunt Virge and Uncle Lou graciously stepped in, obviating me from the more arduous taking of a Greyhound bus, then a taxi, to the campus that I had not yet seen. That morning, we packed up Uncle Lou's car with my things. When saying goodbye to my parents, I noticed Mom was unusually well-behaved. I wondered if that morning Dad had told her to behave or if she had done so of her own volition because Virge was present.

For all four years, I majored in chemistry and biology and was in the school's honors program. Through scholarships and work, I paid for my education. One of my jobs was as a technician at the Endocrinology Department at Indiana University Medical School where I worked twenty to twenty-five hours per week on a study involving alcohol addiction in a special breed of rats.

On my first night at school, I felt so grateful for the opportunity to leave home and study. That night as I lay in bed, I felt like a troop of angels had brought me to this point.

In return, I wanted to give back. So, for my last three years, I volunteered six hours per week as a clinical associate with the Suicide and Crisis Intervention Service—a hotline run by the Marion County Mental Health Association. There I spoke with callers who were depressed, chemically dependent, or in emergency situations such as attempting suicide. For this position, I trained with psychologists for forty hours. Each day of training culminated with the psychologists eliminating people based on how they engaged with practice clients. Also, for all four years, I volunteered four hours per week as a teacher's aide with the Marion County Association for Children with Disabilities at the Noble 1 Center. There I helped teachers of children with autism and Down Syndrome in classroom activities and field trips. Both experiences deepened my appreciation for our humanness.

My freshman year reinforced my belief in myself. I was quiet and shy but knew deep down who I was. All freshmen were required to take a particular math class. In the first class after our math skills were assessed by testing, the professor stood before the class and barked like a drill sergeant, "I want to see Judie Dziezak and Aiden Lokkert in the hall. *Now*." He walked out the door.

That's interesting, I thought.

The girl behind me whispered, "What did you do?"

I shrugged.

Outside the door, the professor told Aiden, whom I had not yet met, and me, "You don't belong here. You had perfect or near-perfect scores. There's nothing I can teach you. I want you to go back in there, grab your things, and scram."

Back at my desk, the girl behind me shot me a quizzical look and repeated, "What did you do?"

I told her, "He told me to scram," and I left. I didn't share that exemption from class with anyone—family or friends.

Dad passed away in November of my freshman year. The morning after learning he'd had a stroke, I took an early bus home. He died that night. Ironically, his passing at 10:00 p.m. coincided with when he would typically say, "Lights out." With his passing, I felt an immense hole in my heart. He was the only one in my immediate family I felt close to because I felt comfortable with him, and we weren't even close. After his passing, I felt I had no family.

At his wake, Mom came up to me, her mouth drawn in a stiff straight line. Leaning toward me, she said, "Faye wants Dad's pin. She said, 'I'm his sister and I deserve to have that.' I didn't know what to say to her."

Mom was talking about a pin bearing a tiny diamond that Dad's employer gave him on his retirement for his forty-two years of service. Dad was proud of that pin. I had never known Mom to be at a loss for words. From her body language and facial expression, I could tell that she felt my aunt was overreaching.

"Tell her she can't have it. I want it," I told Mom.

Mom looked at me. With a bright glint in her eye, she held her head up and marched away. Minutes later, she returned and sat down next to me. "I told her you want Dad's pin. She can't have it." Mom looked pleased.

Before the undertaker closed the casket, he removed the pin from Dad's lapel and handed it to Mom. She turned to me and said, "Here's Dad's pin."

With my hand, I folded her fingers around the pin. "No. This is yours. You keep it. You're his wife."

The look in her eyes evinced appreciation. She tightly grasped the pin, pulling her fisted hand to her heart with her eyes closed. She loved Dad, I could tell, in a complicated way. As I construed it, it was an embattled relationship—with trauma from being violated as a child competing with and eventually overtly defeating that love. Through that relationship and our home, her emotions rolled like unbridled tumbleweed, carried by forceful winds across a vast desert. She couldn't help merging Dad with her attacker, I believe, and forever held that against him. For a second, as the lid to Dad's casket was shutting away his body forever, Mom breached the barricade she had built to protect herself from the rhythm of life: her posture leaned toward the casket as if to express unspoken words of softness.

When I was home for that first Christmas without Dad, Mom's neighbor, Emma, stopped by to talk with me. She, Mom, and I stood in the dining room. Emma reproached me for being "selfish in going to a private college" and "making your mom pay your way." Apparently, no one told her I had scholarships and was paying the balance on my own with no financial help from Mom. Mom stood there with her arms folded across her bosom and her head held high, smirking as if she enjoyed watching me get my due. She said nothing during this reprimand. It was a moment of schadenfreude.

Nor did I. Listening to Emma, glancing periodically at Mom, I took in that Mom was telling neighbors a story deviating from the truth. She made them believe she was paying for my education, not me.

When finished with her diatribe, concluding with "you're selfish," Emma left our house.

Mom stood there momentarily and uttered, "Humph," before turning in to the kitchen.

I said nothing to Emma to disabuse the misinformation she had been fed. I didn't know what to say. I had to process it. Why would Mom lie? Later, I postulated that by claiming she was paying for my education, in her eyes and depending on what she had said, she made herself look good and made me look like a thoughtless, ungrateful daughter, neither mindful of nor caring about her mother's financial situation. We didn't have money. I could see that Emma's rebuke pleased Mom.

I didn't address this with Mom. Ever. By then, I could already hear her response: "Laugh it off."

A Push to "F-A-I-L"

1966 | 1974

Mom tried to get me to fail school. When I was in the fifth grade, she got into my math homework and reworked it. She changed all the answers to incorrect numbers. You could imagine my shock on taking out my homework and seeing her large handwriting, distinctly different from mine, imprinted over my answers. What I didn't expect was for the teacher, Mrs. Wade, to return that home assignment with a huge question mark at the top and a note to redo it instead of giving me an F. Later, from Mom, I learned she had put Mrs. Wade "in her place" a couple of decades before in a church-related group. I assumed my teacher had experienced an aspect of Mom and related that to my peculiar homework submission. I did not tell anyone about that incident. But after that, I hid my homework from Mom.

In high school, I was on pins and needles worried whether Mom would destroy a sculpture I had made of Julius Caesar for an accelerated English class. While I crafted it in the kitchen, Mom came in and stood a few feet behind me, watching silently, for the several hours I diligently worked on molding the clay with my fingers. That night, I didn't sleep for concern that she would damage it before I could get it out of the house. Fortunately, it was still intact by morning.

When I was in college, Mom's effort was more direct. I took statistics the summer I was eighteen. On the day of the final exam, Mom sought to prevent me from taking the test. She blocked me from leaving the house. Standing before the front door, whenever I tried to reach for the knob, she would push me across the living room as she did with Dad. When I started for the back door, she'd grab my shirt and shove me onto the sofa. "You're not taking the test. You're going to flunk. They're going to flunk you!" she exulted, laughing, as she repeatedly shoved me away from the door. This went on for a good fifteen to twenty minutes. She was strong and relentless. And I was not going to submit. She genuinely wanted me to give up.

As if God had heard my prayer, the phone rang. Mom went to answer it, and I ran out the door.

On my drive to school, I was terribly upset. I was trying to process what had just happened. Once I started working on the exam, though, my focus sharpened, and all became well. I got an A.

The Displaced Blessing

1974

Thinking did that for me: whenever I engaged in intellectual or artistic pursuits, it was calming. I learned to focus on my breathing or on a puzzle or problem that needed to be figured out. Books, studying, and sewing became my salvation. Immersing myself in those activities insulated me from the chaos within my home.

I would still feel emotions—the hurt and sometimes a blow to my solar plexus—when Mom would say hurtful things to me, things I had not heard other mothers say to their children. I let emotions within me flow through me, so I would feel them. But I would not let them get stuck within me. I never felt any resentment or hatred for my mom. I saw her as a victim of her own thoughts and self-undoing.

Somehow, though, two things helped soften the blow of her words: 1) not considering Mom a nurturer and having other women from her family step into that role (though on an unsteady basis), and 2) knowing that the things Mom said about me reflected what she thought about herself, not me. It's like walking past someone who is not well and sits on her porch every day, shouting obscenities at people. Eventually, you become inured to those comments. Occasionally, you may feel a tinge of pain from one or two statements, prompting you to search for any glimmer of truth in them and each time concluding, "No, that's not about me. She's talking about herself." With Mom, her words and actions reflected the dissonant world she molded for herself—one where she saw herself as damaged and warranting ridicule. That was her world, not mine.

Even if Mom believed her own words, that did not explain her condescension toward me, her incessant efforts to position me as someone to be laughed at, or her labeling me as "dumb" and "ugly" when that was so far from the truth. She did that from the time I was young. I never saw her talk like that to anyone else. Only to me. In fact, I never heard her call Nita "dumb" or otherwise ridicule her, even though my grades were consistently better than hers. Was that because Nita looked like Mom?

I wanted to get to the *why* behind Mom's behavior. I drew two conclusions. First, Mom seemed to be directing onto me her resentment for Dad's drinking. After all, Dad and I looked alike and were both sensitive, reserved, and gentle-spirited. That could have made me an easy target. I assumed, too, that to some degree, she projected her unresolved feelings toward her childhood attacker onto Dad because of his gender, and that, too, then flowed to me. She often told me, as a young child, that her dream had been to "get married and have two girls." Being in her forties, she prayed to St. Jude, the patron saint of miracles, "for two girls," she told me. I assumed that after her daughters were born, she started seeing her childhood attacker in Dad. Was that part of the reason behind her behavior toward me?

My second conclusion was more concrete. Mom may have felt that I had gotten a "blessing" from her mother that she never received. When I was young—four or five years old—Mom told me that when I was an infant, her mother, Busia, looked at me and said, "Oh, this one is smart. She's very smart."

She said that Busia, who had raised twelve kids, *knew* babies and she'd never heard Busia say this about any other baby. I was bemused because my grandmother's alleged remark was contrary to how Mom spoke to me at the time: "dumb kindergartener" and "dumb first grader."

Mom repeated Busia's comment again a few years later when I was in grade school.

The third and last time she brought up Busia's comment was when I was about twelve years old sitting in the living room watching *The Flying Nun* on TV. A teenage neighbor girl, Valerie, drove past our house. Looking out the window, Mom said, "Valerie just drove by." After a pause, she continued reflectively, "When you were a baby, Busia looked at you and said, 'This one is smart, very smart.'" She paused again, resuming in a loud, disturbed voice: "Awk. You're so dumb. You're so ugly. You're nothing like Valerie. Valerie is beee-uuu-ti-ful. She's beee-uuu-ti-ful, not like you." I was in tears.

Delivered with contempt, that statement stung. But it eerily echoed what I suspected was going on in Mom's mind: *Is she jealous of me? She sure seems to be.* From her frequent bashing of my intellect and looks, straight to my face, I had long suspected that her mother never told her she was smart. Hearing Busia's comment for the third time, now trailed with condescension, I reasoned that she must be playing it over and over in her mind, sharpening it till it has become psychological shrapnel, repeatedly re-wounding her for twelve years. It must have been especially painful, as Mom had the utmost respect and admiration for her mother. She had to feel cheated, like her mother should have said that about *her*, not me.

Mom's fierce jealous streak was undeniable. For example, when Dad made amazing French toast or turned a hot dog into a gourmet meal, or when I giggled with an aunt on the phone or showed delight in being invited to an aunt's home, or when relatives visited, those situations unleashed more than an inkling of jealousy. "Go to the bedroom and don't come out," she'd say before the relatives arrived, seemingly not wanting to share me with them. "I'll tell them you're not home." Mom was intensely jealous of Aunt Virge, who read, had a good vocabulary, was attractive, and played the piano. She was jealous of a friend's mother who sent me home with delicious lemon bars along with the recipe. Her jealousy extended to women who had any attribute Mom deemed missing within herself. She ridiculed and discredited these women and unmercifully criticized them, often calling them names behind their backs such as "barfly," "whore," "dumbass," or "*dupa yash*" (Polish for "dumbass"). She didn't accept that we all have different gifts. Hers was her baking acumen, but in her mind that carried little weight when someone dropped off home-baked goods that made her feel challenged.

That evening when Valerie drove past our home, Mom's criticism, espoused after repeating Busia's comment, screamed that she *was* jealous of me. Busia's remark had to have stung like a slap to her face, I speculated.

From that, I understood why Mom desperately wanted me to flunk statistics class by missing my final exam. In her eyes, that would deface me and deflate her mother's off-handed compliment about me as an infant. Mom's blocking the door was her way, I reasoned, of wreaking vengeance on me for getting the approval from her mother that she never got. It's like someone who directs anger toward a sibling or lies about them because they believe their mom loves that sibling more than she loves them. Or a work colleague who downplays a coworker's success because they feel outshined.

Fast-forward two decades later to a phone call with my Aunt Celia. That call was like a theater's spotlight beamed on the missing clue: it confirmed what I had already figured. My aunt revealed that when she visited her husband's mother, Busia, with whom Mom lived until almost age thirty-nine, Busia "was not accepting of Martha," she said. "Busia 'discounted' what your mom said or did with 'Oh, that's Martha,'" as if my mom were a disappointment, my aunt noted. That disappointment had to seep into my mom's bones. There it sat dormant until activated by a catalyst—Busia's remark about me—and up turned the heat.

A Merging of Two Worlds

1974

It was the summer before my sophomore year. The kitchen sink was a foot away. My thirst needed water. My thoughts were on the dunes, where I would spend the afternoon with two girls from work. They were picking me up in less than an hour. My two-piece swimsuit was already beneath my shorts and top.

Out of the blue, a force from behind hurled me forward. I found myself flat on the floor, my stomach pressed against the dirty, sticky linoleum, a weight atop my back. My mind raced to unscramble what was happening. The answer came fast: it's Mom. Within seconds, she stripped off my summer shorts and pulled down my swimsuit bottom, exposing my bare butt. As if in a stupor, she silently and repeatedly pummeled my butt and lower back with her fists and the palm of her hands. I was screaming, "Why are you doing this? What did I do? I didn't do anything wrong. I didn't do anything wrong! Why are you doing this?" No answer. Tears muffled my pleas for her to stop. I worried she could damage me for life.

A moment before, on my way to the kitchen, I passed her sitting at the dining room table with a mountain of crumpled paper balls heaped before her. She was struggling to write a letter to her family in Poland. Instead of writing a draft of what she wanted to say, she'd write on good paper and when she didn't like what she wrote, she'd crumple it into a ball and toss it to the middle of the table. *She's frustrating herself*, I thought.

As she savagely pounded me, the back door opened. Lisa Bradegovich, a red-headed family personality—Mom's niece's daughter—with close ties to Mom, was at the house, sunbathing in the backyard. She stepped into the kitchen, but my body blocked her path. This was a woman who never concealed her dislike for me.

With a flicker of hope, I looked up. With tears streaming down my face, I pleaded, "Tell her to stop. I didn't do anything wrong. She's beating me for no reason. Please, please? Help me! He-e-lp me!"

Standing there coolly, looking down at me lying there with my mom viciously beating my back and bare butt, she sneered, "Good for you, you bitch!" Her retort delivered the same disdain typically expressed by Mom.

By that point I had no pride: "Please, pleee-e-ease, help me! I'm begging you." She turned and walked out the back door.

A minute or two later, Mom stopped beating me. She got up, silently. As if nothing had happened, she returned to the dining room table to finish her letter.

I rose from the floor and checked for broken bones. I was okay. Hurt, but okay. I pulled up my swimming suit bottom and picked up my shorts. In my shared bedroom, I sat on my bed and tried to compose myself. It was hard. I felt violated, shaken to my core. In the kitchen, I had been so helpless, totally disempowered. I could not extricate myself from Mom's attack. She was a heavy woman, around if not over two hundred pounds—more than twice my weight.

It took me a while to calm down.

Though I had always heard that no emotion is stronger than maternal love, I believe Mom was incapable of love. That day's attack was yet another confirmation of her long-overdue need for help. I phoned my work colleague and told her to count me out for the day. I didn't explain why.

That incident reinforced how I saw Mom: sick and weak. Anyone who needs to use violence, belittlement, or lies to boost themself is weak. *I'm stronger than she is*, I thought. She didn't *do* anything to *me*—to the part of me that, without my body, answers to my name. And my helplessness there did not make me a victim. Victimhood is a mindset, a choice—a club I refuse to join. I am not a victim.

That incident did, however, unveil to me the reality that I truly had no control over my life.

Before then, I believed we each control our own destiny. That beating, however, turned that perception upside down. My mind kept replaying the incident over and over. I was stuck, reeling over how helpless I had felt when pinned to the floor. I could do nothing to stop the beating. It changed the dynamics of how I viewed myself fitting into this world. It stripped away that invisible protective suit that sequestered me from Mom, separating us into two different worlds. Her attack smooshed our worlds together and carved a direct channel for her comments and denigration to hit my heart.

Before that day, I experienced her solely as someone who was seriously mentally ill but separate from me. I felt relatively safe. However, after Mom's attack, I no longer felt safe. I still saw her as ill, but now I felt vulnerable. That attack added a new dimension to our relationship. The lens I viewed Mom through now bore a film of fear that she could irreversibly change my life. She could kill me. I shared this with no one.

I never discussed that incident with Mom either. Nor did I talk with Lisa about her conduct.

That incident taught me about humanity. Before that, I had believed that we as humans, summoned by our hearts and minds, would step in to help another in their time of need. I believed that no matter how we felt about another person—even if we felt they were more gifted, talented, popular, stronger, prettier, or smarter than us—our humanity would prevail. We would step up when needed. Lisa's sneer, laden with epicaricacy, had proved me wrong. It made me realize we could not count on others to act as we would if we saw someone being violently beaten. That day I lost faith in humanity.

I realized I could not count on anyone to step forward to do the right thing for me, should I need help. I vowed that I would not allow Lisa's vehemence toward me to deprive me of exercising my humanity should someone need my help.

The rest of that summer, something peculiar was unfolding within me. It felt like a vaguely imperceptible worm weaving its way within. It manifested as an urge to stuff down food even though I wasn't hungry and to then force my body to emetically expel the contents of my stomach. It was my body's unconsciously guided way to rid myself of toxicity from that experience and to reclaim control over my life that, deep down, I felt I had lost. By the end of summer, I had a new friend: her name was Bulimia.

The Intruder

1975

The summer before my junior year, Uncle Lou, who had connections with the fire department and city hall, offered to get me a job. Though I appreciated his offer, I was independent, so I declined. I needed to find my own work. That summer, I stayed in Indianapolis. There, I found both a job and two girls—a collegemate and a friend of a friend—interested in sharing a place. We leased a second-story, one-bedroom apartment. When I visited the neighborhood, I realized it looked shady. But I needed a place to stay. *I could handle this for three months*, I decided.

However, one girl's parents looked at the place and mandated that she absolutely could not live there, saying it was "not safe." She still paid her part of the rent—it was cheap—and her parents put her up in a nice apartment.

The night my roommate, Kelly, and I moved in, a police car pulled up behind us as we unpacked. The officer asked if we were moving in. "If you were my daughters, I wouldn't let you live here," he said. "This is a dangerous neighborhood. There's a rapist on the loose. You'll stick out like sore thumbs. You're asking for trouble if you stay here." As he pulled away, Kelly and I continued to unpack the car.

For safety, we set up our own security system, one we could afford, to prevent break-ins at night. The entrance to our apartment was one door that led directly outside. It opened inward into a three-foot vestibule, facing a steep staircase of about fourteen steps that led directly to our apartment. Our security system consisted of a four-inch by six-inch block of wood that was cut so it fit snugly between the outside door and the riser of the first stair. When we put the board in place at night before going to sleep, it blocked the door from opening.

That summer, I worked in administration and accounting for an asphalt company. Kelly worked at the zoo, handling animals. Each night, she came home exhausted and complained about harboring animals' fleas. A couple of weeks into the job, she quit. A few days later, she asked me to pick her up from the first day of her new job. The parking lot was full of expensive, high-end vehicles. *Looks like Kelly landed at a fine dining restaurant,* I thought. *She will make good tips here.* I went inside to wait for her. In the small lobby stood several men in suits and ties, waiting for the hostess to seat them. When I heard the hostess' voice, I looked up. Standing before me was a short young lady a little older than me, naked, except for a thong and tassels covering her nipples. I told her I was there to pick up Kelly. "Kelly's up next," she said. "You can take a seat by the stage." Kelly was now a stripper.

Not having a car, Kelly relied on others to drive her to work and occasionally on the clientele to bring her home. A few weeks into her job, her employer started rotating her, with the rest of the girls, through the three clubs he owned across the state. So, with her working one week at each club, I had my own place for two weeks out of three.

I was a night owl. One night while taking a bath at around 11:30 p.m., a familiar rustling sound came from the kitchen. I couldn't readily identify it. Was it the window? *It can't be the window. We're on the second floor.*

The sound came again. It was the window! I then heard Kelly's cat, Noah, screech in the kitchen as if someone had stepped on his tail. He nudged open the bathroom door, widening the gap to about four inches, and came up to the tub.

I told myself I could still be wrong. I knew I wasn't, though. I waited for confirmation. It came in a squeak from a floorboard at the kitchen doorway leading to the hall. Someone was in the apartment! I listened to footsteps slowly make their way down the hall that connected the kitchen at the back of the apartment with the living room at the front. The bathroom was the first door to the left, off the hall.

I froze. Thoughts raced through my mind. There was nothing I could do. *I'm going to get killed!* This was a bad neighborhood. Friends visiting me would toot their horns and wait in their cars for all ninety-five pounds of me to escort them to my apartment. I waited in terror for what would come next. A voice in my head directed me: "Scoot down."

That's strange. That's not my thought. Okay.

I did.

"Scoot down lower."

I did.

"Lower, so only your head shows."

I did.

Please don't let anything bad happen to me.

Outside the bathroom door, the footsteps stopped. The intruder stood there, his face merging with the darkness of the hall. It seemed an eternity that he stood there looking at my wet head protruding above the tub. The footsteps then resumed.

He's checking out the place.

I listened to the footsteps move past the next left—the stair hall leading down to the outside door. A lot of good our security system did. Being on the second floor, I never dreamed that anyone could break in without going through that door.

The footsteps continued past the bedroom I shared with my roommate and faded into the living room. I waited. Silence. Then I heard snoring. Yes, snoring. He was sleeping in the living room, where the phone was! At that time, cell phones were a mere concept.

Quietly, I got out of the tub, wrapped a towel around myself, and tiptoed to the bedroom, which was next to the living room. I pushed a chest against the door, along with both my and my roommate's floor mattresses. I got dressed. Around one leg of the chest, I tied a sheet and to that another to make it look like I had jumped out the screenless window.

Into the cedar-paneled closet I crept. My hiding space was a cubby hole about two feet deep, and equally wide, its base about table height above the floor. Nestled behind a rack of hung clothes, I prayed I could leave the apartment before the intruder found me.

Once a tiny strip of sunlight bled into the closet beneath the door, I grabbed a dress for the office and initiated my escape. Quietly, I opened the bedroom door and tiptoed down the stairs. Removing the floorboard between the stairs and outside door was tricky because that tended to be loud. But I made it outside. As I walked to my car, I noticed a car that was never there before: a long, violet sedan with huge tail fins. I made a mental note of that and recorded its license plate.

I drove to the office, called the police, and returned home. The violet car was gone. One officer went inside to check out the apartment, and another talked to me in the backyard. We noticed a narrow pipe that ran up the back wall not far from a kitchen window.

"There is no way anyone could climb up to that second-story window and get in," the officer asserted. "It's impossible. The window is too high up and that pipe couldn't support the weight of a man," he said. He told me I made this up! He did not believe me. That made it pointless to bring up the license plate number. After the officer inside came out and said it was clear, they left. Inside, I found the toilet seat was up and there was food in the cat's bowl. I returned to work.

When I told my friend Lillian about this, she invited me to stay at her home. I didn't want to intrude on her family, but I spent a few nights there. Her mother was so gracious to me. After gathering my courage and hoping for no repeat performances, I returned home with trepidation.

For a few nights, I couldn't sleep out of fear, but I gradually started feeling more comfortable with being back in my apartment.

How did this guy get in? I wondered. The kitchen windows, I discovered, were so old that they could be easily pulled inside, meaning that from the outside, they could be pushed in and up to bypass the lock. I pounded nails into the frame to block the windows from being opened. One night, it was so hot that I removed the nails to open both windows and didn't pound them back in.

~⌒

Eww! Is that cigarette smoke? Ugh, alcohol, too? That thought flashed through my mind as I realized I was not dreaming. To my right, next to my mattress, kneeled a figure. *He's back!* I feigned sleeping. His breath, reeking of smoke and alcohol, floated across my face. Moonlight filled the room. *He could see me*, I told myself. *Do not move. Dear God, help me.*

Gently kissing my forehead, my intruder whispered, "Sleep well, my love." I feared he would do more. He didn't. He left my room. When snoring resonated from the wall separating us, I again plugged into survival mode, repeating my actions from the last time he broke in. He was not a welcome guest.

The next morning, I drove to work to call the police. They were at the apartment when I returned. Different officers but the same scenario. "No one could possibly have climbed up to that window," said one officer. They did not believe me.

I went inside and again found the toilet seat up and food in the cat's bowl. Distraught and not knowing what to do that night, I returned to work. I didn't tell anyone at work about this.

A week later I awoke on a bright, sunny Saturday morning to loud snoring coming from the front room. *You have got to be kidding,* I thought. Then a female voice whispered something. *He's now bringing his girlfriends to my home? How dare he?* I fumed. *This is going to stop TODAY!* I dressed hurriedly, added a belt, and inserted a string of safety pins across my pant zipper. I grabbed my keys and a can of mace gifted from a friend for protection. I was fired up! I was going to put an end to this. I stormed into the front room.

There on the floor lay the intruder and his friend—my roommate Kelly. She introduced him as Lyle. "He's an ex-con," she explained. Great. This was the first I had heard of him. He learned of our home by dropping her off from work one night.

Lyle had been in prison for felony theft and was on parole. Though he was over six feet tall and muscular, he was adept at climbing and maneuvering his frame in intricate ways from his pre-prison days.

That summer, he popped in and out of the apartment via his inventive entrance, avoiding the door and our elaborate security system. I never knew when he would visit. It was always at night when he came to sleep on the front room floor. I had hoped he wouldn't be a problem, and that was so. After meeting him and seeing his attraction to my roommate, I no longer felt threatened by his presence.

I never inquired about his last name. He became a *de facto* roommate. What I learned from him is that the label "ex-con" does not necessarily mean its bearer is a horrible person to be feared. This uninvited housemate was a respectful, protective, and genuine human being. Meeting him softened my heart toward people who try to rehabilitate but are shunned by society for unfortunate choices and irresponsible decisions they have made.

A Cruel Joke?

1975

In my junior year of college, I was nominated to the homecoming court. When the news broke, instead of being ecstatic, I initially questioned whether it was a cruel joke. *Who, I wondered, would nominate me for homecoming court?*

I asked my suitemate, Cheryl Minks. She said, "You're so nice. Everybody likes you."

What no one knew, as I kept pretty much to myself, is that I had no self-confidence. I did not consider myself attractive. I was skinny, quiet, and bookish.

In my monthly call to Mom, I mentioned the nomination and told her I planned to withdraw. I didn't need to be on the court. It didn't mean anything to me. And if I made the court, I would need to buy a dress for a dance that I didn't plan to attend.

Mom responded, "Awk, no one's going to vote for you. You're not going to make it." Pausing, she continued, "Stay in and see what happens."

Her voice on "Stay in and see what happens" held a smidgeon of pride. That was the closest to a positive remark she had ever uttered. I construed her voice as wanting me to stay in because, if I were elected, it would give her something to brag about. As an enticement, she added, "If you get voted in, I will buy you a dress for the dance."

"You will?" I replied questioningly, surprised she would even say that.

"Yes, I will," she promised. "I will buy you a dress if you get in. But that's not going to happen. No one's going to vote for you."

Well, I made it. That's when what I should have expected happened. Mom jeered, "I'm not buying you a dress! You're not going to have anything to wear. Everyone is going to laugh at you! Hahahahaha!"

I thought, *We'll see.*

My friends came to the rescue, and I wore a beautiful gown to the dance.

Bittersweet Ending of College

My senior year in college is when I felt my world imploding. Each week, I worked twenty to twenty-five hours, volunteered ten hours, and was taking laboratory-intensive classes. I had a boyfriend at a long distance. I was not happy. That year I did not want to go home for Thanksgiving, Christmas, or Easter. My sister and I were distanced. I felt like an orphan, alone in the world.

Being busy with school and work, I lost touch with Mary Keefe (whom I called but not as often), Aunt Virge, and Aunt Mary. Nor had I seen Sister Ann for the past few years; she was in Boys Town, Nebraska.

I felt no joy. I didn't have many friends. I felt I didn't have a family. I told no one about my home life. When sitting quietly, I could feel the tumultuous discord of my early years at home rattle within me, with no release. I continued to express my inner pain through bulimia. Every phone call home followed with me hanging my head over the toilet, but I still called because I felt that was what I was supposed to do.

I had not read about bulimia. Nor had I any training in psychotherapy. For me, that condition had nothing to do with body image; it gave me a sense of control over my life—a false sense. I always had control, but I no longer felt that after Mom's attack.

At the end of the school year, I had my diploma sent to me. I saw no point in going through the graduation ceremony. I didn't feel good inside. Neither parent ever saw the campus.

Bitten by Rats

1977

That August, I started graduate studies in pharmacology at Purdue University under a fellowship from the National Institutes of Health. Did a gap of eighty-five pages mysteriously missing from my new pharmacology textbook portend that this may not be the right thing for me? The thought darted across my mind when exchanging the book.

After I moved to campus, Mom called. "How come you're still in school? Everyone else in your grade is out now and working." I told her that everyone is smarter than me, playing back her words to me. "I need more schooling," I said. She didn't understand I was in graduate school. She ended her inquiry with her mantra, "I hope you flunk"—something I never heard her say to my sister.

A few weeks later, I was delighted to see a letter from Sister Ann. Until I read it. She wrote that as the older daughter, I "should be home" living with Mom and "looking after her," not pursuing graduate studies. Mom was sixty-three and hopping on and off ladders enjoying painting her living room. My sister lived with her. Sister Ann explained that when her sibling Helen left home to marry, my mom had to quit her job as a janitress and returned to live with her mom. "That's the way it's done," she wrote. "The eldest unmarried daughter is supposed to live at home and look after her mom. You already have a college degree. This is what you must do," she insisted. She had enclosed a fifty-dollar bill.

Perhaps that was protocol in our family in the 1940s but that certainly did not resonate with me. After thinking about her presumed "good intentions," I responded. I wrote back telling her that I have my own life to live. I do what I feel is best for me. Though she means well, that principle does not work for me. I don't agree with her recommendation, and I am not going to move back home. That is not in my best interest. I returned her gift of fifty dollars, which I assumed she intended to go toward gas for my return trip.

She responded with a card, remarking that returning the money was a "social transgression." Interestingly, she was notably silent about my intended action. Never again did she tell me how to live my life.

I chose toxicology as my focus. In the pharmacology department, I was one of three or so female graduate students among roughly thirty full-time students.

One day my major professor, Dr. Gary Carlson, led me to a heavy metal door down the hall. Opening it, he exclaimed, "Here are your rats." His voice betrayed an expectation that I should be delighted he got me rats. They were larger than the ones I had worked with at Indiana University Medical Center, each about the size of a chicken and unsocialized, meaning more vicious.

My research centered on evaluating what effect polychlorinated biphenyls (PCB) and polybrominated biphenyls (PBB)—highly toxic pollutants—may have on the metabolism and activity of the drug procaine, also called novocaine, in rats. The experiments involved sticking a tube down rats' throats to deliver an aliquot of vegetable oil to a control group and injecting a diluted test compound into rats' abdomens for an experimental group. I was bitten a few times; I handled the rats with my bare hands as I couldn't get a good grip with gloves. Sometimes when rats were being removed to harvest their organs for analysis, a few would escape into the laboratory, and a technician and I would need to chase them down.

Besides doing research, I also taught pharmacology laboratory classes to fourth-year pharmacy students.

That year, I still struggled with bulimia, which I hid from my roommate.

What I noticed taking shape during my senior year of college now became more pronounced. Something was terribly wrong. I felt that all the negativity spewed at me at Mom's home over the years had punctured holes in my well-being and transmogrified into an impasse, encaging and blocking me from advancing toward my goals. I questioned whether I should have taken the year off to get back on track. But I didn't know how to right my path. The problem was . . .

Repeat: "Do Not Comprehend"

1977

When words on the page devolved into a mush of alphabet soup, I didn't know what to do. My eyes moved across the words, but I could extract no meaning from what I read. I moved to the next paragraph. Same thing. No, it was not dyslexia. Distinct words were clearly visible. However, I could not read what they meant. I was one month into graduate school. I didn't know what to do.

I experienced this when I returned from a visit to Mom's house. She had invited me to her home a few weeks after my letter to Sister Ann. I didn't want to go, but that inner yearning and lingering hope for a connection to some semblance of family persuaded me to accept. For the previous four years, I had not had any meaningful connection with family. My four heart-aligned mothers and I had drifted apart; we had not seen each other for ages. Reluctantly, amid hope intermixed with trepidation, I ignored my gut feeling and accepted Mom's invitation.

As I had since learned to cook, I invited Mom to a dinner that I would prepare at her home and informed her that she would be my guest. "I'm serving."

Mom said she had invited Lisa, the sunbather from a few summers before, to join us. I thought, *That should be interesting*. Almost every interaction I have had with her came with a splash of derision. Years before, she laughed, "You're such a goody two shoes." I wasn't in her league. I recalled that when she was sixteen, she bragged about dating a married man and shrugged off his wife's tearful requests to leave her husband alone. I couldn't understand her impenetrable emotional armor: his wife's tears didn't bother her. So, for my upcoming dinner with Mom and Lisa, I knew two things: one, I had to watch my back, and two, dinner wouldn't be boring.

Mom sat at the head of the dining room table opposite me, her hair still predominately black at age sixty-three. A cream tablecloth of tatted lacework graced the table that I set with Mom's Wedgewood china, along with a floral vase in the center. A slight, perceptible smile settled across Mom's face. This time she sat; she was not waltzing around the table making sure everyone had food. That made me happy.

The conversation veered to the neighborhood, relatives, and local events before landing on food.

"This is good," Mom said, chewing on a piece of beef stroganoff. "How did you make this?"

I promised to give her the recipe. "This is from the cookbook you gave me," I replied, not realizing I had just opened the door to hell.

"What cookbook?" asked Lisa.

"The McCall's cookbook. She slipped it into my bag the last time I was here. It has so many wonderful recipes."

"Martha, you said you were going to give that to me. Why did you give it to Judie after you agreed to give it to me?" grilled Lisa, sounding prickly.

"You can have the cookbook," I said, hoping to extinguish what I sensed was the fomenting of an altercation. "I didn't know anyone wanted it. I only brought a notecard with the recipe copied onto it. When I get back home, I will send you the cookbook."

"Martha, you said you would give that to me." The crescendo was rising. "Why didn't you do that?!"

Mom didn't answer. She shrugged her shoulders and cowered her head. Shrinking into her chair as if to make herself smaller, she looked down, not engaged with Lisa. "I didn't know you wanted it," she murmured unconvincingly.

"I can't believe you didn't follow through on this, you bitch! That was supposed to go to me! You promised it to me. Instead, you gave it to Judie."

Lisa stood up, her plate in hand, holding it by its rim. "You can have your dinner, you bitch! I'm not going to be part of this!" she shouted. With a thrust of her wrist, she flung the food on her plate toward Mom. A mélange of beef, gravy, noodles, and green beans splatted her target, landing on Mom's face, hair, sweater, and dress. Lisa thwacked her emptied plate onto the table and stormed out the door, slamming it behind her.

Silence filled the room. I was shaking. I had not experienced that level of volatility for a while as I hadn't been living there. Mom continued to eat, unperturbed, as if nothing had happened. Into the kitchen I dashed to retrieve a damp dish towel and wiped the wine-laced gravy dripping down Mom's face. I picked off the noodles, green beans, and beef strewed across her sweater. I moved her plate to the side, with gravy and food dangling off its rim. Mom continued to eat as I wiped her face clean.

"Put your fork down, Mom," I urged gently. "You have gravy all over your face." As I wiped her forehead, cheeks, and chin, she looked down. With her fingers, she picked off a morsel of beef nestled among the folds of her dress and put it into her mouth.

"This is really good." Her voice resonated with contentment. My heart sank seeing her eating food off her body as if this were a normal, everyday occurrence.

Tears mounted in my eyes. I took in the disheveled crown of noodles nesting in her hair and a stream of gravy that I had missed, now dribbling down her chin. It hurt seeing her being the recipient of so much wrath but most of all, her normalizing the toxicity of what had just happened. I picked off the noodles, one by one, along with the remaining green beans.

"I didn't know you promised that cookbook to Lisa. I don't need it. I'm sorry I mentioned it. I didn't know."

"Oh, that's okay."

"Stand up and take off your sweater, Mom. You have gravy all over its neckline."

"No, I'm fine. My sweater is okay." I wiped what I could off her sweater. "I will have more of that beef. It's really good." She was calm and composed like she was out at a restaurant.

"Here's a clean plate." I mounded a generous helping of the beef stroganoff along with more noodles and green beans.

"Are you okay?" I asked as I moved my plate closer to her to keep her company. She was enjoying her meal. I couldn't eat. On the inside, I trembled from the toxic drama that consistently seemed to percolate in Mom's home. Being away from my childhood home, immersed in a calm setting, had lowered my tolerance for shouting and drama.

"Yeah. I'm okay. Have some more food," Mom said.

That evening, I cleaned the kitchen. The next morning, on my way back to Purdue, I thought about how Mom normalized having food flung into her face. That was an act of aggression directed toward her. It was not normal behavior to fling food into someone's face. Nor can any reason justify that. I wondered what happened to Mom to totally desensitize her to aggression. That disturbed me. Being in that house disturbed me. It was like a nuclear reactor with toxic energy seeping from its walls, promising to quash any sense of peace and harmony that crossed its threshold.

On my drive back, I decided, *That is not my home. That is not who I am. That is not who I am becoming.*

Unlocking the door to the dorm room I shared with my roommate, I entered the open space. There was no place there for me to be alone and privately process what had happened the night before. I didn't mention it to my roommate. That afternoon, I tried to assimilate back into normalcy, feeling anything but that on the inside.

That is when I tried reading a chapter of a book but got lost in the jumble of words splattered across the page. More and more, I experienced this inability to read. That was most unusual for me. Though I could see the words clearly, it was like smoke obscured their meaning when strung together like pearls into sentences. Their context escaped capture by my mind, floating away like delicate, wispy, amorphous strands of cirrus clouds dissipating high in the vast sky.

My ability to read was evaporating. That frightened me. Recipes were not a problem: I didn't follow their instructions. But aside from that, the meaning of text, irrespective of its source—whether it be in course books, other nonfiction, fiction, magazines, or biochemistry (a love of mine)—was not easily forthcoming.

The Toxicology Lab

1977–1978

I longed to cut ties with family but was concerned about the optics. I was a "good girl," and you just don't cut yourself off from your family, even if you're not involved with them. Instead, I opted to endure the situation, never talking about my family or Mom to anyone, including my boyfriend, best friend, roommate, and classmates.

Life at Purdue dragged on. I never thought I'd ever say that about school; I always loved learning. But now I was struggling simply to read. I finally reached a point where I no longer cared. I lost all interest in school. I had no interest whatsoever in pharmacology or toxicology. I was lost. I was on autopilot. I was dead inside. No one knew.

When I completed the experiments required for my work on PCBs and PBBs, Dr. Carlson listed me as an author on an article published in the journal, *Research Communications in Chemical Pathology and Pharmacology*.

That year, my grades dipped below the GPA required to keep the fellowship. I didn't care. I was like an empty vessel, enveloped in an opaque wrapper guaranteed to hide its contents.

Though my grades dipped, they were still sufficiently high to qualify for a graduate assistantship. My major professor recommended I transfer to the Bionucleonics Department in the School of Pharmacy. He said they could give me a research or teaching assistantship and my coursework would transfer over to that program. That held as much interest for me as drinking ink. I graciously declined as I tried to mask my lack of enthusiasm.

He was such a great guy. He then asked, "If you were going to study anything, what would it be?"

I replied, "Food chemistry."

He arranged for me to meet with the head of the Food Science Department. After the meeting, I decided to transfer there. I was awarded a research assistantship.

I broke up with my boyfriend. When Mom heard the news, not from me, she shouted, "What a dummy you are. Nobody is going to marry you. You're so damn ugly. You're going to be an old maid."

I was only twenty-three, and marriage was not among my goals. My goal was to obtain a master's degree and work in research in a discipline that would trickle out in some meaningful way to help others.

In hindsight, my transfer from the School of Pharmacy was prophetic. It aligned with the views I later adopted concerning medication. Though I believe Western medicine plays a significant role in health care, I also believe our bodies heal themselves in some instances. For example, the needles stuck into our bodies by acupuncturists help bring our energy system into balance and that then allows our bodies to take over the healing process. Amusingly, for someone who studied pharmacology, I favor natural remedies and tend to steer away from medication.

A Turning Point

1978

Welcoming me into my new home at the food science laboratory were my new major professor, a female student from Taiwan starting her master's degree, a female student from California finishing her master's degree, and a male student from Brazil completing his PhD who went on to become a professor at a university in Brazil. Congealing the group was Lynn Miles, a sixty-ish laboratory technician. She was a short, sturdy, inquisitive lady who knew a bit about everything and loved entertaining students and professors with gatherings at her home.

Lynn became a close friend. She had degrees in medical technology and social work. Though she was not a therapist, she asked perceptive questions about my family, and I started opening up about my life. She listened to me and let me talk.

With Lynn, I shared my experience growing up with an abusive, mentally ill mother. What I believe helped me most, I told Lynn, was relying on my own inner compass, assuming responsibility for my decisions, and examining what was behind difficult situations. It also helped never to believe as true anything my mom told me about myself and to accept her not as a nurturer but as a deeply wounded, ill-intentioned three-year-old—as callous as that may sound.

I told Lynn that my mom's hurtful comments and the massive energy she poured into them with viciousness unfurling from her lips, and the toxicity from her attack on me, are what I believe accumulated like dross in my body. At the time of this writing, I also believe it seeped into my energy field. Back then, I didn't know anything about clearing our energy system. Talking with Lynn helped empty the muck that had accrued within.

Near the end of one chat, Lynn said she had met a handful of women—"petals from Mars," she called them. These women, she said, "come across as kind and diplomatic with integrity, grace, and compassion. A few even seem gentle. That's their outer, 'petal-like' expression; that's what people see at first. However, what distinguishes these women," she continued reflectively, "is their core of incredible inner strength, courage, determination, and resilience—that ability to adapt to difficult situations. They are fiercely independent and withstand scorching trials without withering." All this, she told me, is enveloped within that "beauty" of the flower.

Lynn went on to say that what helped these women navigate adversity was a trust in their inner compass, a responsibility they assume for their actions, their resilience in being able to bounce back, and an inner knowing of what to believe, or not, as true of themselves. In the women she knew, those character traits burned with a fiery, Mars-like essence of determination, she mused, much as you would expect from a flower growing on Mars with its petals floating to earth.

Following a pause, she lowered her voice and said, "You're like that. You're a strong, fiercely determined young lady. People may not see that until they know you because on the outside, what shows up first is your gentle nature." She continued, "You could have let yourself wither under the weight of the past, but you didn't. Instead, you tapped your inner strength and steeled yourself. You learned from your past, and you keep moving forward, resiliently undaunted by obstacles."

I was touched. That was the first time anyone had ever said anything kind to me about who I am at my core that I could realistically relate to. I took her comment as a lovely expression of support.

Over that year, things began looking brighter. My grades were good again. I started dating again. My life force was reviving. My bulimia ended as if it had sloughed off on its own, like an outgrown snakeskin, shed to reveal a new, stronger, and healthier me. My life began shifting toward a sense of "normalcy."

My research centered on what were little-known compounds at the time—anthocyanins, colorants that impart the vivid reds, blues, and purples, as examples, to foods such as cranberries, raspberries, cherries, and blueberries. The color of anthocyanins changes with pH. My research involved extracting anthocyanins from plant sources, concentrating them with rotary evaporators, isolating the extracts into individual compounds with chromatography, and looking at stabilizing their color for food applications using spectroscopy.

The head of the Food Science Department, Dr. Paul Abernathy, sat in on a seminar I gave on dihydrochalcones— phytonutrients found in citrus fruit, some tasteless and others responsible for the bitter taste in, for example, grapefruit juice.

He knew I had lost the pharmacology fellowship. After my presentation, he asked to speak with me. Looking me directly in the eye, he asked, "How could you, of all people, lose a fellowship? You're obviously bright and have so much potential." He went on to say kind things, such as that he could see I was driven and had excellent reasoning skills. "School is not a problem for you," he said. "What happened that caused you to lose that fellowship?" He was genuinely curious, I felt, and seemed to care. He wanted to know. He was the only one who probed, "Why?" I tend to be private and not share personal information. I expressed my appreciation for his comments and gave him a watered-down synopsis of how I had been feeling the previous couple of years.

A Magical Christmas

1978

When I was twenty-three, I had the most amazing Christmas. I decided not to spend it at my mom's house. I did not want to have to deal with the ongoing drama of her behavior. My dear friend Ann invited me to her home for Christmas, and that is what I told Mom. It was all true: my dear friend was Mom's sister, Sister Ann, and she had invited me to the convent at St. Pancratius Parish in Chicago. This would be my second stint in a convent, my first visit being a week-long sojourn at a different convent one summer during junior high.

On my way there, I stopped off at Mom's home, gave Mom her Christmas present, and then headed to the convent. There, a myriad of nuns bustled with last-minute packing to meet their rides on their escape to their families' homes for the holidays.

Christmas Eve, I spent with Sister at the convent. We cooked, chatted, giggled, and had a fun time enjoying each other's company. Other nuns floated about the convent in their ankle-length brown habits, topped with partial veils that started at the crown, revealing bangs, or allowing their hairline to peek through. Sister's short, curled, brown bangs sat atop her unlined forehead. Her face had narrowed now that she was sixty-seven years old. Her voice had softened with gentleness over the years.

On Christmas Day, Sister had a surprise: we were going to visit my cousin Sophie, who lived about an hour away. Sophie was hosting an open house for the family. After Mass, Sister Ann, four other nuns, and I piled into the convent's old sedan with Sister Superior driving. Everyone was silent for the entire trip. Sister dropped each nun off at her requested spot with stern instructions to be ready to be picked up at a set time.

Buzzing with merriment, Sophie's home was the perfect elixir for topping off the holiday. Its convivial atmosphere washed over me, as I drank in delightfully spirited conversations with her and her guests. The hours flew! It felt like we had just gotten there when it was time to watch for Sister Superior's car. Sister Ann advised that we do *not* want to keep Sister Superior waiting.

On the drive back, no one spoke. I had to chuckle: When we stopped for gas, Sister Superior got out of the car to fill the tank. As soon as that car door closed, *everyone* became animated and started talking. It reminded me of how kids in grade school come alive when the teacher steps outside the room. As soon as the car door opened, everyone reverted to their silent, stone-faced demeanor, being pleasant if Sister Superior addressed them.

That evening, Sister Ann, the unofficial historian of her family, revealed that my grandmother, Busia, born in 1871, grew up poor, working as a servant girl in a section of Austria that became annexed to Poland years later, in 1918. In the summer, Busia slept outside under the trees, Sister told me.

Yearning for a better life, she signed up to become a mail-order bride. The paperwork went through, and she headed via ship to the United States.

On her trans-Atlantic journey, she met a respectable gentleman, Albert Mroz. Sister Ann didn't mention any blooming romance; she stuck to the sterile facts. When the ship docked at Ellis Island in New York, Busia watched the other mail-order brides descend the gangway to shore with their paperwork in hand. At the base of the gangway buzzed a mass of "excited" and "rowdy" men in a "frenzy." Busia watched "the men grab women like cattle, grab them by their upper arms and yank them off the gangway . . . Some hollered, 'This one's mine.' . . . 'I got this one!' . . . 'Next one's mine!'" No one checked any paperwork to match the mail-order brides with the men who had paid for their voyage. Busia held back from getting off the ship, said Sister. When she did, she walked down the gangway with Albert, the man she had befriended during the voyage, whom she eventually married. He became my grandfather.

I was impressed by my grandmother's gumption. It dawned on me that Busia's action meant that some man didn't get a bride when he had paid for her journey. I wondered if that bothered her. Then I put myself in her shoes and reflected on how I would have decided in her circumstances after witnessing what she saw. If I were in my late teens and saw a frenzied crowd of wildly excited, raucous men grabbing women "like cattle," some perhaps intoxicated, one of whom was to become my husband, I could see myself doing just as she did.

Sister Ann then turned the spotlight to herself. She confessed that when she was young, she made an important decision but did not follow through. It was the start of the Great Depression, 1929. Sister had been in the convent for three years since entering at around age fifteen. Those years proved difficult. For example, when she was tasked with washing a floor, the nun inspecting it would walk across it, soil it, and tell her to "wash it all over again," she said. Her mother was coming to visit. Sister Ann worked up the nerve to tell her that she wanted to quit the convent. She even rehearsed a speech on her decision, she said.

But before Sister Ann could express her desire, Busia, she said, told her she was so proud of her and beaming with pride, handed her a pound of ground beef, saying, "Look what I brought you." On beholding her mother's pride, she couldn't follow through.

The beef part didn't resonate with me at first, but then I thought about how much that must have cost during the Depression. I assume Sister viewed her mother as making a huge financial sacrifice. I didn't question Sister, as I didn't want to seem disrespectful or as diminishing what she considered a significant sacrifice on her mother's part.

I felt sad for Sister giving up on her wishes. *How did she feel about that?* I wondered. I knew she was a good nun and teacher. From experiencing her beautiful, supportive presence, I knew too that she would have made an amazing mother and wife.

Later that night, I wondered why she had shared those stories with me. Her story, I felt, was an implicit nod of approval to me for standing up to her in my first month of grad school, when she told me to move home to look after Mom and I told her I wouldn't because that was incongruent with my long-term goals and was not in my best interest. Both her and Busia's stories were, I believed, her way of relating a lesson about the importance of following your heart and not doing what you think you *should* do to please others.

The day after Christmas, Sister and I headed to downtown Chicago via a bus caught off Archer Street. There we shopped and savored a late lunch at Marshall Field's Walnut Room restaurant. That night, Sister tried to fix me up with a parishioner's son, but I quashed those plans.

The next day while I packed to return to Mom's house, as my schedule allowed one day to spend with Mom, Sister suggested I stop off and visit her sister Marie, the hairdresser—the aunt we knew as Mary in our house. Her apartment in Whiting, Indiana, was on my way. *What a great idea*, I thought. *I would love that.*

As we said goodbye, Sister said she would call Marie and tell her there was a surprise on the way: "Marie, make sure you open the door when someone knocks within the next hour."

Aunt Mary's eyes filled with tears when she opened her door. She squeezed me tightly. She didn't know I was the surprise. My visit touched her heart. After a lovely dinner, we talked and laughed and caught each other up on our lives. At the close of the evening, sitting at her organ, we sang Christmas carols. She gave me a mini singing lesson and explained how to use my diaphragm to increase volume. My aunt was known for being well-read on a variety of subjects. That was such a memorable visit. I loved seeing her.

As I approached Mom's house, she was already on the porch waiting for me. *Hmmm?* I thought. *How did she know I would be coming at this time?* The answer flashed: my aunt, not privy to the secrecy of my visit with Sister Ann, must have called her.

"You lied to me. You told me you were visiting a friend. You saw Sister. And then you went to Mary's and spent the night. You lied, you bitch. You lied," yelled Mom.

"You're right. I saw them, but I didn't lie," I said. "I visited both Sister and Aunt Mary. Both are my dear friends. I like them. I like being around them. They treat me with respect and kindness."

Again, and throughout my short time at home, Mom continued shouting, rephrasing, and shuffling the order of the same sentences but keeping the flow going. "I'm calling everyone and telling them you lied to me."

I told her to do as she pleases. "Say what you want about me. I'm leaving this afternoon to visit another friend in Texas for the New Year." I shouldn't have told her where I was going. At that, my mom's face deepened to an even more brilliant shade of red. I felt sorry for her.

"You can't go!"

I told her, "Yes, I can and I am."

A Police Arrest Averted

1978

It's here. The taxi pulled to a stop in front of Mom's house. It was my transport to the nearby Howard Johnson hotel. There, I would catch a bus to O'Hare airport. On my way to the door, I called out "goodbye." Mom was at the phone, dialing. "Mary!" she yelled, "Judie is a whore! She's going to Texas to get fucked! Tell everyone she's crazy!" When done, she dialed another number. The front door closed behind me.

Settling into the taxi, I took a long, deep breath and thought how lucky I was to have two wonderful aunts I had just seen and to not have to spend the rest of my Christmas break with Mom. I felt sorry for her, but her behavior and verbal abuse were not acceptable and not what I chose to subject myself to.

How interesting, I thought, *that Mom never once told me to my face that I was crazy. Yet she grabs every opportunity to tell people outside our home that.* On the flight down, I pondered why.

I recalled the time she threw me onto the back porch, stripped to underpants that I had to fight to keep on, her laughter audible from behind the locked door. When she allowed me back in, she whispered furtively so as to conceal her role in my nakedness. I then thought of Mom's phone marathon when I was tackling facial acne, shouting into the phone "Judie's crazy!" And the time she arranged rakes and shovels on the dining room table, promising to tell two high school friends coming over that I had brought those in. None of this was normal behavior.

It all aimed, I figured, to convince the outside world that I was the one who was crazy. *Why does she do that? Is it because she herself feels she's crazy? Or has someone told her that she's crazy?*

I ruminated further. *To house guests, did Busia dub her live-in daughter crazy? It sure sounds like she did. Was it so they would understand should Mom act up with angry outbursts, spitting, vitriol, or even near-violent behavior?*

If seven of Mom's family reached out to tell me she is crazy, then yes, I concluded, *she had to have conducted herself like that growing up. And what about Aunt Helen's peculiar question, "How does your mom act at home?" Yes, they all knew she had problems. Amongst themselves, they called her crazy,* I decided.

Perhaps that is why, I determined, *it's so important to Mom that someone else share that label with her. And she is looking to me for that.*

My friend, Robert, picked me up at the airport. Another friend, Leslie, had already arrived. "I have something to tell you before we get to my parents' home," Robert began. "It's not good. Your mother has been repeatedly calling our house. She was yelling filthy vulgarities into the phone. My baby sister answered, and your mom shouted really disgusting things about you. Then she hung up and called again. She kept doing that."

How did Mom get the number to Robert's parents? Oh, she must have gone through my purse, I realized. That was the only place I had it written.

"My baby sister had to listen to your mom's foul language. She's only twelve" he continued.

Yes, my mom could out-cuss any sailor.

"I am so sorry for all that," I apologized.

Cutting me off, he continued. "My parents got involved. This went on for at least an hour, even longer. Your mom calling, yelling at whoever answered the phone, and hanging up. Then calling again and again and again. It was disruptive, to put it lightly."

"My dad wanted to call the police where your mom lives and have her arrested. My mom talked him out of that. After numerous calls, he was able to talk over your mom's voice and get her attention before she hung up. He told her that the next time she calls, he will call the cops on her and they'll come to arrest her. She didn't call back," he said.

"Your mom is sick," he went on. "I'm sorry she is so messed up. I'm sorry you had to live with that. She kept cussing you out, calling you every curse word imaginable—some my dad hadn't even heard of."

I told him those had to be the Polish ones.

"She needs serious help," he said.

"Yes, my mom is gravely ill, mentally," I told him, "and I am so sorry for all the disruption she brought to your household this evening."

On reflection, I was grateful for Robert's mom intervening and averting an arrest. However, on the other hand, I weighed whether an arrest would have been a gift, a lesson, to my mom. She needed a catalyst to awaken her to how others experienced her. Would getting arrested have been a clarion call for her to seek help?

Stance toward Bullies

1980

Someone else's discomfort is not entertainment.

In late spring, I met my new boyfriend for dinner at a German restaurant not far from Purdue's campus. From my vantage point, I watched three male college students, presumably seniors, harass their waitress as she took their order at a table about ten feet away. They didn't look like they had been drinking. They laughed at each other's brash sexual comments about her appearance and peppered her with very personal questions, each one emboldening the other. She haplessly tried to take their order, feigning to be unaffected by their behavior as I witnessed their comments penetrating her armor, making her increasingly uncomfortable. I could sense that she felt violated and did not know what to do as she was *on the job*.

I excused myself from our table. By the time I reached the guys' table, the waitress had just left. The guys were reveling with glee in their testosterone-laden moment of masculinity. Their faces registered surprise to see a thin, petite, blond, soft-spoken woman, slightly older than them, standing before them.

They listened, eyes affixed to mine, as I confronted them about how they treated their waitress. I told them they were coming off like fools.

"How would you like it," I asked, "if someone purposely humiliated you and enjoyed your discomfort? Who would want to date someone who acts like that?" I told them they needed to apologize to the waitress when she returned and to try to act like adults. If they didn't, I would tell management to kick them out. I hoped that if I had to do that, management would support the waitress. They must have sensed strength, for not one of them challenged me as I spoke.

When I returned to my table, my boyfriend asked if I knew the waitress. I didn't. I couldn't sit there and watch those immature boys mistreat her merely because they could. I had to say something. I didn't think twice about approaching them. I felt no harm would come to me in standing up to them. When the waitress returned, I watched them apologize and watched them behave like gentlemen for the remainder of their dinner.

Reflecting on my response to the guys' behavior, I thought about how I would have appreciated it if someone had stepped into the background in that one summer job and put my male coworker in his place.

Eleven years later, when I applied to law school, that boyfriend—now my husband—told me he knew I would someday become a lawyer. By then, I had forgotten about the incident with the obnoxious guys, but he brought it up. He was surprised at how I didn't hesitate to confront what I saw was inappropriate.

Would I step in today to address what I regard as inappropriate behavior? It depends. In today's world, I would, as long as I assessed the situation, felt into the people involved, and felt that doing so would not evoke a dangerous response where anyone could get hurt.

The "Mmmm . . ."

What does a bridal headpiece have to do with a mooing sound?

For my wedding, I opted for a hat instead of a veil. Chicago, I thought, would be the ideal venue to scout for such an item, given its tapestry of shops. After weighing whether to enlist Mom's help on this project, what convinced me to ask her was that we would be in public places, and I could cross one item off my bridal to-do list while having a pleasant lunch with Mom. It would be a mother-daughter day. I hoped.

"Would you mind finding two or three stores in Chicago that sell hats for brides to wear in place of a veil?" I asked Mom. "I will come home at the end of the week, on a Saturday, and we can shop for a hat. Then I will take you to lunch. My treat." Mom agreed to that.

That Saturday, walking onto the bustling street from the underground South Shore train station, I asked Mom, "Where should we go first to look for hats?

"I don't know," she replied.

"Didn't you call any stores to see which have hats for brides to wear?" I asked.

"No," she said.

"I asked if you would find two or three stores here that sell bridal hats that we could visit today. Did you do that?"

"No. I didn't call any stores," Mom replied.

"Okay. Let's try Marshall Field's. They're large and should have a bridal department. Hopefully, they will have something to choose from."

Hearing what I needed, a saleslady set us up in a large dressing room and returned with one hat. Two others, she said, were being brought up. Her entrance interrupted Mom advising that I wear a veil: "Virge wore a hat. She got married in a white suit at city hall."

When the saleslady stepped out of the dressing room to check on the other two hats, Mom asked, "How long is this going to take? I'm hungry." Apparently, the only part of my request that she had latched onto was "lunch."

I would have left the store and returned after lunch, but we had gotten a late start. At Mom's house, my sister's dog jumped onto my lap and urinated on my skirt. As I hadn't brought anything else to change into for my one-day visit, I had to take care of that before we could leave for the train. Mom didn't have a dryer, so I hand-washed the front of my skirt and left the house with it partially damp.

Mom was uninterested in helping me find the right headpiece. When I'd ask her opinion, she would reply, "Get what you want." When the sales lady inquired which hat she liked, Mom responded, "They're both nice." After I tried the second hat, with the saleslady out of the room, Mom said, "Hurry up. You're so damn dumb." Instantly, my fantasized dream that this could be a lovely mother-daughter event dropped like a thud in my stomach. *Why do I keep reaching out to her?* I asked myself.

In the dressing room, Mom used a device, one often employed in the past, that would subliminally trigger her quick-learning daughter to respond as desired. Mom would utter a repetitive "mmm . . . mmmm . . . mmm" noise, sounding like a cross between a revving Mustang motor and a mooing cow, to signal that I was doing something wrong. On that mooing sound, I would know instinctively what to do, depending on the circumstances: be silent, hurry up, or take some other action. Mom would make that sound for about thirty seconds to a minute or longer until I'd respond.

In the dressing room, Mom rustled through her purse, looked at the walls, and shuffled her feet multiple times, as if she were a bored eight-year-old. Then she started to "mmm . . . mmmm . . . mmm . . ." By that point in my life, I had broken that psychological leash she had on me. When the saleslady heard Mom's "mmmm," sounded at speaking volume, she shot a quizzical look at my mooing Mom.

"What are you humming, Mom?" I asked. Mom abruptly stopped, raised her head high, glared at me, and sat there, still, until I finished and made my purchase.

At lunch, she was a peach. She was pleasant and didn't refer to my hat-buying. Nor did she ask any questions about wedding plans.

Notably, never again did Mom "mmmm" me.

Lace Panties

1980

The August after completing my master's program and defending my thesis, I married John, the man of my dreams to whom I am still happily wed. After we dated for a month, I knew he was The One.

At the rehearsal dinner, I watched Mom pull a slim box from her purse and open it. *What does she have there?* I mused.

She pulled out something white and unfolded it.

What is that?

With her powerful, naturally projecting voice, she called out, "Hey, look at what Sophie, Katy's daughter, had a lady make for Judie. These are the underpants Judie's wearing tomorrow when she gets married. Aren't they nice?" She then handed them to my future in-laws.

My father-in-law facially expressed incredulity, like "What is she doing?" Embarrassed to be handling lace panties in public, he quickly pushed them back to Mom as if she had handed him a tampon. Mom nudged them back to him. "Pass them on," she said, gesturing for him to give them to the person next to him. And so started the panties parade around the room.

What could have been a lovely mother-daughter moment where Mom would give Sophie's gift to me in private turned into a spectacle. Why did Sophie entrust Mom with an unsealed, unwrapped box of lace lingerie panties, when she could have given it to someone she knew in the wedding party to innocuously pass on to me? Didn't she know that Mom holds nothing private and has no discernment of what others might consider private? Didn't she anticipate Mom would use this to garner attention? I knew Mom craved attention and would do anything for it.

As the panties began their march around the wedding party and their spouses, I thought of how Mom never hesitated to humiliate me whenever she could. I thought of all the times she threatened, "I'm going to embarrass you!"

Was she now hoping to embarrass me? Or did she truly not understand what some may regard as private? She viewed her own underwear as private and shooed me out when she changed clothes. She didn't want me to see her in her bra, even when I was grown. So, why would she bring panties to a rehearsal dinner?

As I watched the panties parade, past incidents with Mom flashed to mind. I thought back to how I never spoke with Mom about anything important, confidential, or involving my feelings—in fact, anything at all. In high school, I didn't even tell her I was Most Likely to Succeed. She heard that from a relative.

I thought back to the seventh grade when I believed I was the dumbest kid in the class because that's what Mom told me. I believed too that I was the ugliest because of Mom's criticism of the way I looked. She compared me to kids she knew and pointed out how I was not as good or smart or good-looking or as nicely dressed as them. When I looked at my face in the bathroom mirror, I saw a girl with plump Polish cheeks and blue eyes staring back.

If this was the first time I saw her, I asked myself, *would I think she was ugly? No,* I concluded. *Mom is wrong. What if she is wrong about me being dumb and no good? She could be wrong. What is she basing her comments on? We don't talk, so she doesn't know what or how I think. How do you measure "good" in someone? Those are only her thoughts. Is that how she feels about herself?*

By the eighth grade, I realized that what she was telling me was not true. It dawned on me that I wouldn't get A's in all my classes if I were "dumb" as Mom claimed. Nor would classmates ask me for help with their homework. Nor would Sister Bonavita, after asking, "Who worked on the challenge math problem over lunch?" and seeing no one raising their hand, nonchalantly say, "Okay, Judie. Go put your answer on the board," as if she knew I had worked it out. I always did. And they were always the right answers.

In the seventh grade, I learned to carefully weigh what information I shared because Mom would exploit it for personal attention. That year, I confided that I didn't think my classmates liked me. Mom listened intently, which was very unusual, and said to smile more. The next evening, she boasted with derision, "I called Katy, Eleanor, Bertha, [and others] and told them that nobody in your class likes you." She laughed as she said that. "They're all laughing at you." She didn't relate any suggestions, if anyone offered any, on how to be likeable. I remember feeling betrayed as this was the first time I had brought an issue to her. I promised myself to never again talk with her about anything important or private.

As the panties went around the room, I recalled when, lured by a sham hint of compassion, I had broken that promise and regretted it. In that instance, Mom trampled my misplaced trust by repeatedly shouting, "I wish he would have raped you!" That was the only other time I had shared a concern with her.

Outside of those examples, it was easy for me to not discuss personal details with her because we did not have dialogue. We never *talked*. We did not have two-way conversations. I would sit mum; Mom would talk about people, judging them harshly, or she would criticize me and I would walk away. In restaurants or at some relatives' homes, she was most amicable.

The panties crept closer.

I thought about how she could be crass. It was her nature. I recalled her telling me about menstruation. I was eleven years old. It was winter. Mom, wearing a black coat to stay warm as our house was always so cold, crept up close to me in the kitchen when I went to get a glass of water. "Blood's going to shoot out your pee hole," she said.

In response, I reminded her, "I don't like when you talk to me like that." She walked out. That was our mother-daughter moment about the birds and bees. Fortunately, the school hosted an afternoon presentation on menstruation. A few months later, my neighbor Emma saw me on the front porch and came to talk with me about menstruation, as if she knew Mom didn't have the tools to do the topic justice.

Finally, the panties reached me.

Running my fingernail along a strip of ruffled lace, I determined that, yes, all along I have always done what was best for me. That was by not regarding my mother as my mom as she wasn't supportive or nurturing; by not talking with her about personal, private, or sensitive matters; and by not involving her in my life. Those matters were beyond her capabilities.

Passing the panties on was like closing the door to allowing Mom to affect me. What had started out as a *you-have-got-to-be-kidding-me* moment shifted to me seeing the situation objectively: I'm sitting at my wedding rehearsal dinner, holding lace panties made by someone for my wedding day being passed around to the entire wedding party by the woman who birthed me. Nothing here, I realized, reflected poorly on me. What I didn't understand was how Mom could be embarrassed when seen in her bra by her twenty-four-year-old daughter yet feel totally at ease passing around what she herself considered embarrassing.

As I thought that, I looked up at her. What I saw was her signature self—someone who was a character: loud, brash, insensitive, and craving attention. Our eyes met. She thrust her chin up at me. Was that in defiance? She then turned her head to talk with the person next to her. I felt so distant from my family.

Yes, I thought, *I will gift the lace panties to charity, unworn.*

A Delicate Tango

Mom didn't see my wedding dress until the ceremony. Before then, I distanced myself from her for that entire day. I didn't want to see her because I could never predict what her mindset would be. I could not trust that her behavior would be rational that day. I didn't want to experience aggression or a fusillade of verbal abuse, should that be her mood *du jour*. Nor did I want to chance her acting on her pernicious, perennial threat of "I'll embarrass you!" by trying to ruin my dress via dumping something on it or tearing it. No, not on my wedding day. I needed to protect myself from Mom. I sent up a request, "God, please bless Mom with peace of heart and mind."

At the ceremony, I handed Mom a rose. With teary eyes, she accepted, saying, "You look beautiful," with heartfelt meaning. She melted my heart. *That* was the genuine Martha whom I had yet to meet. At that moment, she was like an elusive butterfly that emerged from a jeweled box, soon to retreat back into a blur of chaos.

On stepping back to my soon-to-be husband, I felt compassion for Mom. She had missed out on a large chunk of my life. I construed her emotional outbursts as vehicles of her own form of self-protection—behavioral devices for filling a void within herself, a void that barricaded others from her and blocked her from feeling the love of humanity.

The rest of the evening, I shifted back to the present and savored every delicious moment.

~

Fast-forward thirty years later to Easter 2010. A visit with relatives unexpectedly deconstructed an understanding I had held since I was a child. It revealed that my concerns about my wedding day were not unfounded. Decades earlier, others had similar concerns about my mom's behavior on their own wedding day.

My husband and I took Aunt Virge and Uncle Lou to an Easter brunch. At their home afterward, Lou gently slid a wedding album on their cocktail table toward me as he asked if we had seen their wedding pictures. When I opened the album, my eyes met a surprise.

"Oh? You had a church wedding," I said as I gazed at a photo of Virge in a wedding gown and veil. "And you had a reception at a hall, too."

"Yes, it seems like just yesterday," said Lou.

I was perplexed. Mom had always said they did not marry in church, but in city hall. In fact, she held it against them that they didn't have a church wedding or a reception. She said Virge wore a white suit and hat, with no veil. After marrying at city hall, she said, they went to Busia's house and Busia made dinner for the entire family. What I just now saw and heard controverted all that. Why would Mom say that?

I didn't relate this to Lou and Virge. Earlier that day, Lou didn't remember walking me down the aisle for my wedding, and Virge didn't recall dropping toothbrushes off at my childhood home for my sister and me. They were, after all, ninety-one and eighty-seven, respectively. Time erases echoes of the past.

Leaving their home, I thought about how Mom had behaved on our way to their house when I first met Aunt Virge. It flashed back to me how Mom's family members had independently informed me that Mom was "crazy" and "not well" and how others had come forward later. I recalled how Mom had no qualms about making a scene in public or threatening to spit on people.

Could it be that Busia and Mom's siblings all conspired to protect Lou and Virge on their wedding day from Mom's irrational behavior? Did they fabricate that story about city hall out of concern that Mom would ruin Lou's wedding? My dad would have to have been in on that, too.

I could only surmise what I felt was true.

PART 3

GROWING

Making Bombs

1981

We were in a recession. Companies invoked hiring freezes, leaving no entry-level jobs in food science. After I wrote to one hundred fifty-four companies, relying on my food science, chemistry, and microbiology backgrounds, and turned down a job offer for a microbiologist position, two companies invited me for interviews via telephone. Eerily, their calls came in within five minutes of each other. One was an international chemical company looking for an analytical chemist, and the other was an international pharmaceutical company looking to fill a spot in regulatory affairs.

Both interviews went well. Each company offered me the job via telephone. Bizarrely again, those calls also came in within five minutes of each other. I wondered if my dad, who had passed away years before and loved surprises, was orchestrating the close timing of these calls.

For me, it was important to do what I loved. That was why I accepted the analytical chemist job, though it paid considerably less than the regulatory position.

On my first day at the research center, as we headed into the lunchroom with our white lab coats, I was surprised to see men overwhelmingly outnumber women at the laboratory. Of the few women there, most were technicians; I knew of only two women who were chemists.

My job involved wet chemical analyses, including making bombs (I say that jokingly referring to Parr bomb analysis for bromine) and working with instrumentation such as nuclear magnetic resonance.

Six months into the job, a food scientist position opened at an international food company. Though I enjoyed the work and the people at the chemical company, I couldn't resist the opportunity to use my master's degree.

Growth Spurt in Confidence

1981

At the interview for the food scientist position, management offered me the job, and I accepted on the spot. For the next four years, I worked in several groups, all again consisting primarily of men. In fact, in one group of twelve, I was the sole female.

My work centered on research and product development. It involved developing product prototypes based on concepts provided by marketing, researching various technologies, scaling up the prototypes in the pilot plant, coordinating consumer market tests and evaluating the test results, and optimizing the product for market launch. Writing and presentations to upper management were also integral to the work.

Here again, professional women were a minority.

A few months into my job, a soft-spoken, reserved, senior male manager walked into my laboratory. With a straight face, he asked me to arrange for coffee service for a meeting he was hosting that morning and to bring the coffee up to the meeting room. That involved ordering coffee service from the cafeteria, picking up the coffee cart bearing two large coffee pots, and rolling it down the hall and up an elevator to the far side of the building for his meeting. I estimated that the total time would clock in at thirty to forty minutes, including returning the coffee cart to the cafeteria after the meeting. That time would be better spent doing an experiment, either in the lab or in the pilot plant.

This manager didn't work in my department. Up to that point, my sole interactions with him were a "hello" when encountering him in the hall. I thought he was joking but he was serious. I assumed he thought because I was female, pleasant, and friendly, I would be delighted to fetch coffee for his meeting. Or did he think, "That's what women do"?

I didn't know how to address that situation. I was green. I didn't want him bad-mouthing me, a new employee, to management. So, I reluctantly agreed. After he left, I kicked myself for consenting to that task and especially for not telling him to have his secretary handle it.

The next month, he again walked into my lab and matter-of-factly told me he needed coffee the next day for a meeting. He stated the time and meeting room, expecting me to comply. By this time, I had learned my lesson. I was there as a food scientist, not as a coffee fetcher. None of my male colleagues fetched coffee for managers' meetings. I was straightforward. I told him, "If your secretary won't get coffee for the meeting, you need to take up your request with the cafeteria. Perhaps they can arrange for someone to bring it up for you." I explained, "I have my work responsibilities, and getting coffee for managers' meetings is not on the list. I know you understand that." He looked a bit surprised.

Handling the request that way left me feeling good about my response. I believe it taught him that just because a friendly blond, female scientist smiles with a cheery "hello" doesn't mean she would be willing to waste valuable time rolling a coffee cart to and from a meeting for him. Never again did he ask me to handle his coffee service.

But then again, back then, some men naturally ascribed domestic tasks to women. In graduate school, one male contemporary in pharmacology said he wanted a girlfriend because he was tired of doing laundry: "That's what women do," he said.

Debut into the World of Men

1984

In 1984, I attended the American Chemical Society's (ACS) national convention in Philadelphia. The conference included a host of meetings on numerous topics. One session that intrigued me was a symposium on "Creative Process Leading to New Products," hosted by the Division of Chemical Marketing and Economics. The program included a talk by social psychologist Theresa Amabile on "Managing the Creative Process." I was running late. Five minutes before the program, I made it to the conference room.

When I opened the door, I froze. The entire room was full of suit-clad men. It wasn't their sartorial choice that halted me, as I too was wearing a navy business suit. It was that there had to be at least a thousand men present, with rows upon rows of at least fifty to seventy-five people across. I scanned the room. The only female I saw was a petite lady on the dais talking with a man there.

Okay, I've got this, I thought. *Now, where do I sit?*

I didn't see any vacant seats. One then stood out to me, in the first row, under the speaker's podium. With all the confidence I could muster, I held my head high, walked to the front row with my high heels and briefcase, and grabbed that seat. As the speaker adjusted the mic, an older gentleman next to me leaned in and introduced himself. He followed that with, "I didn't know we could bring our secretaries. Who do you work for?"

"I'm not a secretary. I'm a food scientist and a member of ACS," I countered.

"You are?" His face wrinkled with puzzlement. "But you're a lady. You're a *laaady* scientist?" he asked, as if a penis were a criterion to be a scientist and he was flummoxed at how a female could possibly do that work. "You said 'food scientist,' right?" He then paused as if having an epiphany. "Oh, you must make cookies."

He was serious.

Who, Me?

1983–1984

As a food scientist, I did good work and was often on highly visible projects because of my technical expertise. Though I savored the challenges, I did not like being the center of attention. I also lacked the confidence in a meeting situation to correct someone who unrightfully grabbed credit due me. For example, on one project where I worked with a team, it was my idea and work that solved the problem we addressed. However, as a team member, I regarded the solution as coming collectively from the team, not solely from me.

The R&D director was so pleased with our work that he scheduled a meeting to congratulate us. He met with our team and our respective managers, as we were from different departments. On our way in, one male team member from a different department leaned over to me and said, "I'll do the talking."

I thought, *Great. He's our spokesman.* I was relieved. His speaking would take pressure off the rest of us in talking with the R&D director.

After congratulating us, the director wanted to know how we fixed the problem. Our spokesman swiftly responded. He used the pronoun "I" without any reference to "we" as a team to reflect our collective effort.

The rest of our team exchanged glances. One scientist, not so discreetly, nodded toward me as if to say, "Do you *believe* this guy?"

What was my reaction? I didn't say anything to correct him. Instead, I sat there and listened. I didn't appreciate his usurping credit from our collective effort. Had I spoken, I would have referred to us as a team. I felt he latched onto that approach because his ego needed the attention and this was a rare opportunity for him to shine.

At the end of the meeting, my manager pulled me aside. He was privy to my role in the project's resolution. He told me I was one of his star scientists and I needed to take credit where credit was due.

Though I was confident in my work and competence, I didn't have it in me to speak up and challenge my colleague's choice of pronoun in front of everyone there. Nor did I see the point of interjecting myself into the limelight. I never had problems standing up for others, for the truth, or for what was right. But I didn't see how I could do that in that meeting without marring our self-elected spokesman professionally.

That changed, though, about six months later, when upper management hosted a meeting to discuss consumer test results on one product. The company's statistician had either changed jobs or was on vacation; I don't recall which. One director interpreted the test results as being statistically significant, warranting the replacement of certain manufacturing equipment.

As I had taken several statistics courses, including experimental design, I studied the results and found his interpretation erroneous.

I spoke with that individual about his interpretation, and he would not buy that he had misinterpreted the stats. I explained it to him clearly. He told me he was still going to present on his point, as planned.

At the presentation, I could not let his misinterpretation stand alone. I assembled a counter-presentation with the correct information. I felt that was the right thing to do. As Mark Twain said, "It's never wrong to do the right thing."

My presentation was not on the agenda. I didn't ask that it be included; I wanted to see if the director would change his content after our chat. He did not. He reported that the test results were statistically significant, warranting the replacement of certain equipment. Afterward, everyone voted in favor of that.

That's when I stood up. Unlike today, at that time I was not accustomed to presenting to groups of more than twenty. About thirty or forty people were there. With overhead acetates (Yep, it was a long time ago), I explained the results and demonstrated that they were not statistically significant as just presented.

You can imagine how diplomatic I had to be. Here I was, an associate scientist with a master's degree telling a group that a director with a PhD, several levels above me, had just given them the wrong interpretation. After my presentation, the group took another vote, this time deciding against the proposed action. Afterward, several managers approached me and commented on how I had handled the issue so well and had demystified statistics with my explanation.

In hindsight, my concern about the group acting on misinformation motivated me to take steps that helped further my own personal development. With a nod to Mark Twain, I concluded that when you act on what you know is true, you can't be wrong. It's as if the energy of the universe embraces you and carries you through on the wings of truth.

~⁀

Almost five years into my work as a scientist, I discovered how much I enjoyed writing and speaking, and realized I wanted to do more of that. That's when a classified ad caught my eye. It was for an associate editor position with a monthly technology magazine published by an international industry association. Written as if it were describing me, it *called* to me.

I had a monumental decision to make. Back then, leaving the scientific world was a significant, irrevocable decision: once you left to work outside the laboratory, if you decided to return, you would never again be taken seriously as a scientist.

So, what would it be?

PART 4

BUDDING

A Leap

1985

I decided to follow my yearning. I accepted the publishing position and appreciated the opportunity, as I was now doing what I loved—writing and research.

When hired, I was the sole professional woman on the editorial staff. At some scientific conferences, I would be among the few women there. For example, in 1986, at my first Pittsburgh Conference on Analytical Chemistry and Applied Spectroscopy—called "Pitt Con," though at that time, it was held in Atlantic City, New Jersey—when I walked through exhibits at the convention center, I was the only woman among about two hundred or so suit-clad men in that aisle. Though more women appeared over the years, women were consistently a minority.

Each workday morning, donning tennis shoes and a business suit, I left the house at 6:25 a.m. to catch the 7:10 a.m. train into the city. At the train station, I stood on the ramp waiting for the train to pull to a stop, knowing instinctively to turn my head in the direction of the engine's path to buffer against the blowback flushing out from the train's wheels. Up the stairs I went to the upper level, where I would claim a solo seat. On the ride in, I meditated for about thirty minutes, sometimes attaining a state of bliss akin to floating. What a wonderful way to start the day.

A Bayonet through the Heart

1985

The eighth day on the job, a Wednesday, started out well as they all had so far. I had my work assignments and was busy writing. However, by nightfall, an unexpected act of malice overwhelmed me. It sought me out like octopus tentacles draping themselves around me, wilily wiggling me out of my world, trying to wield me back into a toxic stew of drama.

It was my greatest loss, and it involved my mom. I had long been aware that Mom found it amusing to purposely lie about adults close to her, either to hurt them or to establish her victimhood to others and her domination over her target.

Eventually, that behavior entangled me. Two couples in Mom's family were getting divorced. News of these divorces churned through the family's gossip mill and tickled Mom's desire for attention. To Mom, divorces were juicy stigmas of failure.

On a Wednesday the week after I started working with the magazine, a family member phoned me to ask how I was doing. She said Mom told her that my husband and I were getting a divorce. "Are you?" she asked, sounding concerned.

That was the first I'd heard of this.

According to my mom, I was leaving John because "he is dumb and cross-eyed."

We were five years into our marriage and happily married. Yes, he has a lazy eye but he had that all his life, and he is far from "dumb." In fact, that's not even a word I would choose to describe anyone. I thought, *Where did Mom get that information?* I assumed perhaps it was from a bad dream.

Concerned, that same evening, I called Mom and told her what I had heard. Her response stunned me. Laughing proudly, pleased with herself, she shouted, "I can cause you trouble! I could hurt you! I could still embarrass you!" She went on, yelling, "When you come back home, you'll have to hide your face and run down the alley because everyone is laughing at you!" With her derision, I felt massive amounts of malicious energy hit my solar plexus. I felt sick to my stomach.

I asked whom she told this to. Proudly, she ticked off fourteen names. Later I found she had called more than that. None were people who told me Mom was "crazy."

"Why did you do that?" I asked. "You know that isn't true."

Exhilarated, jubilant laughter was her response. "You should be so embarrassed now." She was elated that she had upset me.

My heart felt like Mom had pierced it with a bayonet. It was not the lie itself that hurt. It was all the animus vehemently flung at me, along with her focused intention to purposely maul me and toy with my marriage via a premeditated lie—a lie that in her eyes indelibly marked me as damaged, a failure, and someone to be ridiculed. I tried to wrap my head around this. I blamed myself for not seeing this coming.

On the call, I tried to maintain composure. I was crying. I told her, "You are a witch. That's 'witch' with a 'w,' not a 'b.'"

I told her that her behavior was hurtful and evil. "I will never speak to you again."

She laughed again. "Laugh it off," she riposted.

When I told my husband about the call, he reminded me, "Your mom is really sick. You know that, right? That's the way she is."

"Yes, she is sick. And she is my mom. But that doesn't obligate me to include her in my life. I can't allow her to keep trying to hurt me with her pathological behavior. It's obvious she needs somebody to subjugate and lie about so she gets attention and could feel good about herself. That's what she did to my dad.

"If I roll over and 'laugh' this one off, as she says to, what's her next act going to be? 'Judie had triplets. They're not John's. The babies are up for adoption. Don't say anything to John. You'll make him cry.'

"No," I continued. "She will keep lying and toying with my life. And yours too. She is pathological. I need to cut her out of my life. She's like cancer."

I went on, "In the past, I handled her behavior by attributing anything she said to me or did as being about her. I didn't regard her words or actions as a reflection of me or who I am. But this is different—she's striking at me, at you, and at our marriage, and is involving others.

"You should have heard the vengeance in her voice. She's trying to rattle my world and turn it upside down. And this time, she succeeded. She hooked my heart," I cried.

John tenderly wrapped his arms around me and held me.

Going on, I sobbed, "She has never been a mother. Because she is sick, she has never loved or nurtured me. I accept that.

I have other mothers who are dear to my heart. I need to move on. I am not going to drown in her drama and toxicity. That is not who I am. God bless her soul, but this was the last straw. I need to stay away from her. I want peace in my life."

John pulled me close. "I am one hundred percent behind you."

I wasn't done: "In fact, I am cutting myself off from the entire family. I don't want to have to deal with them reaching out to judge me as a wrongdoer. She's their problem now. With me out of the picture, she's not going to be able to hold herself together. Let them see the raw, attention-grabbing Martha.

"And if anyone judges me as the 'wrongful' one, they will learn the truth when they pass to the other side." Slowing down my sobbing, I said, "Okay. I'm done talking. Thank you for listening. You're a real sweetheart."

John softly kissed my forehead. He murmured, "You're a remarkable lady. I hope you know that. You've been through so much with your mom—not in a good way—and yet you've come out on the right side. You could have been really screwed up, but you're not.

"And yet you've always treated her with dignity and respect. I don't think I could have done the same." Holding me tightly, he whispered, "I love you, honey."

I was so distraught. That entire evening, I sobbed, hard. Every nerve in my body shook with pain.

To right Mom's wrong, I typed out letters to everyone she said she had called, telling them that this was not true. I wasn't going to let her play with my marriage.

John wrote to my mom of his own accord.

The next day was painful. Fortunately, my job was so demanding that it forced me to shelve my pain until the train ride home. Why would a mother, though I understood she was sick and was not a nurturer, do that to a daughter? Mom had fabricated an entire scenario for the sole purpose of hurting me—by targeting my marriage and in essence, my husband— so she could get attention. Now in the family gossip mill, she could cry, "My daughter's getting a divorce too!"

One lady she contacted was my friend Bev Mollak's mother. Bev did not know my mom, as I avoided having her over because of Mom's volatile and unpredictable behavior. The few times she was over, Mom had channeled the sweetness of June Cleaver. (She did that too when two out-of-town friends visited for a few days.) Bev told me that her mother said my mom screamed and cried over the phone that I was disgracing the family by getting a divorce. She reported that my mom said she was so embarrassed by my divorce. I grasped that this sick plot dished heaps of attention on my mom, something she craved.

One aunt from my dad's side returned my letter unopened. One cousin around Mom's age, who never visited Mom's home, wrote me to say what an awful daughter I was and that my news made my mother cry. She wrote that my mom bragged that "even Judie's garage is clean." *What?* From the "brag" part, I took that it meant Mom bragged about me behind my back.

Months later, after Christmas, Mom called my friend Bev's mom to say that an uncle had dropped off a one-hundred-dollar bill as a Christmas gift, but she was afraid to send it to me because I would rip it up. Hearing that, I wrote Mom and told her to keep the money and use it to buy herself a nice dress, something she really wanted.

Mom continued updating Bev's mother on my estrangement from her. That came to a head one summer day in 1986 when

I met Bev for lunch at Petri's restaurant on LaSalle in Chicago. Bev reported that, according to her mom, mine would scream that she was going to kill herself because I was not speaking to her. (An aunt on Dad's side reported the same.) From that, Bev judged me to be a horrible daughter. As a new mother herself, Bev could not accept that any mother would intentionally hurt her own child. All the years I had kept Mom's mental illness under wraps came back to haunt me. Bev conditioned our friendship on me needing to call and visit my mom, or the friendship would be over. Well, that was an easy choice. I wasn't going to be coerced back into an abusive relationship with my mom to please a friend. So, Bev walked out of my life at lunch that day, with drama and bravado.

After I cut ties with Mom, I felt relief. I savored the peace. It was not difficult to do. I never felt regret or longed to phone her or hear her voice. The way I felt and how my body felt underscored that I had done the right thing. It liberated me from my family's toxicity.

With another friend, also a new mom, I shared what had happened. Before this, I had never mentioned anything to this friend about my mom's mental state. She didn't say she didn't believe me, but I sensed she, too, grappled with trying to understand how or why a mother could possibly do that to her daughter.

Look Out: Female Flying Solo

1985–1991

About a week into my job, the chief editor paid me a visit. He was a short, fiery, action-oriented guy who did not mince words. Standing next to me, he raised one leg to rest the sole of his shoe against the top edge of my desk about a foot from where I sat. That became a standard stance when he wanted to talk with me. Hovering over me, he told me they are not paying me what they pay the "guys." He related a story about a woman who sued a large food company and won. "She got only $250,000 and that's not a lot of money. After that, she couldn't get a job." He told me that if I wanted to sue, think about it: I would screw my career. That's all he said, and then left.

I had no intention of suing. To me, the challenge of the job itself was what I was after, along with a decent wage. Until then, it had not crossed my mind how my salary compared to that of my coworkers. Back then, as long as I got challenging work and enjoyed it, I was fine. Money did not motivate me. I got back to work. Never did my gender block me there from getting some of the most lucrative, challenging assignments. Even so, hearing about the salary disparity disturbingly told me that, irrespective of my abilities, as a woman, I was respected less than my male peers. As I was just starting out, I decided, *Okay, I'll prove my worth.* However, had that happened later in my career, I would have handled it differently.

A key part of my job entailed writing review articles on a myriad of technologies—a task that involved reading a foot-high pile of scientific literature to understand the subject matter and to then follow the thread of its interpretation through the literature. Typically stretching across twelve to thirty magazine pages, flanked by advertisements, the articles I wrote aimed to simplify the science while presenting the information accurately. It was common to travel to conferences and corporate research centers to interview experts in relevant subject matter. In fact, one month I was on the road for three weeks out of four, returning home late each Friday night and leaving that Sunday afternoon.

The chief editor had tremendous respect for my work. Once when I had to stop into his office, he offhandedly told me that I deserved to be given a huge raise because of the quality of my work but his "hands were tied." He said one of my colleagues had to pay for his children's tuition to expensive schools and another had expensive interests. Another time, he said I "would be hard to replace." He told me, "You're conscientious, you know your science, and you're a good writer." So, I know he respected my work and trusted my judgment. After a few months on the job, whenever I handed him a draft of a technology report, he'd thumb through the voluminous document. Looking up, without reading a word, he would say, "It looks good. Send it to press."

Menacing

1987

It's always been easy for me to take action when needed, especially if it involves helping someone in need. One afternoon, breaking my focus was a scream coming from the bookkeeper whose office was next to mine. I thought she might need medical attention. I dashed to investigate. As I approached her door, an unfamiliar man burst into the hall. He shoved me against the wall. Margaret Blanche, in her early sixties, stood in her office screaming, "He has my pocketbook! It has my keys, my ID, my cards, checkbook . . . everything!"

What did I do? Well, I felt he was not armed, and I sensed fear in him. So, I took off after him in my high heels. As I closed the lead he had on me, he ducked into a hall and started opening a wood door that led to the stairwell. I grabbed the back of his leather jacket, stopping him in his tracks. Though I was only about ninety-four pounds, I looked bigger and heavier: I wore three-inch heels, a suit with ultra-generous shoulder pads stylish at the time, and big, permed, curly hair. He was about my size but heavier. When he turned his face toward me, he genuinely looked frightened. I didn't expect to see so much fear.

By that time, Margaret had caught up to us. I knew he wasn't armed. I told him I would let him go if he returned her pocketbook to her. I instructed him to drop it and kick it gently toward her. He did. I told her to check through it and see if everything was there. I assumed it was, as he hadn't had time to rummage through its contents. Yes, it was all there and intact. I then told him I would keep my part of the deal, and I let him go. Back in my office, I questioned, *Did he really see me as menacing?*

The executive director was not happy with me. He summoned me to his office. Shaking his finger at me, he said, "Never do that again." I felt like Maria summoned to the office of Mother Abbess in *The Sound of Music*. I concurred. But deep down, I knew if the need ever arose, I wouldn't hesitate if it felt right intuitively.

Bags

1987

A train ride brought memories flooding back of my mom's behavior toward people who "don't look like us." On the train ride home at the end of one day, I stood in the train vestibule connecting two cars. A Black man, sweating, struggled to move two heavy, monolithic suitcases into the vestibule from the train car. *It looks like he's getting off at the next stop*, I thought. *So am I.* Overweight, he was dressed in a dark suit, white shirt, and a tie; he looked to be in his fifties. Being a people watcher, I observed a few people looking at him; he was the only Black person on that part of the train. Their expressions reminded me of my mom eyeing people of color on the bus.

When the train came to a stop, people were getting out. The man struggled with his bags. No one offered to help. "Excuse me," they'd say as they stepped around this man and his bags.

That's when I decided that someone needs to help this man. His skin color does not define him, if that was, in fact, the issue. From my childhood experience with Mom, I assumed his looking different factored in, to some extent.

I didn't offer to help. Instead, I set my briefcase down in the vestibule by the open door. I told the man to get off the train, stand on the platform, and we will both get the larger bag down. We did. The other I could handle. I carried it off the train and then shot back up the steep step to retrieve my briefcase before the doors slammed shut. The man thanked me. I then picked up his smaller bag, which was huge but not so heavy that I couldn't handle it with my skinny frame.

"Let's go," I said. "I will help you get this to the station."

"Are you sure? It's heavy," he said.

"Yeah. I can handle it," I said, though I was sweating and getting a workout. The bag was *that* heavy.

As we stood on the ramp waiting for the train to pass us so we could cross the tracks to get to the station, a few regular riders in front of us turned around and looked at him, me, and his luggage. No one said anything. I could feel the gentleman's discomfort. I thought back to my mom and the kind bonbon lady on the bus in my early years.

I hoped that perhaps someone would have wished they had thought of helping him.

The Crowbar

1988

The wrong place at the wrong time. That's where I found myself about an hour after leaving a conference on gum technology.

At the end of the conference, I had just enough time to catch a taxi back to the office, switch out my heels for gym shoes, and hightail it to the train station for my ride home.

Outside the door of the hotel where the conference was held, the concierge held open a door to a taxi. En route to the office, about twenty minutes away now with rush-hour traffic, I pulled out a few papers to jot notes about people I had met who would be ideal contacts for a future article. At one point, I looked up and saw we were swinging a sharp right turn. It was still light outdoors.

Suddenly, the light dimmed. We were now on lower Wacker Drive. *Okay, no problem.* I put away my notes, as it was now more challenging to see. The cab pulled up to a stop light. In the lane to our left, about thirty feet ahead, was a white van. Its back door popped open and a huge man resembling a sumo wrestler leaped out. Anger twisted his face as he looked in our direction and began running toward us. *He's coming for our cab!*

The cab driver pulled a crowbar from under his seat, turned to me holding it up so I could see it, and in a heavy accent said, "Don't worry, Miss. I will protect you."

Mr. Sumo was almost to the front bumper of the cab. *What is going on?* "Do you know him?" I asked. "Why is he after you?"

He's coming to hurt the cab driver! I thought. *After he hurts him, what is he going to do with me—a witness? Will my body be floating in the Chicago River tomorrow morning?* I was on the edge of my seat.

What did the cab driver do? He switched into reverse and accelerated, creating space between us and Mr. Sumo. He kept his foot on the accelerator, doing at least forty to fifty miles per hour, deftly weaving in and out of heavy, oncoming 5:00 p.m. traffic. Out the back window, I gaped at the oncoming vehicles. *We're going to get into an accident!* The sound of their horns blasting at us was deafening. It was like a scene out of *The Blues Brothers*.

He swerved a hard left into a deep alcove and, still in reverse, adroitly steered the car to a corner at its far back wall, about a hundred feet from the traffic lane. He turned off his headlights. "Get down," he urged. "We stay here few minutes."

"Who is that man?" I demanded to know, adrenaline still surging through my system. *Could I trust this driver?* My instinct said yes.

"Shhh! Don't talk. I watching."

I regretted not taking note of the van's license plate.

We sat in silence for a few minutes, enough for the traffic light to change several times. He then pulled out and turned back onto upper Wacker Drive. He dropped me off on a corner not far from my office. "No fare. No charge," he said, waving as I exited his cab.

Whew! What an experience!

Back at the office, I phoned the police to report the incident. That's when I realized that I had no way to identify the taxi for them to speak with its driver. There must be a hundred cabs driven by foreign drivers in Chicago. The dispatcher said they would send someone out in forty-five minutes to an hour. I wanted to go home. I told them that was too late for me. I had already missed my train and had about twenty minutes to spare before starting my walk to the station for the next one.

On the train, I sought my usual lair—an upstairs single seat. *What am I broadcasting*, I thought, *to bring this near-violent situation?* Settled in, I parked my ticket in the slot and closed my eyes. *Breathe*, I told myself. *Deep breath in. Deep breath out, taking with it anything that does not serve me.* I visualized white light flowing up from the soles of my feet out through the crown of my head, relaxing every cell of my body on its passage. After four cycles of breaths, I was fully calm.

The next day I shared my experience with the chief editor. He told me to always note the cab number and driver's name posted on the back of the front seat. I realized that I had felt so comfortable that I had stopped paying attention to details around me, contrary to how I was in my childhood home.

I Got This

1987-1989

With a knock on my office door, the chief editor stepped forward. "I'm giving you this manuscript to rewrite. It's way too long—around 100 pages. We can't publish that," he said, flipping through a voluminous stack of papers. "Shorten it so it's about twenty to twenty-five pages long. That's a lot to cut. I know you can handle it."

"Okay. I will take care of it," I responded as he laid the document on my desk and left.

The article was on a scientific topic from a prestigious research center. As a former scientist and one who had some experience in that particular field, I was familiar with the technology and with cleaning up scientific documents to best present their essence.

A few days after I handed the chief editor the shortened, rewritten document, he showed up at my door. In his characteristic direct, to-the-point manner, he nodded, "It's good. Send it to the author for approval." And that I did.

What I didn't expect was the author's wrath. About a week later, the first call after reception opened one morning was from the author. "You ruined my article!" he exclaimed. "It's awful! It's short! You ruined it!" His palpable anger felt like if he could reach through the phone, he'd strangle me.

I responded by first explaining that I can appreciate his surprise in seeing his work being totally rewritten and shortened to a fraction of its original length. Continuing, I explained—as reported in my cover letter—that we had to shorten the article because its original length would have taken more than twenty magazine pages. The revised article would now be about four to five magazine pages long, and it presents the information without changing its teachings.

"This is unacceptable," he countered, his seething temper seeming to settle.

"Let me put you in touch with the chief editor. You can speak with him about what you don't like. He had requested that the article be shortened. He is aware of the revisions, and I believe he will stand behind the revised work," I offered. My stomach was tumbling summersaults. This was a scientist from a renowned scientific center infuriated because of my work product. I had never encountered that before.

"Yes, I want to speak with him," he grumbled.

"May I put you on hold for a moment as I transfer your call?"

"Yes."

With my quick pace, seconds later I was at the chief editor's door to check if he was in his office and available to take the call. "The author of the article I rewrote is the on phone. He would like to speak with you. He is not happy," I said, wrapping my words with a shawl of self-manufactured confidence.

"Put him through," he barked.

Five minutes later, a two-tap knock on my door frame announced that it was the chief editor. "I told him he has two choices: he can have his article published with us as rewritten or he can take it elsewhere. He said he wants us to publish it; he will go with the revisions.

"But I didn't end it there," the chief editor went on. "I told him the rewritten article is quality work. It's much better written than what he submitted. And I told him to wait and see: when it's out, he will get a ton of accolades."

He paused. "I told him that, Judie, because the revised article is well done, so you know."

Fast-forward to a few days after the next issue was out. My phone rang the minute reception opened that morning. It was my beloved author.

"I love the article! I am delighted with the work you did on it. You did a fantastic job. I didn't see that when I last spoke with you," he said with regret trickling through. "All I saw was the short page count.

"I am getting calls from all over the world. Everyone is complimenting me, saying that the article is beautifully written. In fact, so many people are remarking on how clearly written it is," he said. "I was wrong when I spoke with you last. I want to thank you for your work."

Later that week, the managing editor stopped by. The chief editor was not one to gossip about intraoffice dealings with staff members, and I hadn't spoken to anyone about my conversation with the scientist. "You know that article you worked on?" asked the managing editor. "The author ordered five hundred reprints. That's unusual. He must have really liked it. Not everyone does that."

After I was there for a few years, one sales executive contemporary called. "You're making my job too easy," she laughed. "When a prospectus shows that you'll be doing a technology report, the calls pour in," she said, "and advertisers start jockeying for premium pages in that issue." Sent to advertisers, the prospectus solicited ads through its description of the magazine's upcoming issue.

I was not one to seek attention. The technology reports had a cover page bearing the title of the article and my name in a huge font. I didn't need that. The chief editor insisted on the cover page and font size. Most people would have been proud to have that. Instead, I had to get used to seeing that.

Throughout my career there, I wrote numerous articles on a host of technologies. I was fortunate with how well they were received. My work received countless kudos from individuals, corporate executives, and institutions such as the Food and Drug Administration (FDA) in their magazine *FDA Consumer* for an article I did on rapid microbial test systems. As I didn't understand that people write books while holding a salaried job, I turned down a contract with a New York-based scientific publisher that came out of the blue for a book on microencapsulation without discussing that with our chief editor.

Interestingly, decades later I learned that people in the industry were still using my articles. In 2012, when I, as an attorney, spoke at a conference attended by a corporate client, I ran into their vice president of R&D. He nudged me toward a group a few feet away as he said, "I'd like you to meet some people." Introducing me, he mentioned that I had written "that article on microencapsulation."

One man there, not affiliated with my client, said, "Oh, you're the author! That's the seminal article on microencapsulation.

We still use it in our lab today." I found it intriguing and surprising to hear that my work was still of some use.

Though the other editors freely participated in writing competitions, I never volunteered my work. The few articles I submitted were at the behest of the chief editor standing before my desk with a stern expression as he ordered, "You *must* submit something." From the articles submitted, I received several writing awards from competing with individuals who had master's degrees in writing or English. I took all that as confirmation that, *Okay, I can write.*

Tempest in the Teapot

Early 1990

Being one of the first female professionals came with its own challenges. I discovered that a few years into the job when I spoke up about a situation I felt was not right. What transpired was not a reflection on the organization—it didn't suggest anything nefarious about the company or its management—but was instead a reflection of the times and the generational mindset of its leadership. This was a time when leadership across corporate America and associations was predominately, if not exclusively, male, and the men at the top didn't know what to do when a soft-spoken, quirky young lady, with professional men as peers, spoke up.

The entire editorial staff contributed to prospectuses sent to advertisers about the next issue. My role was to take the editors' write-ups of upcoming articles, along with mine, and coalesce them into a finished editorial product before turning it over for page layout. What didn't feel right was when a male marketing assistant, an older gentleman, embellished one prospectus with his photo and a line implying that he alone was responsible for crafting that document. That did not sit well with me. In my opinion, it was unfair to claim credit for everyone's work, especially when authorship was immaterial.

I drafted a memo to the chief editor, copying the marketing assistant and the chief executive officer—an intellectual man in his early sixties—and told the editor, for future prospectuses, to direct all editorial feed to the marketing assistant as he was doing such an exquisite job at it. The chief editor came into my office, looking distressed: "You're still going to do the prospectus, right?"

"Yes, I will," I said. I explained that I felt it wasn't right for one person to claim credit for the work of an entire department. That was the point of my memo.

"Gotcha. Yeah, that's not right," he nodded. An underlying tension always pervaded the relationship between the editorial and marketing departments. After a slight pause, he added, "Let's see how the CEO handles this," winking conspiratorially.

I didn't intend to cause a ruckus. What I wanted was assurance of no recurrences. *How will this play out?* I asked myself.

Responding to my memo, the CEO wrote to the *entire staff*. Each line opened with "Wherefore . . ." A curious early line declared that "we have a 'tempest in the teapot.'"

Who's that? I thought, having a hunch of exactly who it was.

The next few lines confirmed my suspicion: I was the tempest. He wrote that I was upset that the prospectus did not credit *me* for *my* work on the document.

Did he misunderstand my memo? I wondered. That was a twist of facts, sent to people beyond those on my memo, all of whom were unaware of the underlying situation. From his memo, it looked like this is what happens when you hire a woman: she bellyaches that some guy didn't acknowledge her. Boo-hoo. Concluding the memo, he told me to "knock off this nonsense" and "get back to work." I ruminated on whether he would have responded differently if I were male or older.

In the scientific realm, though I observed managers exchange facial expressions about a woman's breast size behind her back, no one marginalized anyone's concerns, irrespective of gender. Nor, as a scientist, was I ever ascribed the coveted title, "tempest in the teapot."

I found the CEO's response nonresponsive. To me, it mirrored how a patriarch might subdue his teenager to maintain harmony in a family. I construed his memo, distributed to the entire staff who knew nothing about the situation outside of the spin he put on it, as a display of power and a silencing technique. However, instead of silencing me, it emboldened me to stand up anytime for anyone who was diminished, discredited, or wrongfully charged.

From his response, I concluded that this situation taxed his leadership capabilities. As I saw it, he didn't know what to do with me—a young-looking female, mid-thirties, in a professional capacity, openly raising what I saw as an issue. He was, in my opinion, "old school" at an organization which, back in the late '80s, and unlike many such organizations today, was totally under male leadership with a mere handful of professional-level women that included me. (Although women have since made progress in the business world, women are still not at parity with men.)

On the positive side, his handling of the situation turned my attention to leadership skills and what defines a strong leader. As I saw it, it's more than the ability to make swift decisions and wield power. I wondered how I would have handled the matter if I were in his shoes. I decided that as I grew professionally, I wanted to embrace respect for the work of others and promote a supportive environment for everyone, irrespective of gender, race, sexual orientation, or beliefs.

In another aspect, this job gave me my first exposure to professional jealousy. As a scientist, I had not encountered that. In this work, most colleagues were like me: It didn't matter if someone else wrote an excellent article. Be happy for them. Next time, it's your turn. Initially, when a colleague made an off-handed jab, I was perplexed but then caught on. That's where my childhood home experience came in handy. It gave me the tools to see past their words and expressions, right into their hearts and insecurities.

For six years at the magazine, I thoroughly enjoyed my work and the people, including the CEO as I didn't hold this against him but attributed his response to a generational mindset. The job taught me to swim and navigate the waters quite well. I had to gracefully surf the flow of old-school, patriarchal thinking that was typical for that timeframe. There, I learned courage, confidence, and more about standing up for myself. For my diplomacy skills, senior staff sought me out to extricate themselves from precarious minefields they became mired in because of ill-thought-out comments. I was grateful for these opportunities.

As I was ready for a fresh intellectual challenge, I decided to leave the world of publishing for law.

PART 5

BLOOMING

Debut into Law

1991–1995

Through law school and my early legal career, I was still estranged from Mom. Reconciling was yet too risky, as I had no indication that she would stop her abusive behavior or that she had even learned anything. Without that, I wasn't going to jeopardize peace in my life, knowing that her unstable behavior could transmute that into turbulence in a flash. Instead, I looked to time as a measure for smoothing the jagged edges of our relationship. Deep within, I trusted and hoped that I would know when to reach out—if ever.

In 1994, armed with a JD from Loyola University Chicago School of Law, I launched my legal career. The year before graduating, I had a license under Illinois Supreme Court Rule 711 that enabled me to practice law in a legal clinic setting, handling court cases under the supervision of a licensed attorney, a professor. During law school, an externship with a federal judge exposed me to the inner workings of the judicial system and accorded me the privilege of drafting court opinions that were published. Under a fellowship that I was awarded for legal writing, I worked with Professor William Braithwaite conducting research for an article on why lawyers lie.

While I was in law school, London-based Academic Press, Ltd. invited me to author two articles for their *Encyclopaedia of Food Science, Food Technology and Nutrition*. These I had completed in 1994, and I updated them through the publication's 2004 edition.

～

My law school class was about forty-five percent women. Yet, in my experience in the legal profession, I roamed in an entirely different world—one dominated by men. And that world had some catching up to do. For example, in law, I had my shortest job interview ever. It was for an associate attorney position and lasted an entire five minutes. The partner of a Chicago-based, intellectual property law firm sat in his leather chair. "Your background is interesting," he said. "One concern I have is that you can still have babies. What assurance can you give that that wouldn't happen?" he probed.

I registered: *He wants to know what birth control I'm on?* "Oh, my apologies," I said, rising from my chair. "I misunderstood the job requirements. Thank you for your time." I walked out of his office, down the hall, and out the door. That was not a place where I would want to work.

During my law career, a male client actually drove to the office to see "what a woman patent attorney looks like" as if on attaining registration, we sprout antlers.

The job I accepted was with a midsized intellectual property law firm. The managing partner, Errol Gorbankowski, seemed pleasant during my interview. On the job, however, he had a different, irascible persona.

A few days after I started the job, he requested that I sign a document stating that I forfeit health insurance. Signing the document was, he said, a prerequisite for the job, though that was the first I had heard of this requirement.

As time went on, his behavior became adversarial. For example, while explaining the firm's calendar system for reminding the firm of patent and trademark office response due dates, he shouted as he slammed box lids like a maniac. I stood there, silently observing his irrational behavior but did not address his conduct. I felt like walking out but feared being fired and having that mar my chances of getting another job. As I was new to law, I stood there. Nothing of substance shouted at me reached my brain. Today I would not stand for that behavior, for it is abusive.

We were expected to come in on Saturdays, and they wouldn't turn on the heat. The office was freezing. Several Saturdays I sat at my desk wearing a coat and scarf, long underwear under my jeans, and heavy socks because it was so incredibly cold. Once when Errol was not there, I asked a senior associate if we could turn on the heat. He advised me not to even think of that.

From the documents at the firm, I came across the name of an attorney whose writing was well-reasoned and well-written, using a variety of sentence structures, unlike the managing partner's rigid pattern of subject-verb, subject-verb. I phoned this attorney, Jordan Sherlock, who was then with a different employer, to inquire about his experience at the firm. I was curious as I had already been in the professional world for more than a decade and had never before encountered a work environment quite like this. He said Errol would berate him, tell him that his work was stupid, and ridicule him for working late. Jordan would leave, then return to the office in the evening and stay until 10:30 p.m. to get more done. He said he became a nervous wreck. Errol, he said, fired him and forced him to sign a document stating he resigned and agreed not to seek unemployment benefits.

I was always at the office by 6:50 a.m. Errol came in early, too, and would go to the cafeteria for coffee. One day he stepped into my office holding a paper plate with a half-bagel smothered with cream cheese. Out of the blue, he began shouting, "Look what you made me do! You *made me eat* this bagel!" I sat there, reticent, bewildered at what had set him off. He went on and on about me making him eat that bagel, letting his anger stream into his hand, giving the bagel flight. It smacked the right upper arm of my navy suit jacket, slapping a schmear of cream cheese onto my sleeve. He stormed out. I got back to work. I did not ask him to cover the dry-cleaning bill because I suspected he'd then fire me. Today, that situation would unfold very differently.

Later, I heard that Errol had told another attorney that someday when he gets "good and drunk," he would tell him a "funny story about Judie." There were no "funny stories" to tell. My law school teachings came to mind where certain crimes require "intent," and intoxication may block the mental capacity to form such intent. *Was that perhaps the point of being "good and drunk" before telling a "funny"—albeit fabricated—"story"?* I wondered.

When I decided to leave after less than one year into the job, I could not in good faith give Errol notice. I did not feel him worthy of such respect. Instead, I sent my letter of resignation by Federal Express, giving ten business days' notice to the lead partner who worked from a different location. The lead partner phoned Errol to discuss my departure. As Errol's office was next to mine, I heard Errol lie. "We had to fire her. She couldn't even write a letter," he said. That is how he learned that I was leaving: via the lead partner. I didn't call him on his lie. Hearing what he said aligned with how I experienced his character.

On my last day there, Errol was out of the office. The accountant, Rita Gladmann, surprised me. She was someone Errol treated respectfully. She vouchsafed that her initial experience at the firm had mirrored mine. She recounted that Errol put her down daily, leaving her depleted by the end of the day. Her husband, she said, told her to stand up to him. And that is what she did. She challenged Errol. After that, she said, he treated her as a peer. She told me that that was my mistake: I needed to stand up to him and didn't.

On reflection, I realized that given his position, I saw him as an authority figure and so treated him accordingly, with respect. Inwardly, though, I felt his behavior at the firm was anything but deserving of respect. To feed his need to feel powerful, he demeaned others—even his peers.

After I left, as I had overheard Errol lie to the lead partner that they "had to fire" me, I consulted an attorney. I was looking for a job and suspected if Errol lied freely about me to a partner, he would likely lie if somehow contacted by a prospective employer. On that attorney's recommendation, I contacted the firm and advised them that I was putting them "on notice" that I was looking for a job and that if they were wise, they would tell the truth about my departure and not lie to besmirch me.

Errol was my only manager who used anger and verbal abuse as a manipulation device to control people. In that respect, he was similar to my mom; he used his energy to try to control subordinates and his work environment. It went beyond being draconian, for it sought to affect and degrade the spirit of people. That, to me, reflects someone with a weak core.

When I left that firm, I was truly grateful for my experience there. In what I felt was a toxic environment, I uncovered a gem for personal development. I learned to look out for individuals who are intentionally cruel. And I learned the importance of calling it quits before letting anyone use me as a masturbation device to boost their personal sense of power.

I learned too that what we experience leaves an imprint in our energy field. Everything is energy and vibrates at a frequency, even solid materials such as steel. That is why we attract to ourselves people, events, and situations that follow a pattern from our past. For example, some people consistently attract an abusive partner. In *Every Memory Deserves Respect*, authors Michael Baldwin and Deborah Korn, a psychotherapist, observe that "Trauma can create an unconscious 'magnetic field' – a powerful attraction to familiar personalities and patterns." (Baldwin and Korn 2021, 132) From that, I reasoned it wouldn't be any different in a work situation. Here, as bizarre as it may sound to those who have not yet been introduced to this concept, I attracted this angry, verbally abusive employer into my life.

After that, I worked on changing my thoughts and not lingering on my past. I hoped I had cleaved that pattern.

An Olive Branch

1995

While working at Errol's firm, I heard about my godfather's passing. I was still estranged from Mom. For more than nine years, I kept my promise not to speak with her. My intention was not to be vindictive or to show that I could hold a grudge. It was to protect myself and my husband, and it was one of the smartest things I had done.

My godfather's death changed that. I thought about our mortality. My mom was eighty years old. One day she would die. Did I want that to be while I was cocooning myself away, even if it was for self-protection? I decided to risk the peace in our life, on a test basis, and call her to offer her a ride to the wake. If she acted up, I would tell her I love her, wish her well, and then hang up.

"Hello?" Mom answered the phone.

"Hi, Mom. It's Judie."

"Who?" She paused. "Judie?" she asked, sounding surprised to hear from me.

"Yes. It's Judie. How are you?" I asked.

"Oh, Judie. Hey, Uncle Joe died," she interjected, as if we spoke daily.

"Yes, I heard." Before I could say anything more, she started talking about his passing and funeral arrangements.

"I'm going to the wake," I said. "Would you like me to pick you up?"

"No, I'm not going to that. I have a ride to the funeral," she told me.

"I'm glad you're going. I know his family would appreciate that. Mom, you and I haven't spoken for years. How are you?" I asked.

"I'm watching TV," she said. "I had a big dinner. I made sauerkraut and pierogi. Oh, it was so good. I haven't made pierogi for a long time. I had a lot to eat. I'm so full. It was good."

"That's wonderful. It sounds like you're eating well. You always enjoyed cooking. How are you feeling?" I asked.

"Good. I feel good. I'm healthy. I walk to church. I take the bus downtown. I still bake poppyseed rolls. I go out and get whatever I need," she said. She talked about my godfather's family and said she was giving money for Mass.

She then talked about her neighbors and a family member who brought a man over to her home to meet. "He has no personality. She's a dupa yash...."

Okay. It was time to end the call. I didn't want to listen to gossip, and Mom was big on gossip.

"I am so glad to hear that you're doing well. You sound good. Take good care of yourself and I will call again soon. Okay?" I said.

"Okay. I'm going to go back to my show now," she said.

"All right. Bye, Mom," I said.

Our call lasted five minutes, tops. Her voice sounded robust. She didn't ask how I was; she usually didn't.

We never had a dialogue, and that apparently hadn't changed. This call had as much depth as our earlier calls. Actually, perhaps a tad less. She didn't criticize me; she stopped that after I married.

I didn't bring up our last conversation, which was about the bayonet incident. As she typically shrugged off responsibility for her actions, if she were to lie about what had transpired on that call, that would have shredded any hope for a reconciliation going forward.

I felt sorry for her. She had missed out on being part of my life.

Reflecting on Loss

Over the nine-plus years of our estrangement, what did I do to deal with my loss on multiple fronts? There was a lot to process: feeling Mom stab my heart for her own agenda, hearing others judge me as being "horrible" and not hesitating to tell me so, losing a good friend, and knowing that Mom was lying to others that I was tearing up money and heaven knows what else.

My grieving process was a long haul. It took months. I talked with my spouse and with another friend about what had happened. I read about mental illness. I shifted my perspective of Mom. I tried putting myself in her shoes to truly grasp what she had been through in life. I tried to see life through her eyes, as someone who had experienced rape as a child and lifelong disappointment from her mother.

In their book, *On Grief and Grieving: Finding the Meaning of Grief through the Five Stages of Loss,* authors Elisabeth Kübler-Ross and David Kessler identify five stages of loss: denial, anger, bargaining, depression, and acceptance.

Looking back now at those stages, I see that with my mom's sword-through-the-heart lie, I went through the denial stage relatively quickly but was stuck in the anger stage for a while. Then I was stuck in the bargaining stage where I felt helpless. I blamed myself for not anticipating this. Its potential was there all the time. That was how Mom treated her sister, Aunt Mary—a sweet, sensitive, gentle lady. I recalled Mom's singsong twisted with mirth: "I made Mary cry! Good for her. Good for her!"

So, why, I thought, *would she not purposely hurt her own child?*

In hindsight, it helped tremendously when my friend Bev dropped me. That stopped the flow of lies I had to listen to. That was when I really started to heal.

It also helped that I had separated myself from the family— that is, both my immediate and extensive family. That gave me space to heal.

It took time to accept these losses. I prayed. I meditated daily. Eventually, I could talk about what had happened with acceptance and without getting emotional. I healed.

From this experience, I began to understand how important it is to hold your own healing space and to be authentic. Until that incident, from everyone—my friends, teachers, and neighbors—I hid Mom's mental illness. Her siblings and their spouses knew, as did my dad's siblings and in-laws, but no one else, not even my cousins. And those who knew and reached out to me in my teens never again broached the topic with me. They opted for silence and allowed my mom, as she was an adult, to shape the affairs of her household, free of their intervention. Everyone did that, aside from Virge in dropping off toothbrushes. From an early age, Mom taught me to hide the fact that Dad was an alcoholic. You hide aspects of your home life that are not normal, because if you talk about those things, people will impute that sense of "not normal" onto you. I learned that from Mom and applied that principle to concealing her behavior and mental state. In hindsight, based on what I now know, today I would not have cloaked Mom's condition with silence.

I learned how critical it is to address mental illness. If untreated, mental illness can be like a cancer, ripping families apart and shredding people's hearts.

I learned that others may have opinions and formulate judgments, and that is their prerogative. What they think is immaterial to you, even if it is about you. It's their belief system, not yours.

Boundaries, I learned, are imperative, even among family members. Sometimes you need to prune people out of your life to honor yourself, I learned. And that, in turn, gives you room to grow and flourish.

I also learned that not everyone will agree with our decisions or actions. The only person who can judge whether someone's decision or action is right is the one making that particular decision or taking that action. In my case, had I not removed myself from my family, I would have endured endless, unproductive, and toxic drama. That would have snuffed out any hope of pursuing my goals as well as every iota of joy, peace, and happiness in my being. By choosing to be healthfully "selfish" and tending to my needs—even if that landed me smack in the middle of gossip—I was able to connect with my soul and direct my focus and energy toward my interests and on helping others.

My losses taught me what pain feels like and how to navigate my way toward healing. Because of this experience, I can relate to how others feel, particularly as to loss associated with relationships, familial dysfunctionality, mental illness in the family, abuse, addiction, or jealousy.

And, more importantly, I learned that there is always hope. Though things may appear grim initially, there is always a layer of hope beneath the gunk. As we heal, the gunk wears thinner and thinner until the hope can shine through brightly.

Have I ever felt resentment toward Mom or family for what I experienced? No, absolutely not. In fact, I am grateful for all the experiences and people I have encountered, including the pain. Pain was my teacher. It sculpted me into the person I am today. It forced me to look within, rely on myself, and cultivate resilience, tolerance, and compassion for myself and others. It gave me a perspicacity into people's psychology and into how some, if allowed, may use or abuse others to fill a hole within their own hearts. It showed me the richness of humanity. It helped me, from a young age, to connect with my soul and to trust guidance from within and from the spiritual world that I choose to follow, for it always leads me down the right path. It gave me an understanding I would not otherwise have had.

Most importantly, I learned it is through our collective experiences that we transform into stronger, resilient beings, more capable of helping others and being of service to the world. For, in my opinion, that is why we are here: to grow into the brightest light we can be and to be of service to the world.

Litigator

1995–1996

When I left Errol's firm, the universe was looking out for me. My next position was with a wonderful Chicago-based litigation firm. Again, the firm's leadership was predominately male, except for one female partner and another female attorney at my level. However, I never saw gender influence the distribution of cases or intrude on an attorney's work there. The people were amazing. Everyone got along and treated each other with respect and integrity. The work was challenging and gratifying. It was the perfect firm.

I was hired as a contract attorney to help specifically on a huge environmental law matter. On that case, I used my chemistry background, working with an expert and identifying chemistry references for him to use to familiarize himself with the requisite science. The work expanded to include trademark, tort, and contract matters, and depositions across the country. The firm kept me on twice longer than the time agreed upon at hiring. It was sad to leave.

Bringing Family up to Speed

1996

Before starting my new job as a litigator, it occurred to me that someone in my family might read about that in the newspaper, as some papers publish the names of attorneys making lateral moves. This concerned me. I had been an attorney for two years and two months, and outside of my husband's family, I had not told a soul in my family that I had even gone to law school. As far as they knew, I was still an editor with a magazine.

Mom was perhaps the sole exception: she never knew what I did. Back when I was a scientist, I asked her, "Do you know what I do for a living?" I had already told her several times before that. She never asked questions and never commented afterward.

To that question, she answered, "Yeah. I tell everybody. You have a good job. You're a foreman at a plant."

I was in a pickle. I had to contrive a means of bringing my mom and family up to speed. So, I called Mom and nonchalantly asked what she was doing, where she went, and whom she heard from. Then, I brought it up: "Mom, did I tell you that I'm an attorney?" I asked in a voice suggestive that "of course I told you this."

247

She met my question with silence, followed by, "Awk, you're so goddamn dumb. What you do that for? You already got so much school."

Quickly, I changed the subject.

Whew! I felt like I had made a home run. However, her "goddamn dumb" remark didn't go unnoticed. It confirmed to me that I was doing the right thing by not rushing into visiting.

What was *THAT?*

Before launching into my next position as a litigator with a well-established litigation firm, I took the patent bar exam. Passing the patent bar is a prerequisite to practice as a patent attorney before the U.S. Patent and Trademark Office.

The afternoon portion of the day-long patent exam involved writing "claims" for a patent application. The claims are the most important part of a patent because they define exactly what the invention is. Courts look to the claims to determine patent infringement. In the exam, these were not short-answer responses to test questions; the test-taker was given a blank notebook and asked to protect a particular invention.

For the claims portion of the bar exam administered at that time, the test taker selected which exam they wanted to take: chemical, electrical, or mechanical. Most people chose the mechanical exam as you could get started right away because you described what you saw. The chemical exam, however, might give you a myriad of compounds and before you could start writing, you first needed to determine what the invention was, based on your knowledge of chemistry. That was the exam I chose to write.

Before the test started, outside the test room, I met a biochemist with nine years of experience and an electrical engineer with thirteen years of experience. We discussed which exam we were going to write. When I mentioned I was doing the chemical exam, both guys tried to dissuade me from that option. They were going to do the mechanical exam, both said, because with that exam, you wrote about the image shown on the test page. The exam was stressful enough and that freed you from having to get the nitty-gritty of the science right, they said.

I studied for both the chemical and mechanical exams. For the chemical exam, I pulled out my college chemistry texts and refamiliarized myself with the material. I tested myself by drawing structures for compounds used in cosmetics and then checked up on the structures I drew. I made sure I knew my chemistry. So, that was the exam I chose.

For the week before the exam and before entering the building, I asked archangels Michael, Gabriel, and Raphael to help me. Back then, I didn't know what Gabriel and Raphael's specialties were, but I included them as I was open to all the help I could get.

Before I could write the exam, I had to determine what the invention was; that is, which compounds were patentable. That took about one hour and seven spreadsheets to funnel down to the answer.

Just as I dotted the final period on the test, I sensed a pushy, masculine energy around me—it felt like it was flying around me—and I heard in my head (not in the room) a strong thought: "Go to page two, line three, third word. It's misspelled."

That amused me. *Okay, that's strange*, I thought. *That's not from me.* Thinking maybe it was my imagination, I went to page two, line three. My eyes widened when I saw the word "methol"—a compound that includes a hydroxyl group. *Methol* and *methyl* are homophones: they are words that sound the same but are different in meaning. So, did I write "methol" but mean "methyl," a different compound?

I went back through the spreadsheets. To my dismay, the correct chemical group was methyl—an entirely different structure with no hydroxyl group. So, this energy's imperative was spot-on. I got a chill and then chuckled, thinking, *After all the exams I've taken in my life, I'm just* now *getting help?*

As soon as I corrected the misspelling, the voice in my head came again, forcefully, "Go to page eight, second paragraph. You left something out."

I thought, *This is so bizarre!* I went to that spot in my bluebook and looked over the seventh spreadsheet. Nothing there. I felt a nudge to "Go back, go back" through the spreadsheets. Successively, I checked the sixth, the fifth, and all the way back to the first spreadsheet. That's where I found I had left out one chemical group.

Right after I corrected my bluebook, the strong energetic nudge returned with "Now go back to the beginning and read it all over." By this time, I'd had it. I didn't like being pushed with that sense of rush, rush. In my mind, to whatever that benevolent force was that was interjecting instructions, I thought, *Leave me alone. I have this.* I was not grateful whatsoever.

On my way home, I tried to fathom what that well-meaning but annoyingly insistent energy was. It was indubitably not me; it was an intelligence outside myself. I didn't believe in divine intervention in the middle of a bar exam, but was it? While I believed in angels, I didn't believe you would actually "feel" their intercession. Because I fixated on the energy's pushiness, the remarkable nature of what had happened escaped me until my drive home.

I passed the exam, earning registration as a patent attorney.

A Surprisingly Warm Family Welcome

September 1996

Though I had spoken with my mom via phone a few times, I still felt it too risky to visit. I let our relationship reform slowly and organically, as I was watching what old behaviors would re-emerge.

It was Sister Ann's Jubilee celebration marking her seventy years in the convent. Running late, John and I stealthily snuck into the church after Mass had already started. Trepidation swirled about in my stomach concerning the post-Mass reception. I didn't know how Mom's family would receive me. Would it be with kindness, or sharp words and judgment? Whatever happened, I decided, I would accept.

After Mass, Sister stood in the church vestibule beaming with joy, surrounded by family congratulating her as they waited for her to lead them to the dining room. John and I were about thirty feet away. I started walking toward the group. With her eagle-eyed vision at age eighty-five, Sister Ann spotted me. I looked quite different from when she had last seen me, twelve years earlier when John and I had spent Christmas Eve with her at the convent.

Suddenly, she excitedly exclaimed, "Judie! Judie! I am so glad you came!" and ran toward me, embracing me tightly. Everyone stood still, silently looking on. She then hooked one arm under John's and slipped her other hand into mine, leading the way to the dining room with the family following. Her conduct, I believe, was a cue to her family on how they were to conduct themselves.

Mom was already seated in the dining room. Her hair was pulled up with a wig affixed to her crown. "Hi. You look nice," she said as I approached.

"So do you, Mom," I said, trying to hug her. She resisted; she wasn't into hugs. "May we join you?" I asked.

"Yeah, that's okay," she said. John and I sat across from her. This was the first time we had seen her since the "bayonet" moment.

Over dinner, I asked Mom about her life. She didn't ask anything about John or me, which was normal. She looked uncomfortable sitting across from me. Her demeanor suggested that she felt vulnerable, as if she was wondering whether I would raise the bayonet moment with her in front of others, forcing her to either cling to her lie or come clean. I felt she was thinking that in my place, she would have exploited that opportunity. From her body language, that's what I surmised occupied her mind.

That day, I enjoyed my visit with those around me, including Mom, who seemed distanced from our conversation and uncomfortable.

Less than two years later, an envelope with Mom's handwriting appeared in our mailbox. In it were a short note, a newspaper clipping of an obituary, and a Mass card from a funeral home. The obituary and Mass card told of Sister Ann's passing two weeks earlier. Sadness filled my heart as I would have liked to have gone to her funeral, followed by a lightness, for I felt she'd be looking after me from the ethers.

Loved the Job

1996–1998

A few days after the patent bar exam, I carried my litigation experience into a new firm where my docket reflected a jigsaw of court calls, arbitrations, depositions (including some out-of-state), dispositive motions, pre-trial conferences, trials, and appellate work. In some court cases, I used my science background—a definite plus. There, I poured myself into my work, with sixty-five to seventy hours per week, and eighty-four hours when on trial, which at the time was not unusual for lawyers, depending on the firm.

The challenges of the cases were my *juice*. As a litigator, I sought that *smoking gun*. It was like trying to solve the math challenges I relished as a child. I felt genuine respect from other counsel and partners there. Despite women attorneys being in the minority at this firm, in day-to-day operations, I never felt impeded professionally because of my gender.

I found myself relying more on intuition. On one wrongful death case, a key witness could not be located for a deposition, and a skip tracer's efforts to locate him came up empty after a month. Within me was a nudge— a strong feeling that I would find him. This was in 1997, before lawyers, who tend to be slow adopters of technology, had computers in their offices. I was considered quirky because I used a laptop. Our office did not yet have access to the internet.

I mentioned to a partner that I would find this witness. He looked at me, bemused. "A skip tracer hasn't even been able to find him, Judie."

Following my instincts, I made a few cold calls to people I didn't know. The missing witness, I learned, had an office in a city close to where I lived. Driving by one building on my way to the grocery store, I got the feeling that the witness had an office there. I stopped inside and noted the business names on the lobby directory; the witness's name was not on the directory. A few more phone calls confirmed that this witness did, in fact, on a few weekdays, work in this building, using an office whose business name matched a name on the list compiled during my visit. Someone mentioned that the runaway witness was there on certain weekdays and would post a sign outside the office door.

One such day, following up on that information, I called an unrelated business there and begged the receptionist to check if a sign was posted outside a particular office on the floor below. Initially hesitating, she agreed to check. A few minutes later she returned. "Yes," she reported, "that name is on a sign outside the door."

I instructed a paralegal to prepare a subpoena for service, *stat*. The partner looked at me as if I were nuts. He was even more astonished when the process server reported the successful delivery of the subpoena to the runaway witness they were looking for.

That's when I learned to appreciate the power of intuition.

I enjoyed this job. I loved my colleagues' commitment to

doing a good job and the firmwide emphasis on ethics. My secretary was phenomenal: she worked with a lead partner and me. However, I accepted the job because I wanted trial experience, and beforehand, I knew I wouldn't use my patent law registration here. After two years with the firm, I reluctantly decided to seek a position where I could do patent and related intellectual property law work and use the experience I had gleaned to that point.

When I gave my two-week notice, the executive director and a named partner with whom I worked closely wanted to counter-offer and exceed the salary of my new position. Though I appreciated the generous gesture, it was time for me to move on.

Of intrigue to me was that the firm's executive director was always on the phone. Every day, as I passed his office, he sat in the exact same position—motionless and silent, like a mannequin, with his feet propped up on a credenza and the phone pressed to his ear, without speaking. Because I suspected he was monitoring attorneys' calls, I communicated with prospective employers via a pay phone outside the office. The day after I gave notice, the firm's receptionist stopped me on my way to lunch. With a baffled expression, she said, "Hmmm . . . It's strange that the phone company was asked to check out only one phone: yours. No one else's, just yours. That's odd. Were you having problems with your phone?"

Again, the power of intuition. We all have it.

The Allure of Ideas

1998–1999

Again, I landed in another good law firm—one that focused on intellectual property law and litigation where I could leverage my full experience.

When a client retained our firm to handle a case on international trade secret theft, the lead partners took about a dozen attorneys who would be working on the case, which included me, to a local restaurant to celebrate. That morning, one partner mentioned a gnarly case-related issue we would need to address. Before venturing out, the thought popped into my mind of how to resolve that issue and a quick internet search revealed just the right approach. At lunch, we toasted, and the key partner ended with something to the effect of "Now, if we could just find a way to get around that issue."

That's when I proposed, sitting near the opposite end of the table, "How about doing X?"

Silence draped the table. The partner looked at me. I thought, *What are you looking at? That will work.*

The partner then exclaimed, "That's brilliant! That's brilliant. That's it. That's our answer."

After lunch, a different partner called my office. He chastised himself for not coming up with that idea. He had been practicing law for fourteen years.

"What were your thought processes?" he inquired. "How did you come up with that idea?" He wanted to know.

I hadn't given the issue any thought. The resolution I proposed just popped into my head, and I then researched the concept to find the ideal approach.

Several months later, a woman attorney there, Vicki Middlebury, and I were chatting about a different case when I mentioned an idea I had for how to knock out a counterclaim against our client. She did not have a chemistry background, so I explained what the publication *Chemical Abstracts* was and how we could use it for that purpose. I mentioned I was going to speak to one of the partners about the concept when he returned from court.

She told me, "That is the stupidest idea I ever heard."

I was floored. I would never say that to a colleague; even if I thought an idea was not the best, I wouldn't nix it. I would credit the innovative thinker with perhaps knowing something I was not aware of. Vicki told me I would look foolish if I brought that idea up to the partner. Well, that didn't deter me. I would talk with the partner when he got back.

About fifteen minutes later, I felt a nudge to get a cup of coffee. The kitchen was across from Vicki's office. The partner had apparently returned without my knowing it. He sat in a chair near Vicki's door. "That's brilliant, Vicki. Brilliant. That's thinking outside the box," he said.

I knew what had happened.

Crossing the hall, I joined the conversation. "What's brilliant?" I asked, already knowing the answer. He explained that Vicki suggested we search *Chemical Abstracts*.

I glanced at her. Her Cheshire cat grin stretched ear to ear. I had already learned this lesson fifteen years ago. I responded, "Oh, that's interesting. That was my idea. I told Vicki about it twenty minutes ago. She didn't know what *Chemical Abstracts* was." I didn't append, "She said it was the stupidest idea and not to raise it with you."

"Well, it doesn't matter who came up with it. It's brilliant," he remarked.

And my idea achieved exactly what I had hoped it would.

From this, I learned two things: first, to *never* share your ideas with a colleague before you claim them as yours to someone who counts; and second, to not trust Vicki.

On the day my colleague presented the *Chemical Abstracts* idea to the partner, I noticed the partner's response didn't go beyond "it doesn't matter." He didn't inquire about facts, as if truth didn't matter. By brushing the exchange aside, he, I thought, missed an ideal moment to touch briefly on the firm's culture and its expectation of how we *both*, Vicki and I, as attorneys were to conduct ourselves to foster a positive workplace. Yes, we are only human, and our egos may sometimes seek attention. But an off-the-cuff quip of "it doesn't matter" sets the bar low for conduct in the workplace—inviting back-stabbing, sabotage, and resistance to collaboration—and, in effect, unintentionally condones those behaviors.

On Secretary's Day, Vicki's first secretary quit on the spot. Her second secretary, who was eight months pregnant, would come to my office in tears from how Vicki spoke to her. I intervened, advising a partner with concern about the lady losing her baby. She could end up suing the firm, I told him.

I wasn't the only attorney there drawing Vicki's favor. She would complain to me about a male associate "messing up discovery" and how she "always had to fix it." She'd say, "He does everything wrong." I thought quite the opposite of his work. A few months later, after that associate was promoted to partner, she stopped criticizing his work behind his back and chummed up to him.

I wondered, *Does she bad-mouth me as well?* I suspected she did, but that was not something I chose to waste my time exploring. I had work to do.

Change in Focus: Mom in Trouble

1999

It was late Wednesday, July 21, 1999, when a cousin, Sophie, called. She said that a teenage boy was on Mom's porch carrying a bat and demanding fifty dollars for the *Times* newspaper subscription, and my eighty-five-year-old mom gave it to him. "Things are not making sense in the house. The dining room has things that don't belong there," she told me. I was concerned.

That evening, I phoned Mom. She insisted no one had come to her home that week, carried a bat, or asked for money. She denied giving money to anyone.

At the time, I was with a Chicago law firm working fifty to sixty hours per week, and I couldn't take off in the middle of the week. That Saturday I visited Mom with my husband to assess her situation. We weren't there long before the doorbell rang. At the door stood a tall, thin young man with unusually fair skin and long black sideburns demanding fifty dollars for the newspaper. Mom's newspaper was paid up; I paid a few months in advance. This was a ruse.

I heard Mom say, "Weren't you just here? Didn't I just pay you?"

When I reached the door, the young man scurried off. I reminded Mom that her newspaper was paid up. The guy was trying to get money from her. As she did not cheat people, cheating was a foreign concept to her. She could not comprehend why someone would ask for money if she was already paid up.

I went outdoors to see where he had taken off to. Walking toward Mom's house, in the parkway across the street, was a heavyset boy about fourteen to sixteen years old. He carried a bat. Apparently, I fit in so well with the neighborhood that he called out to me from about forty feet away, "Have you seen ma fren'?"

"What's his name?"

"Roy."

"Is he tall with long black, sharp-cut sideburns?" I said, gesturing with my hands to show their shape as I crossed the street to the parkway.

"Yeah, that's him. Have you seen 'im? He said he's goin' to the old lady's house to git some money."

I paused. This was a moment of decision. I could go along and have him walk off, or I could contest so he would know someone is looking after that "old lady." I chose to contest.

"That 'old lady' is my mom. Tell your friend to leave her alone. Tell him to stop trying to get money from her or he's going to have his ass thrown in jail." I realized I sounded weak to someone who thought nothing of theft or of exploiting old people. I didn't expect him to have an "aha" moment and agree that his friend's actions were wrongful.

Waving his bat and stepping toward me, he said, "I could break your back."

Okay, technically that may qualify as an assault in some states, I thought from my law school days. As we were still about twenty to twenty-five feet apart, if I had to, I could outrun him. I repeated again, "Tell your friend to leave my mom alone. Let's leave it at that." I turned to walk away from him, hoping he'd do the same. After a few steps, I checked to see where he was. He was walking in the opposite direction.

Inside the house, I called the police to report the incident about the kid demanding money. In the background, they could hear Mom arguing with my husband: "No one came to the porch asking for money! You're crazy!" At eighty-five years old, she still had a powerful voice that carried.

When leaving to return home, I saw mom's neighbor, Angie, on her stairs. I walked up to say hello. She said her husband, looking out the window, called to her worriedly that "some young girl talking to a Black boy with a bat in the parkway is now headed to Martha's house." He hoped she wasn't going to cause trouble for Martha. When Angie looked out the window, she saw a thin, blond girl with shorts, a yellow T-shirt, and sneakers in front of Martha's house. Angie and I chuckled when she identified that "girl" as me. Her husband, in his seventies, seeing me about fifty feet away, thought I was a young girl because of my size. On our drive home, I realized that maybe because I looked young from a distance, that was why the bat-carrying boy called out to me with ease.

After that, we visited every Saturday, making the one to one-and-a-half-hour drive, depending on traffic, and spending the entire day. Each time, we took Mom out for a good, healthy lunch. On our return, we washed her kitchen and bathroom floors, cleaned the kitchen, vacuumed the entire house, dusted, grocery-shopped, and made her a nice dinner with plenty for leftovers. She never asked us to do that; we didn't want her to live in a dirty home.

Her argumentative nature resurfaced and strengthened to the point that she would now readily argue with my husband, perhaps because she associated him with me and saw him as part of her immediate family. Inside her home, she no longer treated him respectfully as she did others such as her brother Lou, who now visited infrequently, according to Mom. With the boundary of respect breached, Mom naturally called John crazy and shouted at him that no one was on her porch demanding money.

With the dinners I made, I found it better if I left the kitchen after plating her food. If I stayed, she would take a bite and yell, "Oh, blahk! This is awful!" Then, with a sound mimicking vomiting, she would spit out her food right onto the floor, look at me, and then repeat that action. If I left the kitchen after plating her food or had my husband serve it with me out of the kitchen, she would clean her plate and tell him, "That was good."

One day, before we switched to my husband plating Mom's food, I noticed Mom's coffee pot had stopped working. After cleaning the house, John and I went out to buy her a new coffeemaker. That evening, she was surprised to see me back on her porch after her mock vomiting on the kitchen floor.

"May we come in? I asked. "I bought you a new coffee pot."

When I showed her how to use it, she was unusually pensive. Standing by the stove, her black sweater drawn tightly around her, arms crossed in front of her, she lowered her voice. "I'm sorry. I don't know why I ack like that. I don't know why," she said, frowning and shaking her head from side to side as if seriously trying to find an answer. I could feel Mom's disappointment in herself. I knew that whatever the unruly force was within her, she was aware that she could not control it. I hugged her, and she didn't resist.

A Stolen Key?

1999

On eighty to ninety percent of our visits, I spent time in the back of a police car. I would be reporting someone demanding money at Mom's door or trying to break in. Once, a group of eight teenage boys gathered on Mom's sidewalk loudly boasting about "pounding on the old lady's door." Before I could go out, a seventy-eight-year-old neighbor leaving his sister's home next door confronted the kids and told them to leave.

And there were incidents I did not report to the police: Mom's wedding ring went missing from her hand, along with her false teeth. We searched the entire house for both. Neither showed up. A few weeks later, she said, "A man gave me my teeth back." Knick-knacks gradually vanished from the house. Initially, I assumed they had fallen from their high window ledge and broken.

I reconnected with Mom's neighbors. She got along with several of them. However, as she aged, she let her guard down and easily expressed contempt toward one neighbor. That relationship deteriorated to the point that they no longer spoke, yet that neighbor remained concerned for Mom's safety.

One night when that neighbor couldn't sleep, she saw Mom's house was "lit up like a Christmas tree" at 2 a.m. and saw a man leave Mom's house "carrying two full grocery bags," the neighbor said. Another neighbor asked what happened to Mom's TV. She had seen two men carrying a TV from Mom's house across the parkway into an alley. When I checked, the TV in the living room was not the one we had given her the previous Christmas; it was an old one from a bedroom. When I asked Mom about the new TV, she explained, "Two men pushed open the front door and said they're going to repair it. I didn't stop them."

We found that food we were buying for her was disappearing alarmingly faster than she could eat it. One next-door neighbor divulged that Mom once knocked at her door and asked, "Could I have some bread? I'm hungry." She gave Mom a loaf of bread and a jar of jelly.

That same neighbor also expressed concern for Mom's safety. "Someone was pounding on her door hard last night. It was 9:30 p.m." Hearing that was disquieting. Mom had to have been scared. It made me question how some of Mom's relatives could counter that her neighborhood was fine.

I never had a key to Mom's house. Ever. And now that she was older, I had to do fancy footwork to get one from her.

One evening after work, I called at 9:30 p.m. After the first ring, a man whispered, "Hello?" When I started speaking, he hung up. I hit redial. The phone rang seven times before Mom answered. She sounded like she had just woken up.

"Do you have company?" I probed.

"No. I'm here alone. Nobody's here. It's late." Her tone blared, "What a stupid question." When I told her about the man answering, she said no one had been over.

I wondered, *Did that man let himself in with a key?*

"Do you let people into her home that you don't know?" I asked.

Sounding annoyed, Mom said, "I don't want to live like a hermit and be lonely." That told me that, yes, she was letting people in. And she was probably falling asleep, which would allow them to case out the place and steal things. When John and I were over, she sometimes fell asleep sitting with us.

On one call, she said a little boy had rung her doorbell that day. He asked, "Do you live alone?"

Mom said she told him, "Yes. I'm eighty-five years old and live here all by myself." The little boy, she said, "was shy" and dashed off.

At night, before going to bed, she routinely left the screen door unlocked. Once when she saw me lock it, angst flashed across her face. She barked, "Never lock this door! Leave this unlocked. Lock only the big inside door."

That confirmed my suspicion: someone had a key to the front door. From the angst in her voice and on her face, she feared consequences if the screen door was locked so they couldn't use their key on the wood door behind it.

Confirmation came in a scrap of paper next to the wall phone. Scribbled on it, in Mom's shaky handwriting, was, "Please: Lock my house. Do not use the back only front & lock it up. Thank you. It was opened all night & that was enough."

The Grasshopper Tattoo

1999

Mom's home was a portal to danger.

At the end of my second visit that July, I was in tears. I hated to leave Mom alone in that house. I started exploring options. One possibility was to hire caregivers—what my family calls "Polish ladies"—to come and look after Mom. I ruled that out on two fronts: 1) I was concerned about something happening to them. The door locks were compromised, and Mom refused to have them changed. Even aside from that, if Mom was opening the door for strangers, why would she stop doing that if a caregiver were there? 2) Who would want to live with my mom? Once the veneer of respect wore down and Mom started verbally abusing the person or became physically aggressive, what if that person retaliated and injured Mom? The only viable option was to find a decent home for her, one where she would be looked after, fed well, taken care of, and treated with respect and dignity. And one that would not dump her onto the street when she ran out of money.

About a month into our visits, early in the afternoon, the doorbell punctuated our clean-up routine. At the door stood two people: Roy—the tall, fair-skinned guy with long sideburns—and another young man who was shirtless but looked clean-cut. I called the police. We heard them badger Mom for money for her newspaper subscription. As I stepped into view, Roy ran off. The other guy started descending the stairs as I came outdoors and tried talking to him. He was smart and glib. He said he was "going to be going."

"If you're not doing anything wrong, why not stay and talk with the police when they get here?" I asked.

He started crossing the street to the parkway. I told my husband, "I am going with him."

The guy shot back a look of surprise, like "What did you say?" He then continued up the street.

I told my husband, "Stay here and watch for the police. Tell the officer whether we go left or right at the crossroad."

John declined. "I'm not going to let you go alone with him."

I didn't know what to do. I didn't want to waste the police call. As I looked up the street, a Hispanic lady was approaching us. I felt like the protagonist in the movie *No Exit*. I didn't know who was a good guy or who was a bad guy. I didn't know if she worked with him or not. I called out to her in a jarring voice, pointing to him, "Do you know this asshole?"

She started yelling at him to leave her mom alone. (Later, I learned she lived up the street.) She heard my exchange with John and offered to watch for the police and flag them down to tell them what direction we took at the cross street. Because of her generosity, I appreciated John joining up with me.

I tried talking to the guy. He was mum. He was too proud to run away. I sensed his worry. He'd never been followed or accompanied by anyone he had tried to heist. He wanted to act like he was in control. Yet, he didn't want to speak to me.

I walked behind him and scoped a tattoo of a grasshopper stretching across his back.

We walked a few blocks, turned down an alley, and went another few blocks. At a crossroad, he pointed to a white garage on the right. "That's where the guy you want lives. He's involved in this. He's the one you want." He turned onto the crossroad and continued down the street. We made a right into someone's backyard. Fortunately, no guard dogs leaped out at us.

The garage door was ajar. I knocked. A woman with a cigarette dangling from her lips shuffled to the door. She looked to be in her mid-forties with tanned, wrinkled, leather-like skin and no makeup, and had a large gap of teeth missing from her upper bridge. Her teeth were stained brown.

"What do you want?" she asked, looking me up and down.

This must be Roy's mom, I mused.

"I want your son, Roy, to stop harassing my mom for money."

"I don't know what you're talking about," she claimed.

"I have photos of a tall skinny guy who has really light skin and long black sideburns that come forward with sharp edges." I gestured. "I am going to show them to the police." At that point, I didn't have photos but did a few months later.

With a cagey voice, quivering on the "can," she asked, "C-a-a-n I see the photos?" as if she was assessing what to do. So, that was her son.

"No, they're evidence. I'm going to show them to the police," I told her.

She opened the door and said, "Come in." I stepped inside, and John stood in the doorway. This was a garage converted into a makeshift home. A TV blared in one corner, explaining the wires feeding into the building. Cigarette smoke competed with the blaring TV for prominence. Papers were strewn across the floor. Worn furniture tossed over with blankets provided seating.

To the left of the door, a thin, wiry-looking man in his mid-to-late forties with marks up his arms, lay on a sofa. To the right sat a young-looking girl, possibly thirteen or fourteen, visibly in her last trimester of pregnancy.

The lady demanded, "I want to see those photos."

"I don't have them with me. If Roy stops harassing my mom, there's no need to show the police the photos. Tell him I don't want him coming by her house again. If he does, I'm showing the police the photos."

She said she would think about it. I thanked her for her time, and we left.

When we got back to my mom's street, the lady watching for the police said she had flagged down the police car and told the officer we went left. But when he got to the corner, she said, the car turned right. He was probably like us, trying to feel who was the good guy and who was the bad guy.

"I'm Maxine Gomez," she said. "You knew me from a long time ago." Then I realized she was my sister's childhood friend from decades ago who lived several houses north of Mom's house.

We started chatting when a police car circled back down the street. Flagging it down, I identified myself as the caller and gave my mom's address. "Get in," said the officer. He drove to the end of the block and parked.

I gave him my driver's license, and my husband did the same. I related our encounter with Roy's friend and mother, and described the colorful grasshopper tattoo across his friend's back. We directed him to the white garage, as he chose to get there via alleys instead of the street. He ran a search for information about the garage's occupants and told us how long they'd been in the area and what was known about them. He then drove back to Mom's house, passed it, and parked again near the end of the block.

Over the next twenty-five to thirty minutes in the car, the officer radioed in a call and had someone on the other end run a search for the tattoo. I was impressed with the wealth of information accessible from inside the vehicle.

Back at Mom's house, we completed our cleaning and cooking routine. Again, it broke my heart to leave her there. She was not safe.

The Money Drip and the Fateful Key

1999

Look at her bank book, the thought came.

I asked Mom if I could see it. It showed increased withdrawals over the previous seventeen days—seven withdrawals coming to an astonishing $7,033 more than her typical withdrawal. On one day, she had made two withdrawals—$300 and $5,930. Mom had no home repairs done or expenses to account for that large sum.

No one is watching her account, I realized. *It's hemorrhaging money.*

I looked at the bank balance and, with my mom, talked with the bank. "What did you do with all that money you took out?" I asked. It was nowhere in the house.

"I needed it," she said. She withdrew money when she needed it and when she saw it was "low."

That Saturday afternoon, after I discovered her account was leaking money, she withdrew three hundred dollars, a sum she insisted on having on hand for church, groceries, and anything she needed. I tried to get her to reduce the amount to one hundred dollars as I suspected someone was coming into the house and taking it.

She won; it was her money. She put it in her china cabinet. About two hours later, when I got home, I called her to check: "How much money do you have at home?"

She checked: three hundred dollars.

That night at around 9:00 p.m., I called and asked, "How much money do you have at home?" She checked: three hundred dollars.

The next morning, I called: "How much money do you have at home?"

She checked: "It's all gone. I have to go to the bank."

Someone was coming in during the night and stealing her money. *How do I stop this?*

Now I was concerned about both Mom's safety *and* her running out of money.

A Crusade for a Cause

1999

Get the neighborhood involved, I thought.

I drew up a flyer. Dressed in jeans and a T-shirt to fit in with Mom's neighborhood, I went door-to-door talking with people about watching out for others in the neighborhood and calling the police if needed. John trailed behind by about a hundred feet to watch over me. I told him to go stay with Mom.

Two neighbors cautioned me to avoid a certain house because "that's where a Latino gang member lives."

One warned, "They kill people."

Well, one thing I learned is that oftentimes people who are spoken of in a negative light—that is, those portrayed as peculiar or evil or nasty or who are otherwise discredited—are good people who are either not understood, eccentric, or so outstanding in some respect that they draw jealousy, dislike, or fear from others. They can, of course, be as they are painted but that had not been my experience.

When I worked in publishing, it was those described by some staff as nasty, harsh, mean, or uncooperative who were the nicest to me. We'd have a pleasant, productive telephone conference and would hang up on good terms. One client's executive, vehemently disliked by some on our staff, even sent me a present because she enjoyed our chat so much.

I also found that some women, discredited by others, were among the sharpest, most competent, and kind-hearted souls I had encountered.

From my background, I decided to forgo the neighbor's warning and give the "Latino gang member" the benefit of the doubt.

By the time I reached that house, my husband had closed in at ten feet behind me and established restrictions to protect his little wife: "You can't go to that house. Gang members live there. Don't talk to them."

What did I do? I said, "Oh, yes I can, and I am," and up the stairs I ran.

Guitar music streamed through the screen door carrying a waft of a beefy-tomato aroma enveloped with cumin. A man in his late forties came to the door. I explained my concern about the neighborhood and handed him a flyer.

He invited me to take a seat on the porch. Before I could point out where Mom lived, he shared that he kept his own watch over the neighborhood. Pointing to a house on the opposite side of the block, he said, "An old woman lives in that house. I think she lives alone. One day I looked out and saw a man pounding on her door, shouting and pulling on the handle, trying to get in. I ran over to that house and shouted to him to leave her alone. He ran off when I started going up her stairs."

"That's my mom's house," I told him. I thanked him for looking after his neighbors, including my mom.

Emanating kindness and humility, he said, "The good you do comes back to you."

"I believe that, too," I told him.

On descending the stairs, I thought, *Yep, I was right. It's often the people most feared or ridiculed or denigrated who are the kindest souls.*

The whole time I was on the porch talking with this man, my husband stood on the sidewalk, looking like a doofus. After seeing no harm coming to me, he left to look after Mom.

As I finished my round on Mom's block, I met a short, elderly Black man walking up the street. We approached each other, and I introduced myself. We started talking about the neighborhood. This sharp-witted man with missing teeth and a frayed shirt with holes in it was a wealth of information. He was aware of incidents where these "hoods," as he called them, exploited old people. He described them as predators. He talked about the breadth of their actions and related stories about losses incurred by several older residents he knew who couldn't rid themselves of the thieves. He took a flyer and said he was all for everyone working together to rid the area of these "hoods."

It was a fruitful Saturday afternoon, even if only a few people started looking out for their neighbors.

Stakeout and "Wanted"

1999

One Saturday in September, after visiting Mom, my husband and I returned to her neighborhood late that night. It was about 11:00 p.m. We had a clandestine plan: we were conducting a stakeout to see what went on at Mom's house at night. Her missing funds and insistence on leaving the screen door unlocked implied someone was getting in at night. We parked our old car, an unobtrusive Corolla, on a corner of Mom's street across the parkway, diagonally from her house. Our lookout gave us a view of both Mom's north-south street and the east-west intersecting street. We had a cellphone, an early model the size of a football.

Sunk deep into our seats, we kept vigil for movement. All was still. A good hour passed. Then we spotted him. It was Roy. He was on the intersecting street heading east, then crossed that street to head north on Mom's street toward her house. With the precision of a bat using echolocation to find its prey, he spotted us. He picked up his pace and kept walking up Mom's side of the street. Momentarily, he stopped in front of her house, hesitating whether to chance going up the stairs. He resumed walking.

We called the police and followed him, reporting his route. When he ran between houses, we lost him. But the police were on the way to his house.

Did we accomplish anything? Well, we were content that, for that night, Mom might not have an intruder.

Was he the one with the key?

∽

Part of my job with the magazine, eons before, involved photographing events and people for the articles I crafted. I wanted high-resolution photos with high-quality, close-up shots. For our home camera, I purchased a telescopic lens and occasionally used it for work. On visits to Mom's house, I'd bring my camera along with this telescopic lens. Anyone walking up to her house, I photographed. When I saw men walking on the other side of the street, I photographed them. On camera, I captured anyone and everyone, should they later prove to have nefarious motives.

In the late fall of 1999, Roy paid Mom a visit while John was grocery shopping. Roy banged on Mom's front door. "Open up!" he shouted. Mom did, and I pushed past her onto the porch. I started photographing him. I was concerned that he'd grab the camera but suspected he wouldn't think that fast. And that was so. He shouted to her, "Give me fifty bucks," as I shot away. Then he took a swipe at me. Fortunately, I'm nimble. I ducked out of his way as I shot yet another photo. What a great shot that was!

I told him, "Get off the damn porch, Roy. Yes, I know your name, and the cops are on their way." In actuality, I hadn't had time to call the police. "Stay if you want to talk to them." He ran off.

On the dining room table, I found a torn piece of paper with Mom's disjointed handwriting: "They call me 'old lady' and talk to me so mean. They call me names. All they want is money. Put him away." That told me she wasn't daft; she knew people were bleeding her of money. I worried they would hurt her, physically. I needed to find a safe place for her.

Exasperated about what to do, I wrote to the Hammond Police Department and enclosed the photos. A few days later, a detective called me at work. He was with the police department's Bureau of Investigation.

"Where did you get these photos?" he asked. "We're looking for this guy."

"I took the photos. You can find the guy at my mom's house. He is on her porch three times a day demanding money."

Over the next few weeks, the detective and I spoke a few times. Several days before Thanksgiving, he called and said they had Roy in custody. "Your mom can relax," he assured me.

The night before Thanksgiving, the detective called me at 10:30 p.m. He sounded concerned. Roy had complained he was sick, he said, and was taken to St. Margaret's hospital. "He escaped. Tell your mother to lock up and not answer the door. We're looking for him."

The Saboteur: A Foiled Stir-Up

1999

In the fall, when my husband picked me up from work at the train station at 7:15 p.m., he asked if I had spoken with Lisa Bradegovich, the sunbather at Mom's house decades before.

I told him, "No, I don't talk with her."

He already knew that.

"Why do you ask?"

"She called our house this afternoon and left a voicemail," he said.

That was a surprise. "What did she say?"

"You need to listen to her message." He paused. "You should stay away from her." I was already doing that.

When I listened to the message, it went like this:

> Hi, Judie. This is Lisa. It was good talking to you today. I'm glad you called me. You're doing the right thing. John is going to be so surprised when you tell him you're leaving him. Take care. Bye.

I was gobsmacked.

John commented, "So that's why, at Caleb's funeral last

year, she asked who checks our voicemail, you or me. I thought that was a weird question. She asked twice. She had something up her sleeve." He continued, "She thinks I'm like her and I would blow this through the roof. She's trying to cause problems between us. Stay away from her."

I didn't call her back to address her fictitious setup. I didn't want to open a dialogue and then have her lie about a conversation we didn't have.

Her message made me curious about what motivates people to malign or discredit another or stir up trouble for them. From that message, I felt sorry for her. It told me that she had me on a pedestal and wanted to kick me off it however she could. Lack of truth was not a barrier.

A Sense of Peace

1999

After investigating several retirement homes for Mom, I decided on one. However, because they were filled to capacity, they put Mom on a waiting list. The home had an integrated assisted living unit and a long-term care unit that Mom could transition into if needed, and it kept patients who went on Medicaid. Most facilities we evaluated did not retain people who ran out of money. Mom's home was valued at less than $30,000 and she had less than that in the bank. Her funds, house sale, and Social Security would cover slightly over one year at the facility.

Through research, I located and spoke with Roy's juvenile officer. I went to the court system to get a restraining order; however, my mom's reluctance to testify quashed that idea. She said she would tell everyone in court that John and I are crazy and that no one asks her for money or comes to her door carrying a bat.

On January 3, 2000, John and I swung past Mom's home on our return from a wake in the area. It was about 8:30 p.m. Mom's street was two lanes separated by a narrow, tree-lined parkway. Her house sat on the northbound side. As I drove south, I saw a man walking north on her side of the street. Was this Roy? Would he pass her house?

With caution, I accelerated and swung around the corner of the parkway, and then again around another corner to head north. The man was walking up her steps. It was Roy. I slammed on the brake in front of the house and got out. "Leave her alone!" I told him.

He ran off, and I parked the car. I rang the doorbell. Mom answered. After greeting her and asking how she was doing, I called the police. When she heard that conversation, she started yelling at John that we were both crazy: no one had been on her porch.

This time, I had with me a letter from the police department concerning Roy. At the time of this writing, I don't recall the exact contents of the letter, but I believe it stated that he was to stay away from my mom's house. I read it to the dispatcher who then verified the information in their records. I told the dispatcher, "He was on the porch a few minutes ago. I chased him away." I gave them Roy's garage address, which they already had after checking, and they sent two cars his way.

The next day, I phoned the nursing home and pleaded— really pleaded—with them to take Mom in. I was so worried for her safety. I told them about Roy's visit the previous night. The director agreed that Mom could move into a room in assisted living that Friday.

With the help of my wonderful husband, we made it happen. I took a vacation day. We enlisted Uncle Lou's help and gave him money to take Mom out of the house for breakfast and to keep her at the restaurant for the morning. We didn't share that information with anyone else, not even my sister, out of concern that it could somehow leak to Mom and she would burrow herself deeper into the house, making it more difficult to get her to move. We had to get her out for her own safety.

We moved furniture—lamps, a bed, end tables, knickknacks, and framed pictures—into her room and arranged it all nicely for when she would arrive. Uncle Lou brought her to the facility. With one glance at her things there, a large question mark loomed over her face. I felt bad that I couldn't have been open with her and had to spring this on her. Before that, each time I asked where she would like to live as she aged into her nineties, she would give the same answer: "I want to stay here, in my house." It was such a challenging decision to make. How do you balance sensitivity to a family member's wishes with the reality that abiding by those wishes could imperil her life?

As she looked around her room, she understood what was happening. Instinctively, I shifted the energy. With buoyancy in my voice, I told her that here she would be safe. She wouldn't have to cook or worry about food. She wouldn't have to worry about people breaking in. She wouldn't be alone.

She started smiling. Aside from her life in a dorm as a janitress at a local hospital, her honeymoon, and the two nights she spent in a hotel for my wedding, she had never been away from home. Deep down, I prayed that she would like it there, that it would bring her peace—the tranquility sorely missing from her home.

The Vanishing Purses Act

2000

After moving Mom in, I realized she didn't have her purses. She loved purses. She would buy them for a dollar or two at rummage sales. I went back to the house to gather them.

All of her purses were missing! *Where did they go?*

A few weeks later, my husband and I finished cleaning both bedrooms at Mom's house. Everything was gone. The floors were now bare.

The following Saturday, we returned to tackle the kitchen. As I walked past Mom's former bedroom, my peripheral vision drew me in: a pile of purses lay amassed in the center of what was previously a bare floor. Someone had been in the house. They returned Mom's purses.

Boy, was I grateful that she was now somewhere safe.

Sticky Matters

2000–2002

Though Mom's safety was no longer of concern, her stay in the nursing home was not without mishap. The first Saturday after she moved in, the phone rang as we walked into our home from visiting Mom. It was a nurse. "It's the center's policy that all residents bathe once a week, on Saturday," she said. "Today is Saturday and your mother refuses to bathe."

"We're on our way," I told her. We drove the two hours back to the facility so I could give Mom a shower. I didn't want them to kick her out.

As I entered her room, Mom was seated in a chair. Her wiglet looked like a bombed bird's nest atop her head. It was the third wig we had bought her. She did not take care of them. Reluctantly, she parted with the messy, misshapen mass bobby-pinned to her crown. She let me bathe her, cursing vociferously the entire time. John could hear her swearing as he sat in her room.

Afterward, she let me cut her beautiful silver-gray hair into a chic, chin-length bob. And she enjoyed a manicure I gave her with mauve nail polish that looked gorgeous with her fresh, silvery coif. Peering into a handheld mirror, she checked over her makeover and nodded approvingly. From that, she learned that ablutions are not to be feared and from then on, allowed the staff to bathe her.

～)

A few months into Mom's stay, she was moved to the dementia wing. There, the staff housed a rabbit in a cage for patients to connect with. On one visit, as Mom looked into the rabbit's cage, she reminisced aloud, "I have a good recipe for rabbit stew." A nurse standing nearby laughed, seeming to think Mom was joking. They occasionally allowed her into the kitchen to make Polish food under their supervision.

I interjected, "She's serious. She cooked our pet rabbits and tried to feed them to us. So, you may want to watch that rabbit. I don't want my mom sneaking into your kitchen and stewing your community bunny."

～)

It was not unusual to come home from work to a phone message such as "There were three altercations on the floor today, and your mother started each of them."

What was unusual was to receive a call to my law office from the nursing director saying, "We have a problem." I knew it had to be serious because it was the nursing director *and* she was calling me at work.

"Okay, what did my mom do now?"

"Oh, it's not your mom. It's one of your family members, Lisa Bradegovich. She's harassing the nurses when she calls.

She unnecessarily keeps them on the phone, ranting that they are not doing their jobs right. She's condescending. The nurses cringe each time she calls."

Previously, I had instructed the facility to share information with my sister, Lisa, and me. I named Lisa reluctantly only because of her close ties to Mom. But this now put a different spin on that. I was concerned that Lisa's harassment could affect the quality of care Mom received. I already knew Lisa would disregard our requests.

I asked the nursing director to handle the situation however she felt appropriate because their obligation was "to my mom and not to anyone else." She suggested using a code word to discreetly let staff know who was calling. I was concerned about that because, as we are only human, eventually someone would slip up.

She was concerned too, but we didn't know how else to stop the caller's disparaging behavior toward the nurses. Understandably, she did not want the nurses to share information and then be browbeaten for their hard, unappreciated work.

The nursing director then went on to say that when she had spoken with Lisa, Lisa—without prompting—volunteered, "Judie is dysfunctional." In the director's rendition of the comment, she elevated her voice and changed its inflection to imitate Lisa. The nursing director said she wanted me to know what Lisa was saying about me.

Yes, that comment would be something one might say to discredit another. My question was *why*? Why would someone want to sully another? What was the motivation behind that?

As anticipated, the inevitable happened. A nurse answering the phone asked the caller point-blank for "the code word." That caller was Lisa. This did not go over well. It circulated through the family gossip mill that I was hiding information about Mom and blocking calls with the nurses. I was the bad guy.

"You Don't Think So?"

2000

How do you handle a situation where someone consistently lies about you? I've found it best to ignore the gossip and let it speak for the one out of whose mouth it flies.

I had been with the firm for about eighteen months when a lead partner stepped into my office. By the time I joined this firm, I had reconnected with family, immediate and extended, and they now knew I was an attorney. Perhaps that was the impetus for a phone call this partner had received. He told me he had just gotten off the phone with Lisa Bradegovich. That was strange.

Lisa, he said, wanted him to tell me what she thought my mom needed at the nursing home, and he did. He then paused and rubbed his head as if trying to figure out how best to relate the next part. "She then told me, 'Judie is dysfunctional.'" He said that part with the exact same inflection and high pitch as used by the nursing director about a month earlier. In a serious tone, he continued, "She said that without me asking any questions."

I tried to process what he had said. *Wait. A family member called my employer? Instructed a lead partner to tell me what to buy Mom? And told him that I'm dysfunctional??*

Without a break, he continued: "I have a brother who has always been jealous of me."

"Oh, this lady isn't jealous of me," I interjected instinctively, as I hadn't in my mind linked jealousy with her.

"You don't think so? My brother has always been really jealous, but he would never think to call my employer and talk with the head honcho and tell him that I'm dysfunctional. Think about that."

I thanked him for letting me know, realizing that I needed to reflect on this.

On the train ride home, I thought about the partner's comment.

Why would Lisa be jealous of me? This was the second time I heard that she had maligned me to others—first with Mom's nursing home and now with my employer. *Who else has she called?* It was as if she was trying to sabotage me. Was she? For her to call my employer, she first had to find out where I worked and then had to look up the firm's phone number.

If Lisa was jealous, that would explain why our relationship had been riddled with potholes for as long as I could remember. From other family members, I'd occasionally hear that she talked about me in a negative light.

I wanted to deconstruct this gnarly issue, to drill down to the genesis of its molten center. Why was she bad-mouthing me? And what did it get her?

Earlier in the year, Lisa had left a voice mail on our home phone demanding I do something for her and if I didn't, she threatened in a sing-song voice, "I'm going to start c-a-a-lling the family." Though benign, that was a threat. From prior instances, I understood it to mean that she would lie about me. I didn't respond. My husband did, though. He wrote her spouse and told him to restrain his wife from calling our home and leaving threats, which, he pointed out, was abnormal behavior.

The year before, 1999, I had called her to wish her well on a new venture and we'd had a pleasant conversation.

The year before that, 1998, we had seen each other at a funeral reception. That was catastrophic. Beaming with pride as if she had done me a huge favor, she approached me as I entered the room at the restaurant.

"Did you hear from Grant, your boyfriend from college?" she asked excitedly. A couple of months before, she wrote me that she had run into Grant, and to get my contact information, she called a cousin but couldn't get my phone number. She sent my address on to Grant, she wrote, so he could contact me.

I told her, "Yes, he wrote me." I didn't add that he said that when he had coincidentally run into her at a train station, she had "insisted" he reach out to me. "Insisted" was the word he used at least twice.

When I was younger, I was a doormat to Lisa, finding it easier to fold than to endure the undercurrents of her wrath. This time, though, recognizing the criticality of boundaries, I spoke up.

I told her that though I understood she may be innocently trying to reconnect us, I didn't appreciate her sending my contact information to a former beau without checking with me beforehand. I stopped there.

My old boyfriend was a good guy. I had nothing to be concerned about. But, it didn't feel right to have someone going behind my back, pushing an old flame to contact me when I'd been married for eighteen years, implying how much I would *love* to see him, and orchestrating a reunion without first checking with me.

At the funeral reception, in response to my saying I would have appreciated her checking with me beforehand, she raised her voice. "How dare you judge me and tell me what not to do! I should have known that you ended that relationship with vitriol." She then whisked herself away amid swirling energy trailing behind her.

When my husband and I looked for seats, wouldn't you know it: the only two available were next to Lisa and her husband. As her charming husband inquired about my work as a lawyer, Lisa cut him off with a cold, sharp-as-a-knife-edge tone, "Thomas, you're interviewing again." The universe must have been winking at me: just as he finished his question, and before her remark to him, my salad fork fell. I bent down to retrieve it. Looking under the tablecloth, I saw her hand on his thigh and as I heard her remark, I watched her dig her nails into his thigh. For the rest of the dinner, he sat there uncharacteristically silent, eating his food like an obedient lap dog.

The end of this reception was when she had asked John twice which one of us checked our voicemail.

Before that whirlwind, Lisa and I'd had a twelve-year hiatus in contact. Our last conversation before that gap ended with her calling me a bitch and slamming the receiver on me after I declined to share my home phone number with her. Before that, the few conversations we had all pretty much ended with her calling me a bitch, and often with me in tears and her blaming me for something out of the blue, like not telling her that a recipe she found in a cookbook—one I had never made—would come out dry, or for somehow knowing that her former boyfriend would be abusive and not telling her so.

So, yes. She bore some hostility toward me.

And now she was calling my employer to influence my reputation there.

~

Thirteen years later in the spring of 2013, from the family gossip mill, I heard about a new story told by Lisa. This time, she was telling people I had "stolen two rings" from Mary Keefe with "diamonds the size of golf balls" and "one was supposed to go" to her. What she didn't know was that Mary had only one ring with a so-so diamond that had gone missing decades before I reconnected with her. When I did, Mary Keefe was in a nursing home on welfare. She didn't have clothes or shoes (everything was donated), and she'd lament that she couldn't even keep twenty dollars or a bottle of nice hand cream (my gift) in the three drawers that housed all her possessions. They would go missing by morning.

How do you handle someone lying that you're a thief? I didn't know what to do.

Once, when I addressed a full-frontal lie, Lisa shot back tauntingly, "Yeah. So, what are you going to do about it?"

I learned that some people feel no guilt for their conduct. They want their behavior to disturb your peace of mind. With people having such mindsets, instead of going round and round without resolution, I find it more intriguing to unravel the *why* behind their behavior.

What I came up with is that some people—though I have met fewer than a handful—feel so bad that they are not moving forward that, instead of looking within to develop themselves to attain a level of "mastery" they perhaps perceive in others, they spend their time contemplating how to bring down those whom they deem to be successful.

Because our words and actions broadcast who we are, whether we want that or not, when someone lies or bad-mouths us, that's a way for the person to project onto others how they themselves feel—whether that be jealous, threatened, unsuccessful, or discouraged. If we tend not to get jealous, we may miss that as a motivator in others. Momentarily, their comments may give them a shot of espresso in confidence, magically elevating them—in their mind—above their target. But that confidence fizzles quickly because it's not solid: it's not based on truth.

When bad-mouthed or lied about, I find it best to ignore the comment or action. Trust that truth will eventually come out. Along the same vein, worrying about what others will say about us, even if it is a lie, drains energy that we could otherwise funnel into something positive and productive, such as working on a project, planning a vacation, going for a run, or chatting with a friend.

We can, as I see it, accomplish so much more if we champion positivity. If we embrace truth and focus on developing ourselves, we won't get caught up in how so-and-so is more successful, loved, prettier, or smarter than us. And we won't then allow jealousy to wrestle with our souls, compelling us to smear muck on another's reputation in order to feel better about ourselves. If we focus on developing ourselves to be the best and brightest light we can be, that is all that matters in the end. It is also important for the present; the more we work on ourselves, the more of that positive energy we attract to ourselves.

So, that comment made to the "head honcho"—as he deftly dubbed himself—rolled off my shoulders with a call to the universe to bless the caller and help her see her inner beauty and greatness. Thirteen years later, on hearing I was now being branded a thief, I again sent out the same blessing.

Transitioning of Mary Keefe

April 2000

Mary Keefe was dying. When I paid her my final visit, her face looked so peaceful despite the tubes. Her eyes were closed. When the nurse announced I was there, she and my husband said that Mary's lips curled into a slight smile. I missed that; I was taking in the tubes. Holding her hand, I thanked her for sharing her life with me. Though infrequent, our visits were quality time for me.

The next day, I returned and sat with her as she slept. The doctor said he expected her to pass within a week. Squeezing her hand, I said my final goodbye.

I recalled how Mary Keefe and I had lost contact, and how I had searched to no avail to find her. My Aunt Mary's funeral in 1982 was the last time I saw her before we lost touch. About six months after the funeral, I called Mary Keefe's apartment, and no one answered. Multiple times, I asked Mom if she knew where Mary Keefe was. She said no one knew. Mary stopped picking up her nurse's uniforms from the lady who washed and pressed them. Over the next two years, I asked Mom several times if there was any news about Mary Keefe. Each time, Mom said she didn't know.

To find her, I called nursing homes and hotels, and roved the internet, all to no help. Then one day in a chat with a relative, by happenstance she disclosed where Mary Keefe was and said my mom visited her all the time. It was a nursing home I hadn't called.

In 1983 at age sixty-two, Mary Keefe was admitted to a medical facility and three years later, she was scheduled to be released. A prank denied her that opportunity: when she rose from a chair to use the restroom, a fellow patient stuck her leg out to trip her. Mary fell, breaking her pelvic bone. After surgery, the staff encouraged her to walk, but she lost interest in life. After that, she was confined to a wheelchair.

By the time we reconnected in 1995, Mary Keefe had been in the facility for twelve years.

At our agreed-upon time, she rolled up to the front desk, her legs looking atrophied in her wheelchair, her hair the same gray-white I remembered as a child, her smile radiating kindness. I recognized her instantly. Her wit and humor were intact. She was sharp cognitively. Reading and keeping abreast of the news filled her days. She was informed about politics and world events.

We talked about our lives and past fun times and got each other caught up. Midway through our visit, Mary Keefe ruefully related how a fire at her apartment had destroyed her possessions and forced her brother who lived with her to move. This happened shortly after she was admitted to the nursing home.

We were so engaged that we lost track of time. The nursing staff had to show my husband and me out.

Throughout her last years, she always thought of others. On Sunday dinners, a man seated next to her unfailingly grabbed crackers off her plate where the menu invariably consisted of salty chicken soup, soda crackers, and pudding. The first time I saw that, I started to speak up. "It's okay," she whispered, gesturing with her hand for me to stop. "Let him have those."

As with holidays and her birthday, for what was her last Christmas, I brought an entrée she liked along with all the accoutrements and enlisted the help of the facility's kitchen to heat up her food. As I carried a tray to her room, several nurses stopped me. One forewarned, "Mary's not going to eat that. She refuses to eat. She's not sick, she just refuses to eat." They had her on an IV.

"She'll eat," I winked with a smile as I kept moving toward her room. When she saw me, her eyes lit up and we began chatting. I asked if she would like dinner; she could see I was carrying a tray decked out with food.

Her response resounded with delight. "Oh, yes!" Because Mary Keefe's arthritic fingers were curled in, preventing her from holding a fork or spoon, John fed her as we all talked.

Outside her door stood a group of nurses watching. I heard one exclaim, "Well, I'll be!" Others could be heard excitedly chiming in: "She's eating! She's eating! Look! Mary's eating!" They were astonished.

It was a Tuesday when Mary Keefe died. The nursing director called me at work. I wrote her obituary and arranged for burial services. Her passing hit me hard. That surprised me, as I had been to many wakes and funerals without shedding a tear. When I was a child, wakes were Mom's time to socialize, and I'd accompany her. But for Mary Keefe's wake, I could not stop crying. I felt such a loss.

Something Amiss

April 2000

O n our way home from Mary Keefe's funeral, my husband and I stopped to check on Mom's vacant house that we were preparing for sale. As I walked into the backyard, I almost threw up at what I saw.

It was not the wildly overgrown lawn that bore a hole in my stomach. It was the bereft state of Mom's landscaping: all her bushes and plants—her pride and joy—were gone, except for yews in the front yard and some small plants along the south side. Someone had dug up everything else—a huge lilac bush, phlox, and many other bushes from the backyard along with eighteen to twenty bushy, mature foundation plants that graced the north side. Who would cannibalize her landscaping?

I suspected one individual and thought back to my last conversation with him.

The month before, we had asked a cousin to help us pull up Mom's carpeting to showcase the wood floors beneath. My cousin brought his brother with him.

With my two cousins, John, and me, it took the four of us less than one hour and thirty minutes to pull up about three hundred sixty square feet of carpet from the living and dining rooms and an adjoining hall, and carry it to the alley along with an old bed frame from the basement, with a bit of time to chit-chat. We so appreciated their help.

At the end, the brother asked if he could take "two or three plants." I told him, "Yes. Take whichever ones you want." Never did I suspect he would return and clean out the place.

Neighbors filled in the details. Angie, two doors down, said that in early April, she had seen a man at Mom's house for three days in a row—from early morning to early evening. As she and her husband drove past his pickup truck parked in front of the house, her husband remarked about its back end overbrimming with green leaves from bushes the man had dug up. He suggested they call the police but didn't want to get involved in case I had hired the man. Another next-door neighbor, Emma, corroborated that the man had come by three days in a row and was there from morning to early evening. She thought it strange that each day he brought a lawn mower because "the grass had not yet started growing back," she said. "It didn't need to be mowed." Each day, he left the lawn mower on the side of the house while he dug up bushes and plants. When Emma came out, he'd start mowing the grass; when she went indoors, he'd stop and continue digging. She found his behavior "suspicious," she told me. She thought about calling the police, she said, but didn't want to get him in trouble if he was there legitimately. A third neighbor, Irma, said that when she looked out her back picture window and he saw her standing there watching him, he'd put down his shovel and "pretend to tie his shoes." She remarked that he did that whenever he saw her watching him. She said she thought about calling the police but didn't know if I had hired him.

I had to address this. I knew who the man was. He was the brother of the cousin we asked to help pull up carpet. I decided to forgo filing a police report as I didn't want to get him in trouble with the law.

I called his mother, my Aunt Faye. We had a good relationship. Apparently, she was expecting my call.

When she heard my voice, instead of her usual welcoming tone with "Hi, Judie," she asked brusquely in a monotone, "What do you want?" That was a first.

Her icy tone spoke volumes. It told me she not only knew but implicitly approved of her son's taking nearly all of Mom's bushes and plants. *Is she trying to protect him?* Beyond the glacial freeze, I recalled he lived with her and realized he would be planting my mom's bushes at his mother's home. So, she had something to gain from his mischief.

I told her I wanted to speak with her about her son taking nearly all my mother's bushes and plants when we were trying to sell the house. To that, she pretended not to hear me: "What? I can't hear you. What are you saying? I can't hear you." That was odd; she never had a problem hearing me in the past, nor as the conversation progressed.

"Your son asked if he could take 'two or three plants,'" I related. "I told him, 'Yes, take whichever ones you want.' That, however, was not authorization to take ALL my mom's plants and bushes."

"Who do you think you are talking to?" she responded indignantly.

Ohhh, she is in on this too. She *wants to keep the plants for her yard*. I realized I needed to be firm.

"He can keep three plants of his choosing," I told her, "but I want him to return everything else he dug up. We are trying to sell the house, with the money to go to my mom's care. You know that." I continued, "I want him to restore the landscaping to its original state, aside from the three plants or bushes he can keep of his choosing."

"No, he's not doing that," she countered. "What I would be willing to have happen is for him to return only those plants that he has not yet planted. Besides, he mowed the lawn and worked hard pulling up carpeting."

That was not the response I had expected. My attention snagged on her words "what I would be willing to have happen" and her control over what her son would do. *Did she direct him to clean out my mom's property? She sure sounds like she had a hand in this,* I thought. *She now wants to negotiate what gets returned?*

After our call, my aunt pumped the family gossip mill. She phoned Lisa. Casting the plant theft as "a miscommunication," she said that I was blowing this out of proportion.

Even if it were a miscommunication and, assuming her son did not hear me correctly or assuming—worst case scenario— he actually thought I told him it was okay to take all of Mom's bushes and plants, I was stupefied that a grown man would clean out his eighty-five-year-old aunt's landscaping when he knew the house was up for sale and the proceeds were needed for her care in a nursing home—especially when the plants and bushes were not extraordinary.

I felt if this were truly a "miscommunication" and I were in my aunt's shoes, at the start of the call, I would have responded to my niece in my typical tone when hearing her voice instead of bluntly and frozenly asking, "What do you want?" I would have expressed surprise at hearing about the plants. I would have been apologetic and more than willing to work with her to return her mom's landscaping to as close to its original state as possible. That, however, did not happen. I would not have excused my son's theft with "He mowed the lawn and pulled up carpeting." Nor would I have tried to negotiate what I could keep of my sister-in-law's property.

But instead, my aunt fought me on the return of my mom's own property and, to save face, controverted the facts to others. In the end, my Aunt Faye's house got a landscape facelift at my mom's expense.

I wasn't totally surprised by this. Earlier, she had demanded certain furniture pieces from Mom's house on grounds that "I deserve to have that. I'm your Dad's sister." And decades before at Dad's wake, she had insisted on getting his lapel pin for the same reason.

A few weeks later, I visited Mom's house. Her son did plant one skimpy row of sparsely spaced, tiny, three-inch plantlets, each about a one-sixth divide from the original plant, along the north side of the house. But apart from that, the landscape was still bare. At least now both sides of the house had some greenery. My mom had taken pride in her home and if she had known how her property looked when being sold to others, that would have gravely upset her.

No one cared about facts; they're not sexy. Instead, my family opted to ditch facts in favor of the gossip mill, embracing it as truth like it had the power of a reality show. The gossip mill churned the situation as "only a miscommunication." No one did anything to try to rectify it. They all were copasetic with this man's actions.

Inside, I felt torn. It felt like I was the only one looking out for my mom's property. I felt "family" had let her down. First with the theft, then with their fight to keep Mom's plants, then with the tale of "miscommunication," and then with whitewashing the situation without seeking any facts about what was left at Mom's property in the end. It felt like I was the only one embracing truth and what was right, while everyone else threw their hands up in the air with "Who cares? Let's eat."

I realized, too, that I was not without fault. In hindsight, I had made an egregious mistake in not filing a police report.

Years later when this aunt passed away, no one from her family contacted me. I found out via Mom's former neighbor, one of the three who had contemplated calling the police. My cousin who dug up the plants returned my sympathy card, unopened, for objecting to his plant theft. I was now the black sheep. But sometimes that's a blessing.

All of this distracting static was playing out behind the scenes while I worked fifty to sixty hours per week in a demanding, high-detail job, dealt with the passing of Mary Keefe, and helped Mom acclimate to the nursing home. At the same time, I was also trying to close on her home when the prospective purchasers kept pushing back the closing date and failed to show up for closing. The universe must have been smiling on me, for I always said, "I love challenges."

Tying Up Loose Ends

2000

During my two years at the firm, Vicki, the attorney who had earlier scoffed at my "dumb idea" but later took credit for it, gradually took on my persona, presumably out of admiration. It started out with her inquiring where I bought my clothes. She then began dressing like me, including wearing clothes identical to mine. She started wearing earrings like mine and cut her hair short like mine, replete with highlights like mine. For her first few months there, she walked to her office without smiling at anyone, sometimes muttering a dry "hi" to the secretaries. But then she adopted my morning greeting to secretaries with the same inflection as mine: "Good morning. How are you?"

One afternoon as the attorneys going out to lunch together gathered in the foyer, the receptionist exclaimed, "Oh my god! You look like sisters." I glanced up into the mirror before me and saw Vicki smiling back at me. It was true. By our attire, hair, and jewelry, we did look "alike," though not the same.

After two years, I felt I needed a fresh workspace. I accepted a position with a large intellectual law firm that made me an offer I couldn't resist.

Two weeks after I gave my notice, when packing up my things, Vicki knocked at the door. She wasn't smiling; Vicki didn't smile at me if others weren't around. She walked to my desk and, without sitting down, in a matter-of-fact tone stated, "Your idea to search *Chemical Abstracts* was a good one. Because of that, we got the counterclaim dismissed. I want you to know you were right." No sooner than saying that did she turn and start walking to the door.

"Vicki, thank you. Good luck to you," I said.

"Yeah, to you, too."

I didn't expect Vicki to credit me with the dismissal of the counterclaim or to clean up her earlier assessment of my concept as "the stupidest idea … ever." She was trying to wipe the slate clean. She didn't acknowledge usurping the idea as hers, but her retraction that the idea was "stupid" counted for something. She gathered the courage to speak with me when she could easily have chosen not to. That told me she had a conscience and more importantly, she had already thought about her actions and learned something from them.

One summer day a few years later, as I walked from the train station to work, I encountered Vicki jogging. We nodded to each other. She flew past me, then braked. "Judie. Do you have a minute?"

"Yeah. How are you?"

"Fine. You too?" she asked.

"Yeah, things are going well."

"Good." She got right to the point. That was her style. "Back when you were at the firm, I lied about you to a partner to make you look bad and I blamed you for a mistake I made." Pausing a second, she continued, "I worked so hard. Because of your ideas, you were getting attention. I didn't want you to take everything I worked so hard for away from me."

"O-o-k-a-ay. I always suspected you lied about me there in some respect, in a big way, but I didn't know about what specifically. It doesn't matter now. I appreciate your telling me this."

Nodding, she finished up, "Okay. I'm running late. I have to go." She turned and jogged away. That was the last time we connected.

Wow! I gave her credit for owning her actions. Most people would not have had the courage to do what she did. I don't know if she ever came clean to the partner, but I do commend her for telling me what she did. I didn't expect that. Her taking ownership as she did told me that, in retrospect, she regretted her actions and was trying to address them.

A Dance with My Soul: Taking a Stand

2000

After leaving the laboratory and the publishing world, aside from a handful of legal jobs, I longed to find a law firm where I felt I would want to settle in for good. I wanted a place where I would be intellectually and personally challenged in ways that would promote my continued growth. Where people respected each other for who they were and were recognized for their intrinsic value and competence, rather than how they might outshine another by disparaging others to gain visibility. Where integrity was the norm. Where people worked in a spirit of mutual cooperation and harmony. Where we would teach and learn from each other and be receptive to perspectives and ideas that challenged our established views and understanding. Where we would take responsibility when our humanness colored a situation. That was my dream job.

The first prong—a growth-fostering environment that provides intellectual and personal challenges—was easily met. It was the rest of the attributes that I sought.

~つ

In starting my new job with the law firm, I hoped for a long relationship. My work there spanned the full realm of intellectual property law and included work that drew on my diverse scientific background. The firm treated men and women alike. It felt like a good fit, from the attorneys' dedication to their work and clients, strong work ethic and character, and the thread of integrity that permeated the firm.

About three weeks into my position, I stumbled upon something in a file that made me question whether I had erred in my work when drafting a client status letter for a partner's signature. The letter had been sent out. What prompted my question was noticing that the partner had made significant changes to the substance of my letter. Though he didn't say anything to me about it, I wondered how I could have gotten the matter wrong. I probed through the file and saw that my content was correct, but the partner's was not.

Later that week, the partner requested I write a letter to another client's general counsel detailing the status of various other patent applications. When completed, I left the letter on his desk for review and signature. The next day, the client's paralegal called and asked to speak with me because the partner was out for the day. As I had been with the firm for only a few weeks, I had not yet met her. She inquired about the status of a few patent applications; they hadn't received a status report for a while. I brought her up to date and told her that a letter regarding their status was in draft form, awaiting the partner's signature, and would be going out shortly.

The next day, I updated the partner on the client's inquiry and the update I had provided. He was sitting behind his desk, peeling an orange, with stock market chart trajectories on his computer screen behind him. As I spoke, he looked up with a flash of fear immediately dashed by anger. He flung the orange into the wastebasket as he shouted, "Don't fuck it up! Don't fuck it up!" I was new to the firm. People didn't yet know my work quality or ethic. He headed into the hall, shouting, "Don't fuck it up!"

His conduct baffled me. It did not make sense. *What did I do wrong?* I answered the paralegal's questions about the status of their company's patent applications. They had a right to that information. After all, they were paying for us to provide a service. That same information was in the status letter that was going out. If I had hired someone to provide such a service and called for an update, I would expect to receive one.

His behavior got me curious. Maybe it wasn't me he was concerned about. Over the next few hours, for which I didn't bill, I combed through this client's patent applications that I had not handled. There, I saw letters relating actions that did not make sense, in my opinion. *What is this about?* I wondered. *Maybe he and the client have some understanding I'm not privy to. I am not going to get involved in this,* I decided.

I recalled one other partner earlier wondering aloud how this partner had so much power and brought in so much money when he spent far less time than other partners at the office.

Later that afternoon, I confronted the partner about his conduct. It was not commensurate with what I related. I told him too about what I had come across in the files. What did he hope to accomplish? His response was that "sometimes you have to lie." He didn't have to worry about me saying anything incorrect or wrong to clients, I told him, because I was not going to lie. That didn't go over well. It only made him more resolved to try to force my hand. He insisted that I follow along. "I'll cover for you if you get caught," he explicitly told me. To me, that had as much weight as a flea. It didn't matter if someone "covered for me." I was not going to lie to clients.

I took the matter to a liaison between partners and associates, as I was a senior associate, and told him I was going to turn this partner in. The liaison cautioned me: "Are you sure you want to do that? If you do, your life here will never be the same. Do you want that?"

"It doesn't matter. I come first. When I look in the mirror, I have to like the person I see. I'm not going to lie. And I am not going to be bullied into doing so," I responded.

If I turned the partner in, I knew they could fire me and mangle my professional reputation as this partner was quite the rainmaker. Anticipating that, I retained an attorney who practiced in attorney ethics matters. I wanted to know my rights for retaliatory discharge. I was not going to be deterred.

On a Monday morning when I came in, I noticed that a file stack on my desk looked shifted. *That must be from the cleaning staff,* I thought. When I opened the top desk drawer, it looked messed up. *Oh, I must have slammed the drawer shut when rushing to catch the train.* However, when I opened the desk file drawer, that drawer was also messed up. That's when it all became clear: someone had gone through my things.

I held my breath as I moved the files aside to access the one I had prepared on instruction from my attorney. That file detailed the matters I had worked on where I had noticed discrepancies, along with communications from that partner. It held "evidence." It was missing!

Later that day, I overheard two paralegals chatting about their surprise that the partner was in the office that weekend. "He never works on weekends," one said.

In Illinois, law is a self-policing profession. Attorneys have an obligation to turn in counsel who lie. I decided to turn this partner in; and I did, to the firm. I did not turn him in to the Attorney Registration Disciplinary Board as I was supposed to. Without the details noted in the mysteriously missing file, I knew it would be my word against his. And, as he was a huge rainmaker, I suspected the firm could craft a case against me to discredit my allegations. Deep down, though, I also knew that from what I had seen of the firm's strong moral compass, principles, and integrity underlying its operation—outside of the immediate situation—it would not tolerate this partner's conduct. It would deal with him harshly and directly. So, I directed my report to the firm's executive director.

After I made the firm aware of the partner's actions, their attorney—who represents them in court when they are sued— paid me a visit. Drawing imaginary circles on one corner of my desk, she said, "That partner brings in a *lot* of money." As we continued speaking, her facial expression and tone of voice reflected no-nonsense, genuine concern, and intolerance of the partner's conduct. I could feel her disappointment in him because his conduct reflected back on *all* the firm's attorneys. Her presence told me the firm would not give this matter short shrift. They were taking swift and serious action to quash the partner's conduct so as to preclude recurrences. I knew I had made the right decision in taking the matter to the firm.

Afterward, from various partners there, I learned that the firm had a lot of respect for me. They disciplined the partner, I heard, and curtailed his activities. He retained his job, for a while at least. I never regretted my action.

A Hit on My Life

2001

As the glowing embers of the issue with the partner faded, another unusual, poignant experience unfolded.

The firm decided that a new attorney and I would share an admin we would jointly select. Of the candidates interviewed, one lady had prior experience in intellectual property law, presented professionally, and passed a mini-test on patent and trademark procedures that my colleague had prepared. After Human Resources checked references and hired her, Fiona sat at the admin station outside our offices.

Within a few days, Fiona walked into my colleague's office with crocodile tears. She shared that her ex-con partner was abusing her. My colleague, having a big heart, lightened up on the work she gave her; I did the same after my colleague informed me of Fiona's situation. My colleague may have talked with HR about the situation, but I don't recall.

After a couple of weeks, my colleague and I started to gradually give Fiona work—not much, one or two projects. Fiona, though, was not getting my work done. When I would ask about the status of a project, she'd apologize and attribute the delay to my colleague keeping her "so busy" that she hadn't been able to get to my work. As I had shared admins in the past, sometimes with two other attorneys, it did not seem realistic that one attorney could keep this admin that busy.

At lunch with my colleague, I brought up that we both shared Fiona as our admin and that the operative word was "share." I noted that we each needed to be mindful of that. I told her Fiona was "not getting my work done because she says you're keeping her so busy." The look on my colleague's face exposed our admin's skullduggery: She wasn't doing my colleague's work either and had told her the exact same thing about me—that I was keeping her too busy. Fiona was deluding both of us.

We devised a plan. We would give her two weeks to conform with her work obligations. If she didn't, we would turn her in to HR.

Fiona was not the most ambitious person. Her work ethic did not come out in the interview where her professional demeanor, appearance, and test scores shone. She had no intention of working. We had no choice but to talk to HR. At that point, they were aware of Fiona's situation with her ex-con partner.

HR set up a work plan for Fiona to follow. She resisted.

On a day that I had planned to take as a vacation day, a partner in licensing asked me to work on a contract for a client. I was going to do it at home and fax it in but then decided to reschedule that vacation day. That Friday, I took an earlier train in (the 6:18 a.m.), printed out the licensing partner's email, and went to retrieve it from the printer.

When I read the document in my hand, I blushed. It was an email from a man outside the firm to Fiona, talking about her being naked and in handcuffs. I looked at the first few lines and couldn't even finish reading the message. *How did this get in here?* I wondered. My document was behind that. Later that day, I finished the contract and submitted it to the client.

On my train ride home, I started wondering what was going on with this admin. Whenever I approached her desk to retrieve something from the printer, she would switch to her screen saver and stare at it intently. I could stand there for four minutes reading over a document, and her eyes would be glued to that screen saver the entire time.

The following Monday, I showed my colleague the handcuff document; I had not shown it to HR just yet. When Fiona was at lunch, my colleague—retrieving a document from the printer—picked up the admin's bag to move it. Readily viewable on Fiona's computer were her emails. After Fiona left for the day, this attorney came into my office. She wore a solemn expression. She said she thought Fiona was a call girl after hours: her computer had emails to and from guys setting up appointments after work, she said.

The attorney added, too, that Fiona "is packing heat."

I thought, *Packing heat? Did I hear that correctly?*

"Judie, she's carrying a gun in her knapsack," my colleague snapped. She postulated that Fiona probably carried it to protect herself in what looked like an evening gig.

My colleague and I took the matter to HR. They needed to work with her. This was beyond our purview. A few weeks went by, and Fiona started doing some work.

One afternoon, I was surprised to get a call requesting a meeting from a litigation partner with whom I worked on a few patent matters. The meeting had nothing to do with my work. He started off by telling me not to be concerned. He said he knew I drank coffee and occasionally soda.

How does he know that? I wondered. *He's on a different floor.*

Word, he said, had come out that Fiona may try to put something in my coffee or soda. He advised that when I leave my office, if I have not finished my beverage, "Go get another cup. Do not drink what is left on your desk."

This is getting surreal, I thought in the elevator, returning to my office.

Whenever my colleague was at a client's office, Fiona occupied her office and used her phone, door closed. She'd be in there for an hour. I had work to do and was well-adept with typing, formatting, etc.

Once, after returning from a client's research center, I decided to find out whom Fiona spoke with from my office, as I assumed she used my desk too when I was out. I got into the habit of checking callbacks on my phone. Invariably, it was Walgreens that would answer.

That made sense.

One afternoon when I called Fiona into my office to give her a light assignment, she traipsed in and leaned over my desk, wiggling her breasts at me. Sitting down, she looked "off." I told her she needed a pen and paper. She retrieved them and returned. She laid one leg—not just her foot but the entire leg—across my desk perpendicular to me. I asked, "Are you high?" She wobbled her head affirmatively, as her face evinced that she was in a different world.

A few weeks later, my colleague announced she was changing jobs. Coming in to say goodbye, she handed me a can of mace. She told me that Fiona was telling the secretaries that she was "going to take Judie out."

Is she that ticked about being turned in to HR? I declined the mace. I told her I didn't need it.

She reiterated, "Fiona is going to come in here and try to shoot you. When she comes in, hit her with mace." Though I appreciated this attorney's concern, I questioned whether it was over-concern and perhaps hyperbolic.

I decided to find out. I asked Myrna, the secretary who sat next to Fiona and was Fiona's closest friend there for a short while. That friendship had since expired. "I hear Fiona is telling people she wants to take me out. Is there any truth to that?"

"Oh my god! I'm so glad you brought that up!" she exclaimed. Myrna said that whenever Fiona went into my office, "all of us stop and wait" for her to come out. "I'm on pins and needles whenever she enters your office. I'm so worried about you. We all are." Okay, so there was something to this story.

I took this up with the second in command, the assistant executive director. I told him that rumors had circulated back to me that Fiona was going to try to kill me. He was shocked. I related that HR knew that Fiona came to work armed with a gun. He was flabbergasted. He didn't know what to say. I told him that by talking to him, I was putting the firm on notice of this, and should anything happen to me, I had already spoken to several people both within and outside the firm about this matter. This could have serious consequences if anything were to happen to me. He told me he would call the HR director. That did not feel reassuring.

I spoke with the HR director. "Why can't you just fire her?" I asked. He told me they needed me to make a case against Fiona. He explained that the emotional trauma she had suffered at the hands of her ex-con partner when she started her job raised disability issues. That could be problematic if they were to fire her now, he said. To fire her, they have to make a case, and they needed me to make it. He told me to document issues as they arose. I was there to practice law, not to track my admin's mistakes or defiance.

As a practice, I don't wait until the last minute to file a document with the court or the U.S. Patent and Trademark Office. I had been waiting for Fiona to finish an extensive trademark response that I had completed and that needed only formatting and exhibits. She kept promising she would get it to me. The day before it was due, she said it was done; she only needed to proof it. The morning it was due, I was at a client's office. When I returned, she said she hadn't started it, smirking.

That's what I had suspected. I replied, "Fiona, I will take care of it."

She followed me into my office demanding, "Fire me! I want to go on disability. I want you to fire me."

I told her I did not have that authority.

"Fire me. I want you to fire me!" she exhorted. I would have liked to say that I would gladly fire her, but I didn't see any point in that. Again, I told her I didn't have the authority to do that.

Fiona was visibly upset and saying things that drew my concern. I was not going to disregard her behavior. I told her to sit back and relax, and I would talk with HR. I called HR and told them what had transpired, expressing my concern. They said they were "in the middle of a crisis" and told me to take care of it. I told them I didn't have time for that. "I have a trademark response that is due today. Fiona didn't get it done. I am going to finish that. My law license is on the line.

You need to handle Fiona's situation. This is an HR matter."
They came up and escorted her down to HR.

With the help of a paralegal, we got the trademark
response filed.

It's hard to brush aside others telling you that your admin is
talking about wreaking harm on you. Even when I intellectually
dismissed it from the forefront of my mind, it was still there,
hovering in the background: "what if?" That low-grade buzz
interrupted an otherwise healthy work environment. Perhaps
that was part of Fiona's intent.

Over the next week, Fiona was away from the office. I told
HR I wanted to work with a different admin. The previous
week's episode was over the top, and this drama and toxicity
were impeding my work. Again, I was told no: I needed to
make a case against this admin.

That response was unacceptable.

I reflected on all the drama. I had an admin boasting she
was going to "take Judie out" and HR wanting me to make
a case so they could fire her. This came right on the heels of
a partner expecting me to lie, all the while cooing "I'll cover
for you if you get caught." This was not what I had signed
up for. Other than the issue I'd had with the partner—which
had since been extinguished—and this admin's overt threats,
this firm was perfect. I loved the work, my colleagues, and
my clients.

During the week that Fiona was out, several admins stopped
by to express their concern for me. One secretary in her mid-
thirties, who was attractive, took care of her body, was married
with children, and whom I didn't know well but would say hello
to, told me that Fiona had asked her if she'd be interested in

participating in a threesome after work sometime. That fit in with one attorney's hypothesis about an evening call-girl gig.

Yes, about six months into my work, the firm did give me a very generous five-figure raise. But less than one year into this job, I ruefully decided to find a new employer. The potential that I could be physically harmed on the job shaped that decision; I wasn't going to gamble with my safety.

I connected with people I knew at another firm that did intellectual property law. They offered me a position, as they had just fired an attorney for submitting fraudulent expense reports. If I took the job, I would have his office and all that yummy energy.

On my last day when I approached the partner who had vouched to "cover" for me to wish him well, he blurted out, veritably ecstatic with an ear-to-ear grin, "She died! That paralegal died! She had cancer." He was talking about his client's paralegal, with whom I had spoken earlier in the scenario that unleashed the "I'll cover for you" muck. He was thrilled. His words told me that had I decided to pursue this matter before a professional tribunal, it would have been his word versus mine, and he could have made this look like it had never happened.

What I realized, as I moved through these last few firms, was that I was adaptable and resilient, and I was being challenged in ways that fostered my personal development. But drama and bending the truth are not within my core. I learned that some people try to shine at the expense of others, and some feel better when they make other people's lives miserable. I also learned that sometimes people, as we are human, do things for which their rationale is incomprehensible. I learned to prioritize my well-being and leave when rumor suggests my safety may be compromised. And just as I had learned growing up, when the situation gets tough, that's when we need to mine our inner strength: to go deeper within, for there is even more there than we could imagine.

The Teensy Fish—An Augur?

2001

To accept that job offer, or not? That was the question. I asked this prospective employer to arrange a meeting with other attorneys there so I could better assess the firm and gain perspective on its people.

The meeting was a lunch with a partner and several associates—all men. We took two taxis to a long-established Greek restaurant. The partner riding with me paid the driver and jumped out to join his colleagues in the second taxi as I was exiting our cab. They walked into the restaurant together; I made my way in, solo. Everyone was already seated. The waiter, a macho-looking man, took the men's orders first and mine last.

On one tray, the waiter brought out everyone's plate, each overbrimming with food. As he set down the last plate, I was the only one not yet served. He had to return to the kitchen for my plate. On it sat an exceptionally tiny piece of fish, so small that I could have swallowed it in four bites. As I stared at the remarkably teensy piece of fish, I dismissed a visceral knot forming in my torso. Offhandedly, I mused whether that tiny morsel of food, the visceral knot, and the serving of all men before me were metaphors for my future experience at this firm. At the time, I didn't believe in "signs."

The meeting and lunch went well. Yes, the attorneys at the firm were predominately men, but that shouldn't pose a problem, I thought. I had always worked in predominately—if not exclusively—male environments and assimilated well without encountering issues. So, I dismissed my speculative question as whimsy and accepted the job offer.

On my first day at the job as a senior associate came another potential sign. A woman identifying herself as a manager took me out for a welcome lunch. At lunch, she said that she supervised the admins. That felt peculiar. Why was the supervisor of admins my host for a welcome lunch? When she discovered she didn't have money or a card to pay, she asked me to cover the cost of our meals. I did and the next day, in my top desk drawer, I found her envelope reimbursing me. A few days later, several attorneys treated me to a second welcome lunch.

None of my previous law firm employers openly discussed gender when referencing an applicant's attributes. However, a few months on the job, a male partner tapped me to convince another female attorney to join the firm to help increase their number of women attorneys. From the partner's request, I suspected that I was hired for my gender, not my credentials.

A few months later, I sensed a whiff of inequity: the firm declined partnership for a highly talented, female associate attorney who had more experience than a few of the partners there. She was an exemplary attorney, an extremely good writer, and an articulate speaker, and she had a good head on her shoulders. Yet, she was denied partnership. A few years later, when the firm finally promoted her to partner, they did the same with several male attorneys who had substantially fewer years of experience than she.

Subtle indicators began to emerge that this firm was not a good fit for me. Never before had I encountered the particular issues I kept running up against at this firm—all with the same three partners.

Mixed Messages

2001

How do you handle a situation where someone in power bad-mouths you to cover his own butt? I understand this happens in workplaces but never before had I experienced it personally.

At the request of Phil, a partner in the firm, I prepared a memo looking into issues intertwining particular aspects of law and science. Two days later when I asked him about the document, he said it was "fine."

The next week, however, a different partner told me that in a partners' meeting, Phil said I "did a bad memo." That flummoxed me as it contradicted Phil's earlier comment.

Because I value integrity in communication, I approached Phil and told him what I had heard. "What specifically did you not like about that document? In what way was it 'bad'?" I asked.

A flash of shock splashed across his face like he was wondering, "Who told her?" As he shifted uncomfortably in his chair, his inner turmoil registered on his face as, "Oh shit, I've been caught." He looked like he'd welcome the ground swallowing him up. That informed me that I didn't need to probe for the "why" behind his contradictory statements. His behavior confirmed that he was intentionally untruthful to one of us. His discomfort broadcast that it was to the partners.

I silently awaited his answer. Phil's response came uncharacteristically inundated with "um's" and "uh's," unlike his naturally fluent speech. "Uh, uh, the memo *was* fine," he said emphasizing "was" and quieting his voice. "There was nothing wrong with it. Um, uh . . ." He then launched into an explanation of how he had left the memo on a table before a meeting with clients and someone had read it before he could.

Okay, that was an "unintended circumstance" but certainly not something that would make a work product "bad" in itself.

Reading between the lines, I figured that because Phil wasn't prepared, he didn't know how to answer questions, and because of his unpreparedness, he came across poorly and he knew it. To diminish negative feedback about himself trickling back to his colleagues, it was easier for him to pin it on a "bad" memo—and mar another's reputation—rather than take responsibility for not reading the memo before showing up to the meeting.

I had to decide how to address Phil's response quickly, as a fellow attorney, standing at his doorway talking with someone, was about to step into his office. I finished up with "In the future, I want you to be honest with me and everyone else on matters that involve me."

Sidelined

2001

I worked with a colleague on a project to research information needed for a client. By that time, given all the scientific and legal research I had done, I could do research with my eyes closed. I came upon a patent that was pertinent. In a group meeting, when I showed it to the partner in charge, he dismissed my discussion: "No, this isn't even relevant."

The next day, he summoned me into my male colleague's office. Handing me the patent I had discussed the day before, the partner said, "Look what he found. This is really good. This is what I'm looking for." It was the exact same patent the partner had dismissed the day before.

I looked at it. "I showed this to you yesterday," I told him, "and you said it wasn't relevant. So, yesterday it wasn't relevant, but today it is? Why is that?"

Following that incident, I wondered if other male partners marginalized women. *Is that why there are so few women attorneys here?*

This attorney's conduct is what I later learned is called a microaggression. Psychologist Derald W. Sue of Columbia University defines the term as "everyday slights, indignities, put downs and insults that people of color, women, LGBT populations or those who are marginalized experience in their day-to-day interactions with people." (DW Sue, 2010) How does one handle that? It's one thing to read about, but another to experience. And this was the first time I had encountered that professionally to this significant extent.

I had been on the job for only a few months. *Give the place a chance*, I concluded.

Needed: A Woman's Presence

2002

On another occasion, a women-owned company contacted a partner about retaining the firm. The partner asked me to attend a consultation with this prospective client to help influence their decision. The meeting was scheduled for after-hours as that was when they were available. He openly disclosed, "I want you there so they know the firm has women attorneys."

"They're here. We're in the conference room," said the partner phoning my office. As I entered the room, my eyes scanned the mass of banker's boxes containing discovery materials cluttering the entire tabletop. Near the middle of the long, mahogany table was a cleared space, allowing just enough room for the two lady executives to be seated on one side and the partner opposite them. Stacks of boxes at both of his elbows blocked me from sitting across from the ladies.

After introductions, he instructed, "You can sit at the end of the table," pointing to a seat about nine feet away where the tabletop had been cleared—a seat separated from everyone else by a mountain of stacked boxes.

"No. I will move some of these boxes. It's not a problem."

"No, no. You don't have to do that. Have a seat there," he said emphasizing "there" and pointing again to the end of the table. Agile as I am, from one side of him, I pushed a mass of boxes away from the center. As I settled into a seat next to him, across from the ladies, I couldn't help but wonder: *Are you serious? Would you participate in a meeting seated a gazillion feet away from everyone else, your face and body obscured behind a mass of stacked boxes?* It was obvious he didn't want me to participate. He wanted me there solely to be seen for my gender. Then I realized that was exactly what he had said to start with. If I were male, I would be redundant.

At one point when I presented an idea, he quickly discounted it before I could even develop it: "No, that's not a good idea." To that, both women—who I believe saw through his visibly unnuanced behavior—leapt at it. One said, "I want to hear more on that," and the other added, "I like that. Go on." I felt that if the partner could have kicked me to be quiet, he would have.

Shortly after that, the firm was taking executives of a large corporate client to a hockey game. A dozen or so attorneys—all men—from the firm were going. Late that afternoon, a male partner stepped into my office. "You're going to the game tonight." He told me he had just found out that a woman executive from the corporate client was coming. "We need a woman there."

I had no intention of changing my evening plans on last-minute notice, solely so my presence could demonstrate that our firm had women. "Count me out. I have plans for this evening."

That did not sit well. "You need to be there. Plan on it."

I countered, "No, you will have to find someone else." I wanted to say "find another vagina" but thought that in vulgar taste. "This is too-late notice. In the future, if the firm wants me to attend an evening event, you need to let me know ahead of time so I can plan accordingly and include that on my calendar," I told him.

These incidents of being trotted out to show that the firm had women felt disempowering. But if I were to leave, I believed, my resume would look like I don't set down roots.

Today's Winning Concept Is . . .

2002

One partner I worked with typically started late, around 5:00 p.m. Meetings with him were invariably after hours. Late one day, this partner asked me to draft a response to the U.S. Patent Office for an application for his client. It was a straightforward response, due in a few days.

The next day, again in an after-hours meeting, he looked at the response I'd prepared, jotted some notes on it, and questioned the rationale for one section: "That doesn't make sense. Why don't you talk about X argument here instead?"

I thought the argument he proposed was weak and explained why. He disagreed and insisted I use his argument in place of mine.

At our next meeting, he looked at the revised document, pointed to the argument he had recommended at our last meeting, and said it didn't make sense. "Here, you should be discussing Y instead," where Y was my original argument.

Fortunately, I had brought with me the first draft where he nixed my Y argument. Pointing to it, I asked, "Isn't this your handwriting saying that this argument didn't make sense?" I then again explained why I believed the Y argument was stronger than the one included at his insistence. He didn't counter that, but he told me to use the X argument instead. I told him I would craft the response as I saw fit.

"If we write it up with what you are proposing, the client, quite frankly, will think we don't know what we're doing. No disrespect intended. That's the reality as I see it," I told him.

"Okay." He paused, then added, "I know you got this."

By that time, I could see through his shenanigans. I pointed out that our communication on projects followed a distinctive, repetitive pattern: I would present an idea, he would diminish it, and then he would resurrect it as his own. I told him I would appreciate his professionalism on future projects. He didn't try to defend himself.

On returning to my office, I wondered if he behaved like that with the male attorneys.

All this unnecessary, after-hours work recurringly resulted in taxi rides to the city's post office around 8:00 p.m. to 9:00 p.m. to drop off documents, which could easily have been done a few days earlier during office hours. That meant catching the 9:30 p.m. train and getting home at 11:00 p.m.—all for what were typically simple, straightforward matters that were not rocket science.

A few weeks later, the partner asked if I would step in to teach licensing at a patent law course hosted by a national education institute. As it was last minute, I declined.

Interestingly, about a month later, at the end of the day, on running into him on my way to the train station, he told me he had a confession to make. Casually, he blurted out, "I'm jealous of you. You have it all. You really do." That told me he genuinely respected me and my work.

The Gaslight

2002

In a chat, Karl, a partner in his thirties, commented about an entry on my resume and another entry about my former work as a scientist.

Shortly after that, in a meeting with another associate and me, he instructed me to write a patent application for one of his clients. It related to an aspect of my scientific background. As the other attorney sat there, Karl explained the invention and handed me a stack of documents offering more detail on the underlying technology. He said he needed the application done before the end of the following week. That weekend, I finished it.

In his office, I handed Karl the completed document, along with the supporting documents he had provided. In a calm, unquestioning, monotone voice, he remarked, "Why did you do the patent application? I did not authorize you to do that." His voice and facial expression were devoid of any element of surprise. It was as though he had rehearsed his response at least mentally beforehand. His remark left me thunderstruck.

"Yes, you did," I replied. "You, Fred, and I were in a meeting last week when you asked me to do this patent application. You explained the invention and handed me these documents to familiarize myself with the technology. You do recall that, right? And you said you needed the application this week."

Karl ignored my questions. Calmly, he reiterated his earlier statement. "Judie, Judie," he said, shaking his head as if I were a confused dotard, "I didn't authorize you to write this patent application. I don't know where you got the documents to write this. You can go now. I have a phone conference. Leave everything here."

"No, we talked about this in last week's meeting with Fred. How else would I have known about the invention or even that such an invention existed?"

In a monotone voice, he repeated, "I didn't authorize you to write this patent application."

As he reached for the phone, I told him, "We need to discuss this. Let me know when you're available."

"No, we're done. There's nothing to talk about. I didn't authorize you to do the patent application. You can leave now. I have a call I need to get to." He began dialing.

What a liar! I thought.

I didn't know how to address this. Karl clearly shut himself off from further communication on this issue.

This was serious on multiple levels.

On returning to my office, I passed by Fred's office, the attorney who was present at that meeting. Popping my head in, I asked, "Last week when we were in a meeting with Karl, did you hear him tell me to write a patent application on [client's] invention?"

"Yeah," said Fred. "He told you to work on it and said he wanted it done this week. He talked some about what the invention was and gave you some documents to look at."

"Right. A few minutes ago, I gave him the completed patent application. He told me he did *not* authorize me to do it. *And he said he didn't know where I got the supporting documents.*"

Fred grimaced. "What?" he said, sounding incredulous. "That's not true!"

"I know. Something is off!"

I wasn't going to ask Fred to come to my rescue.

Karl's claim of "not authorizing" meant that the time I had spent writing the application would not count toward my annual billable hour requirement—a key criterion used by firms for evaluating attorneys.

I thought about taking the matter to the executive director but decided against that. From what I had seen, he was more of a figurehead than someone with genuine power. Plus, any follow-through would mean dragging my colleague into a kerfuffle with this partner, and I didn't want the situation to devolve to that point.

So, I reluctantly decided to drop the matter. This experience, however, colored how I perceived that partner thereafter. Anyone who gaslights is not to be trusted and has serious issues with power.

A teaching from my childhood then dropped in: explore the why. It occurred to me: *Why did he tell me to leave all the documents? That includes the patent application I wrote. Is he going to use it?*

The Switcheroo

2002

The lead attorney on a litigation matter requested that I write a trial brief and give it to a junior partner who was handling that phase. The junior partner was also instructed to prepare a trial brief. I followed through.

As I hadn't heard from the lead attorney, I got a nudge to check in with him. When I got him on the phone, I asked, "Did you have any questions about my trial brief?"

"Judie, your trial brief was pretty bad," he said slowly as if delivering bad news. I didn't expect that.

Something did not feel right. Flipping through the copy of my brief in front of me, I asked, "What did you think about the argument concerning [xyz]?"

"I didn't see that argument," he said.

Stymied, I asked, "Did you read the brief or skim it?"

"I read it."

"That argument was midway through," I said, and gave him the page number.

"Hold on a second. I have your trial brief right here on the corner of my desk." Flipping through it, he said, "No, that argument isn't in the brief."

How could that be? I wondered. "Does the document you are looking at have a heading on page [w] that reads . . .?'"

"No," he responded.

"How about a heading on page [y] that reads . . .?" I asked.

"No," he told me. "That's not in the brief."

I asked about another case referenced in the brief. He said that one was not cited in the copy he had.

I read the start of the second paragraph from the end. "Is that on your copy?" I asked.

"No, it's different on the document I have," he said.

"Does the document you're holding have [z] pages?" I asked.

"No, it's a different page count," he replied.

That's not the document I wrote, I concluded. "I didn't write the trial brief you are looking at. That is not the one I wrote and turned in," I said.

"Your name is on the top page," he responded, matter-of-factly.

I told him I'd like to look into this. He wasn't interested; his focus was on getting the job done. Following up on this side issue was not a priority.

On hanging up, I realized that the junior partner must have thought highly of my work. It certainly sounded like he had put my name on his brief, and I assume his on mine. This same partner consistently left me off on emails advising of team meeting dates for that litigation matter. And each time I'd raise the issue with him, he'd grin and say he'd check into it or disclaim ignorance: "Gee, I don't know how that happened." It was obvious he did.

∽

A few years later at a cocktail party, I was chatting with an attorney in his mid-sixties who worked for a different firm. Our conversation turned to our experience in firms. I told him about this incident. He stepped closer, hushing his voice as if sharing a confidence. "People don't talk about that when it happens to them."

"Well, they should," I replied. "Looking the other way or treating that like it's a mark of defeat works against fostering a positive work environment, don't you think? Would you want those values in your home?"

Momentarily, he mulled over my comment. Nodding affirmatively, he uttered, "You a have point. It's a good one. I hadn't thought of it that way."

∽

I felt like I was constantly dancing on eggshells, frequently running into situations that required fortitude and resilience where I would have to confront the same couple of partners over and over. The occurrences weren't the occasional, mundane, garden-variety slip-ups where someone says or does something unintentionally. Instead, a pattern existed, replete with thought and intention. The conflicts—and in some instances, a subtle, underlying hostility from one partner—were huge distractions. Still, though, I nixed escalating the situation as I didn't want to alienate the problematic partners and pour fuel onto the fire for future interactions.

Each energy-depleting scenario taxed my performance and suffocated the joy my work typically gave me. Not every interaction was tinged with negativity; the ones that were, though, felt like a vacuous black hole.

Nor did I feel like I belonged. Even a male paralegal would tell me he was booked for the day; yet a minute later, within earshot, he'd respond "yes" when a male attorney asked, "Do you have time today to do . . .?" None of this felt right. I needed to leave.

Intelligence + Competence = Fired

2002

A bright young lady was assigned to work as my admin. She was intelligent, socially adjusted, convivial, conscientious, and highly competent. She reminded me of myself when I was younger. She was attractive as well. Her supervisor—the lady who had hosted a welcome lunch when I joined the firm—had a problem with her. A few weeks after the admin's start date, that person assigned her massive amounts of work besides her handling my work. My heart went out to the admin.

I watched her transform from being chirpy and doing amazing work to starting her day looking overworked, downtrodden, and overwhelmed. I sensed that her supervisor was jealous of her and purposely overwhelmed her to make her job unpleasant. I told her she needed to talk with her supervisor. "This isn't right," I said. "You're doing far more than any of the other admins." I volunteered to accompany her. I didn't like what I saw. I wasn't going to go behind her back and speak with her supervisor. I felt so bad for her that I came in one Saturday and spent four nonbillable hours, filing away documents relating to my clients' matters so my files would be up to date, and freeing up space from her to-be-filed piles. She was so overworked that she didn't even notice her lightened filing pile.

One day, I had to speak with her supervisor on an unrelated matter. I hesitated to address the issue about my overworked admin but did, thinking they would appreciate hearing they could lose an exceptional employee. I told her that this admin was excellent and conscientious but was way overworked. "She is too good for the firm to risk her quitting," I explained. "She is doing far more than any other admin here *in my opinion*," I added so as not to step on any toes.

Well, I must have scrunched her supervisor's entire foot: she fired the admin that afternoon. After that, for about a week, as I walked down the hall, the other admins successively stood up as I neared their stations and turned their backs on me—a shunning that I believe none would have attempted if I were male. They apparently blamed me for this talented lady's job loss.

I felt horrible about my admin losing her job. I went back to her supervisor to ask why. She wouldn't say.

About a year later, I met a female colleague for dinner. She asked if the fired admin had said "fuck you" to me. I was surprised she would even think that.

"No," I replied. "She was not that kind of person. She didn't talk to me like that."

Looking puzzled, my colleague asked again, "So, she didn't say, 'Fuck you'?"

"No. She was respectful. She didn't talk like that. She never said that to me."

My colleague was surprised. She told me the rumor circulating around the firm was that they fired my admin because I reported her for saying "fuck you" to me.

I thought, *What?* From that, in my perspective, what I saw was a fabricated reason for eliminating an exceptional employee because of personal jealousy or a sense of inferiority.

Final Visit and the Cemetery Call

2002

In May 2002, my mother passed away suddenly. She had been in the nursing home for twenty-nine months.

When the home called with the news, I felt sad but relieved, for she was now at peace. It touched my heart that for the past year, she had been the happiest I had ever seen her. I wondered if she ever revisited the trauma she carried through life.

The last time I saw her was Easter of 2002. From then until her passing was the longest that I had not visited, though I had called. For Easter, John and I arranged a lovely dinner in the home's private dining room. We met her in the activity room where a nurse helped nine ladies from the dementia wing select crayons to color pages of Easter scenes.

As I walked toward my mom at the far end of the table, I passed the other ladies, each diligently coloring in Easter bunnies, baskets, and eggs on their papers, taking care to stay within the lines. Mom didn't see us walk in. As I reached her, I saw that she was rhythmically and hurriedly running a fuchsia-colored crayon up and down across the entire page, as if in a race, washing over the multiple images on the page with a single color, oblivious to the concept of coloring within the lines. She was the only one doing that.

"I'm done!" she shouted merrily as she waved at the nurse. That's when she saw us. It was obvious she had no interest in coloring.

"Hey! Let's blow this popsicle stand and go eat!" she called to John and me.

With another nurse who joined us, we walked to the private dining room.

I recalled how her first year there had been challenging. Even the outside world had reached within to wreak havoc. A prospective buyer of Mom's house had probed one of Mom's neighbors for where she lived. A reverend from a church that the prospective buyer belonged to then visited Mom, covertly bypassing their security system. Sneaking in with a visitor for another resident and lying (as the nurses had to buzz people into the dementia wing), he evaded the nurses and asked residents to direct him to Mom's room. Ear-piercing screams from Mom's room brought the nurses running. There, they found the man holding a Bible, trying to force her to sign a sales contract for her house for a lower price than agreed upon. Threatening to call the police, they escorted him out and called me. It took hours to calm Mom down.

Over the previous year, she had evolved into a happier, spirited self—someone I had not seen before. Yes, she was still nasty: to one reserved, gentle lady on her floor, she would stamp her feet and doggedly bark, "Get out of here, dumbass!" as the lady approached me, wanting me to walk with her down the hall. Several nurses had commented that for Mom's first year there, she cursed and called a few of them names, requiring some to retreat to the nurses' station to catch their breath. One nurse said that my mom thought she was me, would call her "Judie," and would allow her to bathe her. Apart from her foot-stamping at the one lady, for Mom's last year there, she had acclimated well. And they loved her for her vivacious spirit.

In the dining room, Mom was the same person I had always known. Except, she had now softened and was happy. Gone was her inimical behavior toward me. Supplanting it was respect and kindness. She was pleasant to be with, without requiring strangers nearby for her to strike that demeanor. I sensed that she had made peace with herself. It felt like she had shed the demon that had been devouring her from within. What now shone through was the genuine Martha—a beautiful, content soul.

Fortunate is how I felt that this home had taken her in, though she didn't have much money and went on welfare. They provided a place where she was treated with dignity, kept safe, looked after, fed well, bathed, and genuinely loved by the staff.

Gratitude is what I felt for Mom, for it was through her that I had developed resilience and taught myself to mine my inner strength—qualities that I continued to apply in my professional life. Because of my early interactions with Mom, I taught myself to connect with my soul, though at the time I didn't know I was doing that.

At her wake, John and I sat outside the parlor room waiting for the undertaker to open the door, commencing visitation. I didn't know anything about mediumship as I had been raised to fear ghosts. What was I to make of what felt like Mom's vibrant energy? It felt like her spirit was flying around the funeral parlor, I told my husband, "as bizarre as that sounds." And, I told him, it felt like I could hear her in my head, raving ecstatically, "I'm beautiful! I'm beautiful! Oh my god, I'm beautiful!" The energy would fly off and then return. We were eager to see how she looked in the casket. As he and I approached, it was as if my mom were flying alongside us, continuing with her astonishment at how stunning she looked.

She did look gorgeous. I had never seen her look as nice as she did then. Her hair was freshly cut and perfected coifed. Her makeup was exquisitely done with foundation, eyebrow pencil, a touch of mascara, lipliner, and lipstick—an expanded repertoire over Mom's beauty bag of rouge and lipstick. I wanted to take a photo of her but decided against that as people were now streaming in and I wanted to greet and thank them for coming.

Mom's burial attire was also sophisticated. From the three outfits we purchased, she selected the one she wanted to be buried in along with new jewelry, as hers had gone astray in the nursing home. There, residents meandered into each other's rooms and innocently helped themselves to sweaters, earrings, and underwear. In Mom's closet hung clothes bearing the names of two other women on her floor.

Several of the firm's attorneys visited the funeral home—a thoughtful gesture. A few commented on how the wake, with its din, revelry, and vibrancy, felt more like a wedding celebration than a funeral. It was my mom's robustly dynamic energy infusing the room.

The next day, one of the firm's attorneys called my cell. He knew I was out of the office for my mom's funeral. "May I call you back? We just pulled into the cemetery for my mother's burial, and they are about to take the casket out of the hearse."

"No. It'll be quick," he said. He didn't see my notes in a client's file about a meeting I had with them.

Yes, I was annoyed as this was my mom's burial. But it didn't matter to him. I regretted answering the phone. He was clearly insensitive to the fact that I was at the cemetery waiting for my mother's casket to be removed from the hearse. His questions could have waited until the next day or that afternoon. Noting his insensitivity, I decided to get him out of the way so I wouldn't have to call him back.

The call took longer than I expected. My husband whispered, "Judie, they're taking the casket out of the hearse. Let's go."

I responded, "One minute."

About a minute later, John again said, "Judie, we need to go. They just got the casket out of the hearse. Come on, let's go."

I held up my index finger, "one minute." I was explaining to this attorney where he could find the notes to further answer his question.

A third time, my patient husband said, "Judie, they're walking the casket to the grave. We're going to miss the burial." I ended our call.

This attorney's sense that it was okay to call a colleague during her parent's burial, as if it weren't a big deal, and my foolishness in answering the call were a reality check. I had worked with other attorneys who were so entrenched in their work that they thought nothing of sidelining their families. I recalled witnessing the hurt etched across the face of a colleague's wife who came to the office to meet her husband for a planned dinner date, and how he cavalierly told her, last minute, that he was going to stay and work. I could feel her pain as she stormed out of the office.

I was grateful for being able to be fully invested in my career without sidelining my husband or elevating my work as being more important than significant, potentially life-changing, or auspicious events in another person's life. Respecting what happens in the lives of others is just as important as respecting what happens in our own life. I vowed I would never fall into that trench.

I didn't fit into this firm. And there's the finale . . .

Two Weeks' Notice

2002

All this drama, compressed into seventeen months, realistically boiled down to one question: is this a firm I want to stay with? My answer was immediate and instinctive: no. I decided it was time to leave. There was too much game-playing, intermixed with jealousy and alternative facts, for my preference.

One mistake I made was that I had become concerned about what people thought—something I typically didn't care about. But here, for some reason, I took that on. I don't know why. Was it attrition of my stamina from dealing with one drama after the other, or the continual need to stand up for myself, or the attempted gaslighting? Or was it the cumulative footprint of all the above?

I gave the executive director two weeks' notice of my departure. He asked if I had another job. I didn't want to say no. Doing that suggested that this job was a shitty experience. It was shitty—in fact, beyond shitty. But I wanted to play it "nice"; I didn't want to burn any bridges. I told him I had a job offer, though I didn't. As soon as I said that, I felt a thud in my solar plexus. I had lied. I felt awful. I felt I had become like the others. I had let myself down.

I didn't know what I was going to do for my next job. I enjoyed practicing law. But a niggling thought kept surfacing. If I joined another law firm, how much unseen drama lurks behind their facade of prestige?

I started questioning why adversity kept popping up, with different colors, in this and the last firm. *Am I attracting this?* I asked myself. Because I try to mine every challenge for its teaching, I probed why I was encountering these interpersonal challenges. At my last place of employment, I had stood up for values and honored myself by leaving after learning of a threat to my physical safety when it felt like it had become a "let's-wait-and-see" situation. In the scenarios I had run into here, I experienced what I concluded were values not aligned with mine, marginalization, disempowerment, jealousy, and gaslighting.

So, what could I learn here? On a broad, over-arching scale, my biggest takeaway was to always honor myself—that is, to treat myself with the same love and respect I show others. Here, that meant to unequivocally trust my Self, my competence, and my instinct, and to walk away when my values are irreparably not aligned with those of others. That, I found, was the most significant teaching from this—and one that, in retrospect, applies to all my prior challenges, including those from my early years. It comes down to a simple choice: honor yourself or submit. And each time, I will choose to honor myself, for that unlocks the door to moving forward.

Moreover, I was aware of the chameleon effect—where people interacting with others for a long time often unconsciously pick up each other's behaviors, mannerisms, and expressions (think "long-time-married couples"). I recognized that I wouldn't want to adopt some behaviors I had experienced in this environment.

The Friday before my two-week notice period was to expire, I ran into yet another situation I had never before encountered. My admin refused to type up a document called a PCT because, as she put it, "That is not my job."

Paige had been my admin for a few months, since the unjustified firing of my last admin. A pleasant lady, she tended to try to squeak out of work. For example, one morning when asked to make a ten-minute phone call for something I needed for a presentation I was giving that evening, she declined: "I'm typing a patent application for Pierre"—a task with an open-ended deadline. Since working with her, I had already pulled correspondence and several other projects and handled them myself.

So, one week before my last day, Paige refused to prepare a document I needed. "That is not my job. Hannah, the admin down the hall, does PCTs. Talk to her."

I was flummoxed. I had never heard of an admin refusing to do a task that other admins are doing. Paige knew I was leaving the following week. Was this a ploy to push the envelope and see if I could *make* her work?

Diplomacy always wins out, I thought. I explained how the firm handled PCTs: the admins prepared the paper documents (this was before electronic filing), and Hannah then sent them to the appropriate patent office for filing.

Again, Paige countered, "That is not my job. I'm not typing it up."

Okay. How do I handle this? I didn't want to call her supervisor right then. The last time I spoke with her, she responded by firing my remarkably exemplary admin. I told Paige I would check with Hannah as I thought that would get the project moving. *Maybe the firm changed the way it handles PCTs and I wasn't aware of that,* I reasoned.

Hannah confirmed that my understanding was correct.

Going back to my admin, I told her I had checked with Hannah and repeated how the process worked. "I understand you were not made aware of that during the hiring process. I would appreciate your taking care of this."

"No. That's not my job. That's not what I was hired to do." She was adamant.

I kept my cool. Now I had no choice but to turn to my last resort. I told her I would speak with her supervisor, and she could explain the responsibilities. "It sounds like that point wasn't clear when they brought you in."

I phoned her supervisor and asked her to stop by to speak with me. "Paige," I said, "contends that typing up a PCT is not her job."

Trying to get this project squared away was gobbling up my time. This was like a little kids' squabble, unlike the typically positive, mutually respectful relationships I had enjoyed with admins in my previous careers.

The supervisor talked with Paige before knocking on my door. Her response to me was bewildering. "You need to tell Hannah to do the PCT. The admins don't do those. Hannah does."

I felt like I had been beamed into an alternate reality. "I've already spoken with Hannah," I responded. "She said she doesn't prepare PCTs. To do that for all the attorneys here would be a herculean task. Hannah said the secretaries prepare the documents, they give them to her, and she then submits them to the appropriate international patent office."

"No. You're wrong. Take this up with Hannah," she instructed. This was turning into a mindless powerplay.

I was stunned that the supervisor of admins was not aware of how, procedurally, these documents were created and handled internally. "It's not done the way you are proposing it is," I said. "You can ask any of the admins here or Hannah. In fact, please do that, because that then will help you understand what the process is."

Raising her voice, she reiterated, "That's not Paige's job. She is not going to type up that document for you. Take it up with Hannah." And she stormed out.

I was flabbergasted by the supervisor's comment. Why was it that other admins prepared these documents, but according to my admin—and now the supervisor of all the admins—that was not my admin's job? In my twenty-year career, I had never had an admin contest that something document-related was not their job when their peers were doing that very same task. Nor had I ever had to escalate a matter to an admin's supervisor as to whether something was or was not the admin's job. *This doesn't make sense*, I thought. *What is going on here? Is it because I'm leaving and this is an opportunity to strut power?* The question floated by: *If I were male, would this be happening?*

Let the matter rest until Monday, I decided. I knew how my past employers would have handled this situation. None of them would have given an admin or a supervisor of admins the authority to block an attorney, associate editor, or scientist from getting their work done.

Ten minutes later, the executive director stepped into my office. "You upset your admin. You have a week left on your two weeks' notice, but you can't stay till the end of that. Leave now," he demanded.

Okay, Paige's supervisor talked to the executive director. What did she tell him? There has to be more to this than that. I've heard admins being ticked off with their attorneys about having to do rush jobs or take on a huge project they didn't want to do. This wasn't in that camp.

The executive director said they'd pack everything up and send it to me. Eyeing all the art and professionally framed licenses and certificates in my office, he then retracted as the firm didn't want to assume liability for damage. "You can pack up, and then leave."

A handful of admins, excluding Paige, dropped by to say goodbye. Earlier in the week, I had told one associate, the IT department, and Paige that I was leaving. The partners already knew. I planned to tell everyone else the following week.

As I had commuted by train that day, my husband drove out to retrieve me and my belongings. Waiting for him, flashing to mind was that incredibly tiny piece of fish on my plate at lunch with the attorneys before I had accepted the firm's offer. I also thought back to the first welcome luncheon where the admin's supervisor was my host, and I again questioned why the supervisor of secretaries was tasked with taking me to lunch. *Did they decide that because of my gender?* And I recalled how I had paid for our luncheon because she didn't have money or a credit card. In hindsight, these incidents truly were metaphors for my experience at the firm.

Doing It My Way

2003

Working in the world of law at firms owned by others was markedly different from being in the publishing or scientific arenas. In publishing and science, irrespective of whom I worked with, I felt respected, appreciated, and valued for my competence—despite my employers in these fields being under patriarchal leadership at the time and despite the singular conflict in publishing where I was dubbed a "tempest in the teapot." Aside from my disappointment in the chief editor's remark about my salary falling short of the men's, not once was I made to feel "less than" in day-to-day interactions or have my ideas rejected or experience resistance from management.

By contrast, in law, where I continued to work in male-dominated environments, I didn't always feel that same level of respect or appreciation, depending upon the firm. And where that was the case, it tended to be an unusually harsh environment.

It was through professional and interpersonal challenges at these firms that I learned more about the art of finessing resilience, embracing courage, and standing up for myself.

The adversity I encountered taught me to think on my feet. As an attorney, I also learned more about professional rivalry from both men and women, unfortunately from the position of being the target of poisoned arrows.

What I learned, too, was that sometimes people take latitude in their interactions with others, particularly men who say they want to boost the representation of women in a business. That interest, I found, sometimes conflicts with what seems to be an implicit survival need to safeguard their own personal power, which some protect by projecting supremacy to make sure women beneath their management tier know their place.

So, I couldn't fathom going to another law firm. One point crystalizing over the past few years was that I knew more about law than I gave myself credit for. On several occasions, on teachings of law, I corrected misunderstandings of colleagues who had been lawyers for significantly longer than I had, some two to three times longer. And one thing for sure: if I didn't know something, I always figured it out.

I started my own law firm where my practice centered on intellectual property law and FDA regulatory matters.

One synchronicity opened after another. Clients found me before I started marketing. I loved the work, and I set a strong foundation for my firm. Gone were the ancillary distractions and challenges that had colored my previous professional experience. With my firm, my professional and personal lives flowed effortlessly, making the experience even more delicious.

What was clear was that I had now found the perfect job. All went well, aside from one perilously serious challenge . . .

A Near Miss

2007

F our years into my firm, the complexion of life's challenges
shifted back to my personal world. Here, the biggest challenge
was to my personal strength. It stopped me in my tracks.

April 25, 2007, was day three of my husband's three-day
business trip to Phoenix—short compared to his usual two-
week international trips. He was a food scientist scouting
new technology. The first night of his trip, John recounted
his flight out where a man two seats away had been visibly
sick and sweating profusely as he sat collapsed forward for
the duration of the flight. He was too sick to be on the plane,
noted my husband.

Walking into the house from the limo, John held up his
hand, signaling me to stop. "Don't kiss me! I have the flu."

In the middle of the night, I awoke. John was talking to
himself in his sleep as he sometimes did. I rolled over. That's
when an alarm blared in my stomach. A voice in my head
coaxed, "Get up. Get up. Don't go back to sleep. You'll regret
it." I got up and went downstairs.

The sense of alarm surged through me. Trying to figure out
why, I checked the gas stove. It was off. *Maybe it's John. Maybe
he's sicker than I think. Maybe I should take him to the emergency room.*

Seeking guidance and being spiritual versus religious, I implored, "Dear God, please tell me what to do." About a minute later, I was surprised that John had come down to the kitchen. I could feel him standing to my left. What was odd was that I didn't hear the clop-clop of his house slippers. However, when I looked to the left, no one was there. But I could still *feel* someone standing right next to me.

A lady's voice then spoke into my left ear. I could hear the voice inside my head; it wasn't audible in the room, just in my head. The voice quivered, "Ta-a-a-a-k-e h-i-m-m-m N-O-O-O-W!"

I thought, *Wow! That was strange. What was that? Someone up there must think they have to hit me on the head with a two-by-four to get my attention.* Given the circumstances, the impression of an emergency quickly eclipsed my sense of awe. *Okay. I will take him to the ER.*

When I turned to dart upstairs, words poured out of my mouth, bypassing my brain. I didn't know what I said. That had never happened before. The thought came: *Repeat it. It's in two parts.*

I opened my mouth and the first part tumbled out, again without me engaging my brain: "Oh my god, that's his birthday." *What?* I thought. *Some being—who? an angel? or was it my intuition?—tells me to take my husband to the ER and I am now talking about his birthday? That makes no sense.*

Then I saw it: the LCD on the microwave. It was 2:26 a.m., the month and day of John's birthdate. A chill rolled down my spine. The sense of alarm returned.

What's the second part? I knew it had to do with death. Okay, here we go: "If I don't do something, he could die." I repeated that to distinguish if it was "could" or "would."

Without wasting a nanosecond, I shot upstairs to wake John. There he was, sleeping like a baby. I shook him gently, "John, sweetie, wake up."

He peered at me through half-opened eyes. I told him, "Put your clothes on. We're going to the emergency room."

He sat up abruptly, concerned. "Are you okay? What's wrong?"

"I'm okay. Let's take you to the ER and get you checked out."

"I'm fine. I only have the flu. I'm not going to the ER. Go back to bed," he said, nestling back under the covers.

"Come on, John. Get up and get dressed."

"No, I don't need to go to the emergency room. Go back to bed." I was not going to tell him what had just happened. That would freak him out.

Laying his clothes on the bed, I said, "John, put your clothes on now, or I'm calling an ambulance."

"What's with you? I've never seen you like this. You're overreacting. What's wrong?"

"Honey, humor me. Okay? Please? Put your clothes on. Do that for me. Humor me. Go along with me on this, okay? Please?"

He looked at me as if I had three heads. "I don't understand this at all." He was getting dressed, as was I. He was not pleased.

Downstairs, I called out, "John, are you coming?"

Slowly, he ambled down the stairs like he had all the time in the world. "What's the big hurry?"

I can't tell you, Sweets, I thought. It was not good, I felt.

The ER was not busy. Within five to eight minutes, he was on a cot, answering standard questions—name and address. I looked at my watch. We had made good time. It was 2:56 a.m. I had sped.

The cadence of his answers changed, I noticed. John didn't answer the third question, prompting me to look up. With his hands clasped together above his head, his entire body jerked violently. He was having a seizure. He had never had one before, and he did not have epilepsy.

Someone shouted, "He's seizing! He's seizing!" More medical staff poured into the room. They injected him. Another shout, "He's seizing again!" Another injection. Then he was out, unconscious.

"We're admitting him to intensive care." It was 3:06 a.m.

As I waited for John to be set up in ICU, I thought back to the lady's voice I had heard less than an hour before. I felt so grateful for that. *Was that an angel? Or was it my intuition?* The instruction given was an imperative coming from some intelligence outside myself. Its urgency—conveyed with the louder, stretched-out "N-O-O-O-W"—proved to be prescient. My sense of awe returned. What had happened at home felt eminently profound. It was as if John were being looked after in an inexplicable, subtle, nuanced way by the Divine.

At about 7:30 a.m., the attending physician, a tall man with an Eastern European accent, walked into John's room. He explained that something—they didn't know what—was attacking my husband's brain. It had caused his sodium to plunge, prompting the seizure. "We now have it under control." As if on cue in a soap opera, a nurse dashed in, interrupting with urgency, "Doctor, his potassium is dropping fast!" The doctor pulled aside to speak with her outside the room.

Thirty minutes later, the doctor returned. He stopped about three feet into the room. Without even glancing toward John, he nonchalantly declared, "I'm going to intubate your husband," as if that were routine hospital protocol for all patients.

"You are going to do no such thing," I retorted. "You mean to stick a tube down his throat so he can breathe, right?"

"Yes."

"He's breathing fine," I said. In my mind's eye, I had an image of the inside of John's throat, raw and bloody from a tear from the tube being forcefully lodged in.

"Look at your husband! He can't breathe. He's struggling for air!" The doctor raised his voice in both pitch and decibels, gesturing frantically, emoting a need to act fast. *He's still standing near the doorway*, I noticed. *Okay, now he finally glanced at John.*

I walked to John's bed. He had a cannula beneath his nostrils delivering oxygen. He was serene, breathing like a baby. His chest rose gently and descended gently. No struggle there. The doctor's words and actions did not feel right. Something was off.

The doctor approached John's bed. Now waving his arms wildly, he continued, "He's struggling. Look at him! Are you going to deprive your husband of breathing? Is that what you want?"

He's trying to bait me into agreeing with him, I thought. Again, I looked down at John. Stillness and peace emanated from him. *I have to do what I feel is right.*

"You need to look at him, doctor," I said. "His chest is rising and falling, gently. See that? He's not struggling to breathe. But here is what I would agree to: you can remove the tube that runs beneath his nostrils (at the time I didn't know it was called a cannula) and if he struggles for air (I felt and believed John would be fine), then you may intubate him." I hoped I hadn't made a mistake saying this.

The doctor removed the cannula. John continued to breathe just as he had been before.

"He's breathing fine. You can see that, right?" I pointed out. Looking the doctor directly in the eye, I told him, "I do not authorize you to intubate him, doctor."

I didn't relate the rest of what raced through my mind: *You should lose your medical license. What you just pulled is unethical, and you know that.* I thought back to the legal world, where firms gauge lawyers on how much they bill. *Is it the same for the medical profession?* I wondered.

The doctor left the room without saying a word. At the nurse's station, I reported what had happened. "I don't want to see him in my husband's room again. I want him off my husband's case." I didn't know if my words carried any weight or if that was even how it worked in the medical field.

At about 11:30 a.m., the neurologist walked in. He asked questions; I gave detailed responses. Apparently, too much detail. He responded, "I don't need details. I'm a neurologist."

I could have retorted, "I'm an attorney, doctor. And details are how we win cases," but I didn't. I noted his hubris, glad that I didn't conduct myself that way.

He imparted, "Your husband is stuck between reality and a coma. He's in an altered state. He's not in a coma." Maybe that explained why John was chanting with a distinctive cadence. The neurologist had no idea how long John could be in that state. If John survived, he could be a vegetable, he told me.

"This is a puzzling case." He paused. In a shift to a softer, compassionate tone of voice, he concluded, "Your husband is very, very, very sick. It's time to gather the family. I don't think he's going to make it." I froze. I couldn't imagine life without my dear husband of almost twenty-seven years. "I'm sorry," he said, and left.

That afternoon as I stood at John's bed listening to his chants of brisk staccato sounds delivered in packets of three to six syllables, each packet cleaved clean by a pause, I experienced something unusual. It felt like a powerful, benevolent force in a spiritual context abutted each of my shoulders and continued around John's bed with a magnified sense of that power set at his head. It was as if I were standing, shoulder-to-shoulder with a fleet of angels. That feeling of awe lingered for a few minutes.

At the end of visiting hours, I asked if I could stay. The nurse said I couldn't. My husband had an infectious disease yet to be identified. I pleaded softly, "He is my husband. I'm not leaving him. Please?" She was a sweetheart. She scooted a comfortable chair in for me to stay in that night. I didn't sleep; I watched. The pump—his lifeline to a cocktail of pharmaceuticals—stopped working, and I summoned a nurse to replace it.

Over the next two days, a series of mishaps colored my husband's care. In addition to the attending physician trying to sneak in an intubation, his neurologist strutting "I'm a neurologist," and the pump going out with me being the only one to inform them of that, someone lost his urine sample on its way to the lab, the phlebotomist screwed up on a blood draw sparking John—not knowing what was going on, given his state—to go into fight-or-flight mode and resulting in him being put into a strait jacket, and they lost his shoes. And that is only what I was aware of.

Since that time, the hospital is under new ownership and operates under impeccable standards.

A second neurologist visited late on the second day. She expounded, "This is an unusual, puzzling case. We've never seen anything like this." With her help, I had my husband transferred to the neurology wing of a major medical center—a task that took a lot of arm-twisting and political finessing.

In the second hospital, John came out of his altered state. He was in the hospital for eight days, six in intensive care. Neither hospital identified what microbe had attacked his brain. With rest and recuperation, his brain health returned to normal.

At home, as his legs were weak, we danced his strength back to physical health.

Evolving: 180-Degree Shift

With my firm, opportunities outside of serving clients opened. I took and passed the Regulatory Affairs Professionals Society (RAPS) exam and earned a RAPS certification—a nice addition to being a Certified Food Scientist. I was admitted to the U.S. Supreme Court bar. And I was invited to speak at numerous conferences and meetings, including the International Union of Food Science and Technology's Twelfth World Congress of Food Science and a few other conferences that I declined.

Practicing law was my passion. In fact, I couldn't imagine leaving law. However, after practicing for more than two decades, I reached a point where I wanted to have more of an impact on people—on individuals—versus helping corporations protect their intellectual assets or comply with FDA regulations.

I felt called to work on a level that intimately speaks to our inner self.

How I would channel my professional experiences and the knowledge gleaned from them into meaningful work on this *self* level was not clear. One thing I did know was that to continue evolving and being happy, it was time to move on, to leave law. Though it was unclear what exactly my new focus would be, this time, my path, I recognized, was outside the conventional, professional world where I felt comfortable.

For guidance, I looked within.

Eons ago, I regarded people who talked about energy, intuition, auras, and chakras as *woo-woo*. In fact, if someone had told me they honed their intuition and studied energy, face reading, space clearing, or other related disciplines, I would have thought they were—*ahem*— "interesting." When a friend, a reiki practitioner, excitedly told me she used energy channeled through her hands to heal people, I privately doubted that. *She's so smart. It's a shame she believes that*, I thought.

I was such a skeptic! That was despite having had a number of bizarre experiences—several highlighted in this book—just as you may also have had.

What I didn't expect was that one day I would become one of *those* people.

So, what happened?

PART 6

BLOSSOMING FULLY

One Step Forward, Two Steps Inward

E mbracing change and being open to exploring new concepts introduced me to a new vista: spirituality, soul work, and personal transformation. Spirituality initially called to me, not in a religious context but as an intellectual pursuit before it spoke to my heart. By spirituality, I mean the understanding that we, as humans, are so much more than our physical bodies. Equipped with a soul and a spirit, we are part of something greater than our individual selves, something divine. We are all connected as if by invisible threads to each other, to each living thing on this planet, to our universe, and beyond. Related to this are the concepts that everything is energy and vibrates at a set frequency; that thoughts, having an energetic frequency, are powerful and can change the direction of our lives; and that our consciousness creates our reality. To some, this may sound peculiar, as it did to me early on.

Additionally, a few experiences, particularly during my legal career, taught me that wisdom—divine wisdom—is available to each of us. And while still practicing law, I had a few experiences (not disclosed here) that convinced me that we do not die—our souls do live on.

My focus on soul work brought awareness to the importance of working on ourselves; that is, to develop ourselves to be the best expression of who we can be while on this earth plane. That, I found, is the secret to finding happiness, peace, and success in our endeavors.

That became my new world. And I use my experience, along with a variety of modalities—outside of psychotherapy—to help others with self-development and professional challenges that they feel hold them back. This work is a way for me to inspire others in their transformation into empowered beings.

What Have I Learned?

With significant adversity now behind me, my past opened like a tome for self-reflection.

I believe all the obstacles encountered in my personal and professional lives had a purpose. Through each experience, some painful, I grew and gleaned teachings not otherwise available in books.

In my early years, I compared myself to others and would see myself as falling short. This, I believe, was because comparisons were the currency behind my mom's communication with me. That's why it's so important to know who we truly are so that another's comments about us slide off our energy system instead of becoming kneaded into our mind and buttressing the development of mistaken, negative self-beliefs.

This, I found, is particularly true if we have people in our life who need serious help and whose self-loathing compels them to project their feelings of falling short onto us, so they are not alone in their self-manufactured imprisonment. If we place others above ourselves in an imaginary hierarchy as being more accomplished than us, more competent, or *better* than us in some respect and believe that to be true, it will become true. Our subconscious will make it so.

What we tell ourselves is a private matter, safe from any eavesdropper. No one outside us hears what we say to ourselves. Our subconscious does, however. It listens. It cannot distinguish between real and make-believe, or true or false. So, what we tell ourselves has the potential to unlock doors to a better future or to spiral us downward into a dark place. I could have told myself what my mom said to me—that I am "dumb," "ugly," "no damn good," or a "whore." Had I done so, however, I would not have evolved and progressed as I have. Instead, I told myself an entirely different story, one projecting success and confidence.

What we experience with others is not about us, I observed. From all my experiences, whether it was a criticism or someone's judgment of what I did or said or how I acted, or someone claiming credit for my work, or even when my mom orchestrated events to affect others' perspective of me, never did I regard those as being done *to* me. Instead, I felt that in those situations, the individuals were expressing how they perceived themselves or what they would have liked for themselves, or what they disliked about themselves. It was quite telling, really. Sometimes, we're fortunate to experience people at their best. Sometimes, it's at their worst, where the person's feelings or wishes get transmuted into words that come flying out of their mouths or are otherwise expressed in their actions.

Apart from constructive criticism, I learned never to blankly accept negative or critical comments as being about me. Instead, I see them as gifts that allow me to feel the speaker's self-perception of their own weakness and to use that as a tool to help that individual, over time, to learn about their strengths. So those moments that might not have been pleasant for me were an inchoate step for me to help someone move into their greatness—one they had not previously known.

It wasn't until I stepped away from law that I realized how valuable my experiences with my mom were to my personal growth. Each time her mental illness tore at my heart, searing it with pain, it was like I gained a droplet of insight that I don't believe I would have had, if I'd had parents or nurturers who validated my thoughts or actions.

My childhood home, I realized, was a playground—albeit a rough one—that taught me, from a young age, what it means to be human and stand firm in my personhood. It taught me to rely on myself. It taught me the importance of connecting with my soul—my inner self—and of accessing my inner strength and believing in myself. That is, thinking and acting from a place of unshakably knowing who I truly am and what I stand for irrespective of the circumstances around me, even if I didn't present as confident on the outside to others. I believe I got through my early years by doing just that, though I didn't realize that was what I was doing at the time. It also taught me to guard my self-beliefs against negative influences, whether they be from others or from what I choose to expose myself to. It taught me resilience.

In reflecting back, I realize that throughout my life, no matter what the situation was, I never wished I were someone else or had someone else's life. Our life is like a fingerprint: it's unique, special, and precious. No one else in the world has the privilege of walking in our shoes, even if it means experiencing a rocky road or shoes full of holes. From adversity, pain, and struggle can come resilience, grit, and focus along with compassion and forgiveness, if we allow it.

What I also learned is that no matter how a situation unravels into a negative experience, it does not help to play it over and over in our head. That only reinforces the negative in our subconscious mind, and that has the potential to draw more of that particular negativity to us. What matters is how we choose to respond to those situations, for that determines whether we grow as a person, stay stagnant, or spiral downward. By our response today, we are ultimately charting the course for our future. That is where our power lies.

Adversity is a catalyst for self-transformation. Facing it head-on—with some varieties presenting more challenges than others—allows us to grow and align with who we are at our core, and to express our true essence with grace, integrity, diplomacy, and inner peace.

As I personally had to learn to value myself and to believe in myself while growing up and in my early professional years, I know we are all capable of enveloping qualities such as self-compassion, self-love, and empowerment.

We each have within us the seeds to be magnificent in our unique way, the gifts to evolve into masterful beings, and the light and inspiration to attain success, happiness, joy, and whatever it is we seek. No matter what our past has been, it is not our destiny. Before us, we have an open book in which to write the future as we wish it to unfold.

My wish for you is twofold: that any adversity you encounter melts into grace and imbues you with strength, resilience, and wisdom for leading a richer life, and that your light within shines and guides you into a meaningful, purposeful life.

AFTERWORD

AFTERWORD

A Reflection on Trauma in a Parent

When I was young, my mom and dad's families characterized my mother as "crazy." I pathologized her behavior from the time I was a toddler. I could see something was wrong with Mom. What I didn't know was what it was. The answer to that question didn't come until later in life for me, too late to make a difference in my mother's internal struggles.

I postulated that she had some form of psychopathy. She lied a lot (in my teens, her brother Tony said he never believed anything Martha told him), she took pleasure in hurting people, she never expressed regret, she had no empathy for the pain she inflicted on her siblings and others, and she had frequent episodes of uncontrollable rage and occasional depression.

It wasn't until I read a few publications on what childhood trauma looks like in adults that I understood her behavior, though only peripherally. I am not trained as a psychotherapist or psychologist. As a layman and her daughter, I believe that at least part of her behavior stemmed from unresolved trauma she had carried since being raped at age five—a horrific act.

Her mother and siblings cradled her assault as a family secret. They didn't work with her to get her to see that she was not an object of shame for the family, as she seemed to believe she was. That wasn't done in the 1920s. So, she never accepted that she was not the one at fault. This construction is through my eyes.

Throughout her life, my mom perhaps dissociated many times. In a few instances when I referred to a recent past behavior, she had no recollection of it. The times she smashed cookies or beat me during a break from her letter writing—both instances done in silence with the same rhythmic and vigorous pounding and fighting-type hand movements—was she dissociating? I didn't discuss those incidents with her. Our family did not have the tools for that level of communication.

My mom was inherently wounded. Many of us incur trauma to some degree as we go through life. Hers was deeply rooted. It sculpted her perspective of herself and of others, and it opened for her an avenue for exploiting the authority of her position as a mother and wife to prey upon those she saw as gentle fodder. Her cruelty crushed my father's soul.

Society has advanced remarkably in its understanding of mental illness. What was taboo in the past is now discussed openly on talk shows and is even embraced as a badge of honor by some. Society still has far to go, though.

If you know someone who is struggling with mental illness, please try to encourage them to seek help and investigate healing protocols. Try to help them understand and embrace their self-worth as they work through their challenges. And, if that individual is responsible for children, try to step in and model for them what support, respect, and love look like so that they can incorporate those qualities into their being and how they lead their lives. By doing that, you can not only help the one struggling with mental illness but may also change the lives—profoundly for the better—of those in close relationship to that person.

Acknowledgments

The word "gratitude" does not come close to how appreciative I am to all who have played a role of any capacity in my crafting of this book. A huge thank you to those whom I have interacted with, favorably or otherwise, whether still on this earth plane or not, and from whom I learned something worthy of writing about here, for you were my teachers. Because of you, I am the person I am today. Thank you to those who took the time to read my manuscript and offer comments on it, and a special thanks to Jane Vaninger. Thank you to my loving husband for his patience and for indulging me in that "one more cup of coffee, please." And I am grateful, too, to Capucia Publishing, LLC for the privilege of flying among their skein of geese, carried along with that energy, and for their mastery in the design and publication of my words on these pages.

Resources

Baldwin, Michael and Deborah Korn. *Every Memory Deserves Respect – EMDR, the Proven Trauma Therapy with the Power to Heal.* New York: Workman Publishing, 2021. p. 132.

Brewer-Smyth, Kathleen. *Adverse Childhood Experiences: The Neuroscience of Trauma, Resilience and Healing throughout the Life Course.* New York: Springer, 2022.

Chapman, Daniel P., Shanta R. Dube, and Robert F. Anda, "Adverse Childhood Events as Risk Factors for Negative Mental Health Outcomes," *Psychiatric Annals* 37, no. 5 (May 2007): 359-364.

Felitti, Vincent J., Robert F. Anda, Dale Nordenberg, David F. Williamson, Alison M. Spitz, Valerie Edwards, Mary P. Koss, and James S. Marks, "Relationship of Childhood Abuse and Household Dysfunction to Many of the Leading Causes of Death in Adults," *American Journal of Preventative Medicine* 14, no. 4 (May 1998): 245-2587.

Iacoviello, Brian M. and Dennis S. Charney, "Psychosocial Facets of Resilience: Implications for Preventing Posttrauma Psychopathology, Treating Trauma Survivors, and Embracing Community Resilience," *European Journal of Psychotraumatology* 5, no. 1 (October 1, 2014): 23970, https://doi.org/10.3402/ejpt.v5.23970.

Jackson Nakazawa, Donna. *Childhood Disrupted: How Your Biography Becomes Your Biology, and How You Can Heal.* New York: Atria Books, 2015.

Kübler-Ross, Elizabeth and David Kessler. *On Grief and Grieving: Finding the Meaning of Grief through the Five Stages of Loss.* New York: Scribner, 2014.

Merrick, Melissa T., Katie A. Ports, Derek C. Ford, Tracie O. Afifi, Elizabeth T. Gershoff, and Andrew Grogan-Kaylor, "Unpacking the Impact of Adverse Childhood Experiences on Adult Mental Health," *Child Abuse and Neglect* 69 (July 2017): 10-19, https://doi.org/10.1016/j.chiabu.2017.03.016.

Mullen, Paul E., Judy L. Martin, Jessie C. Anderson, Sarah E. Romans, and G. Peter Herbison, "Childhood Sexual Abuse and Mental Health in Adult Life," *The British Journal of Psychiatry* 163 (December 1993): 721-732, https://doi.org/10.1192/bjp.163.6.721.

Sue, Derald Wing. "Microaggressions in Everyday Life." 4:24 mins., John Wiley & Sons, 2010, www.youtube.com/watch?v=BJL2P0JsAS4.

About the Author

Judie Dziezak is a speaker, mentor, and intuitive who draws upon the spiritual arts and her former careers in law, publishing, and science to guide people to step into their personal power, evolve into the best expression of themselves, and reconnect with their inner wisdom. She is a former registered patent attorney and litigator who practiced in all aspects of intellectual property law and food and drug law; before that, a science technology writer and editor; and before that, a food scientist and chemist. An engaging speaker, she has spoken before industry conferences,  women's groups, corporations, and universities. Judie enjoys reading, hiking, yoga, and Pilates. This is her first book.

Learn more and connect with Judie at judiedziezak.com

Follow-Up Note to the Reader

I hope you found this book interesting.
If you have a few moments, please post a
review at your favorite online retailer.
Your feedback helps potential readers and me.

Made in the USA
Monee, IL
18 September 2023

42929269R00226